VARIATIONS ON A THEME

Happy 80th Birthday!

Hg

The Didsbury Lecture Series

VARIATIONS ON A THEME

King, Messiah and Servant
in the Book of Isaiah

H. G. M. Williamson

THE DIDSBURY LECTURES 1997

paternoster press

First published in the UK 1998 by Paternoster Press

04 03 02 01 00 99 98   7 6 5 4 3 2 1

Paternoster Press is an imprint of Paternoster Publishing,
P.O. Box 300, Carlisle, Cumbria CA3 OQS UK
http://www.paternoster-publishing.com

British Library Cataloguing in Publication Data

A catalogue record for this book is available
from the British Library.

ISBN 0–85364–870–0

This book is printed using Suffolk Book paper
which is 100% acid free

Cover design by Mainstream, Lancaster
Typeset by Photoprint, Torquay
Printed in Great Britain by Clays Ltd, St Ives plc

Dedicated to Peter and Anne Bustin

Southwold 1984–1997

Faithful servants

Contents

List of Abbreviations

AnBib	Analecta Biblica
AOAT	Alter Orient und Altes Testament
ASTI	*Annual of the Swedish Theological Institute*
ATANT	Abhandlungen zur Theologie des Alten und Neuen Testament
ATD	Das Alte Testament Deutsch
AThD	Acta Theologica Danica
AV	Authorised Version
BETL	Bibliotheca Ephemeridum Theologicarum Lovaniensium
BEvTh	Beiträge zur evangelischen Theologie
BhistTh	Beiträge zur historischen Theologie
BHS	*Biblia Hebraica Stuttgartensia* (Stuttgart, 1983)
BibSac	*Bibliotheca Sacra*
BiOr	*Bibliotheca Orientalis*
BKAT	Biblischer Kommentar, Altes Testament
BN	*Biblische Notizen*
BWANT	Beiträge zur Wissenschaft vom Alten und Neuen Testament
BZ	*Biblische Zeitschrift*
BZAW	Beihefte zur *Zeitschrift für die alttestamentliche Wissenschaft*
CBQ	*Catholic Biblical Quarterly*
CBQMS	*Catholic Biblical Quarterly*, Monograph Series
CBSC	Cambridge Bible for Schools and Colleges
ConB	Coniectanea Biblica

DNEB	Die neue Echter Bibel
EB	Études bibliques
EF	Erträge der Forschung
ET	English translation
EvTh	*Evangelische Theologie*
	FAT Forschungen zum Alten Testament
FOTL	The Forms of the Old Testament Literature
FRLANT	Forschungen zur Religion und Literatur des Alten und Neuen Testament
FThL	Forum Theologiae Linguisticae
FzB	Forschung zur Bibel
HAR	*Hebrew Annual Review*
HKAT	Handkommentar zum Alten Testament
HUCA	*Hebrew Union College Annual*
IB	G.A. Buttrick *et al.* (eds.), *The Interpreter's Bible* (New York and Nashville, Abingdon 1956)
ICC	International Critical Commentary
JANES	*Journal of the Ancient Near Eastern Society of Columbia University*
JAOS	*Journal of the American Oriental Society*
JBL	*Journal of Biblical Literature*
JSOT	*Journal for the Study of the Old Testament*
JSOTS	*Journal for the Study of the Old Testament, Supplement Series*
JSS	*Journal of Semitic Studies*
KAT	Kommentar zum Alten Testament
KHAT	Kurzer Hand-Commentar zum Alten Testament
LecD	Lectio Divina
LXX	The Septuagint
MT	Masoretic Text
NCB	New Century Bible
NEB	New English Bible
NedGTT	*Nederduits Gereformeerde Teologiese Tydskrif*
N.F.	Neue Folge
NICOT	The New International Commentary on the Old Testament
NKZ	*Neue kirchliche Zeitschrift*
NRSV	New Revised Standard Version
OBO	Orbis Biblicus et Orientalis

OT	Old Testament
OTG	Old Testament Guides
OTL	Old Testament Library
OTS	*Oudtestamentische Studiën*
PIBA	*Proceedings of the Irish Biblical Association*
RB	*Revue biblique*
RHPhR	*Revue d'Histoire et de Philosophie Religieuses*
RSV	Revised Standard Version
RV	Revised Version
SBLDS	Society of Biblical Literature Dissertation Series
SBS	Stuttgarter Bibelstudien
SBT	Studies in Biblical Theology
SJOT	*Scandinavian Journal of the Old Testament*
SVT	Supplements to *Vetus Testamentum*
TDNT	G. Kittel & G. Friedrich (eds.), *Theological Dictionary of the New Testament* (Grand Rapids, Eerdmans 1964–74)
TDOT	G.J. Botterweck and H. Ringgren (eds.), *Theological Dictionary of the Old Testament* (Grand Rapids, Eerdmans 1974–)
ThB	Theologische Bücherei
ThWAT	G.J. Botterweck and H. Ringgren (eds.), *Theologisches Wörterbuch zum Alten Testament* (Stuttgart, Kohlhammer 1970–)
ThZ	*Theologische Zeitschrift*
TLZ	*Theologische Literaturzeitung*
UCOP	University of Cambridge Oriental Publications
UF	*Ugarit-Forschungen*
VT	*Vetus Testamentum*
WBC	Word Biblical Commentary
WMANT	Wissenschaftliche Monographien zum Alten und Neuen Testament
ZAW	*Zeitschrift für die alttestamentliche Wissenschaft*
ZDMG.S	*Zeitschrift der deutschen morgenländischen Gesellschaft*, Supplements
ZThK	*Zeitschrift für Theologie und Kirche*

Preface

It was an honour to be invited in October 1994 to deliver the 1997 series of Didsbury lectures. Although it is usual in such circumstances to adapt the form of lectures as delivered into a form suitable for publication as a book, I have on this occasion worked in the opposite direction. I first wrote the book in order to try to do justice to the topic chosen, and then based the lectures on the results achieved in a form which I hope proved more palatable to the audience at the four lectures, on 6–9 May, 1997. I should like to place on record my gratitude to the Principal and staff of the Nazarene Theological College for the welcome and kindness they extended to me during those few days.

Part of chapter three is based on a section of the Ethel Wood lecture I gave in the University of London on 5 March 1996, repeated as a guest lecture in the University of Uppsala the following month. I am grateful to my hosts on both occasions for their warm hospitality.

In the tradition of this lecture series I have tried to make the discussion accessible to a wider circle of readers than fellow academic specialists alone. It is, nevertheless, no secret that some of the topics covered are among the most

controversial in scholarly study of the Old Testament. It
has not been easy to steer a path between these competing
interests, but my hope is that the main text will be widely
intelligible, and that the footnotes will provide more advanced students with some of the necessarily more technical details of argumentation and bibliography. The
English translation of the Bible used throughout is that
of the New Revised Standard Version, unless otherwise
indicated.

Because of pressures of other commitments and the
requirement to complete this book before the lectures
were delivered, the time available for writing has been
shorter than ideally I could have wished. Although the
main outlines of the argument are the fruit of longer
reflection, and so would probably not have changed significantly even if more time had been available to me, I am
aware that I have not been able to master all the abundant
literature on this topic, and that to have done so might
have resulted in minor changes of detail and presentation.
I apologize to any who feel that their contributions have
been unfairly overlooked. Even so, the book has turned
out to be rather longer than I originally envisaged, and I
appreciate the indulgence of the publishers in accepting
the overgrown result. I am also grateful to my colleague,
Dr David Reimer, who made a number of helpful suggestions on my first draft.

Most of the book was written during a term of sabbat-
ical leave between Christmas and Easter 1997, two sea-
sons in the year of the Christian church which, together
with Lent in between, have afforded abundant opportunity to reflect on other and wider ramifications of many
of the passages analysed here. This period has also seen
the retirement of Peter and Anne Bustin after twelve years

of distinguished service in the parish church of St Edmund, King and Martyr, Southwold. Their ministry has provided a practical example of what it means to live as servants of the Lord in today's world. The book is therefore fittingly dedicated to them, in appreciation.

One

Statement of a Theme

Academic study of the book of Isaiah has gone through a remarkable transformation in recent years. One of the few results of critical biblical scholarship which seems to be known, if not always accepted, outside professional circles is that the book was not all written by a single prophet in the eighth century BCE, and for the past century or so the various parts of the book have generally been studied in complete isolation from one another. Recently, however, scholars have been impressed more by the number of ways in which the various parts are connected with one another. Attention has focused primarily on phraseology and themes that span the whole or substantial parts of the book, though there have also been suggestions about the integrating nature of overall editorial work.

In the context of these recent developments it is, perhaps, somewhat surprising to find that the topic of messianism has not been given sustained attention.[1] Older studies, as well as those which have continued since to

---

[1] An exception to this generalization is the recent programmatic essay of R. Schultz, 'The King in the Book of Isaiah', in P.E. Satterthwaite, R.S. Hess and G.J. Wenham (eds.), *The Lord's Anointed: Interpretation of Old Testament Messianic Texts* (Carlisle, Paternoster/Grand Rapids, Baker Books 1995), pp. 141–65.

adopt their conservative critical stance, gave this subject pride of place, and passages from all the major parts of the book were combined to develop a portrait of the Messiah whom, it was believed, Isaiah expected. The recent approach to the study of Isaiah does not allow us to return directly to this position, as will be demonstrated more fully below, but it seems that this is nevertheless a subject worth revisiting in the new climate of opinion. Whether it proves fruitful in taking the study of the book as a whole further forward can only be judged after the analysis is complete. At the very least it would seem that the topic deserves to be explored.

If we are to do justice to the breadth of our subject, however, it is necessary first to take a step back in order to examine something of the wider context of Isaiah's theology within which his understanding of kingship must be located. That is the task attempted in this first chapter, and the suggestion will emerge that there is a fundamental point of principle – a theme – in the thought of the prophet whose application, by way of a series of variations, can then be taken up in the remainder of this book.

Apart from the formulaic headings in Isaiah 1:1 and 6:1, the first character in the book of Isaiah to be called king is 'the Lord of Hosts' (6:5). He is portrayed as seated in exaltation on a throne in his palace (*hêkāl*), probably in royal garb (6:1),[2] and surrounded by his royal attendants in the heavenly court.

---

[2]   For a cautionary note on this see M.Z. Brettler, *God is King: Understanding an Israelite Metaphor* (JSOTS 76; Sheffield, Sheffield Academic Press 1989), pp. 79–80. He is certainly right to point out that the main focus of the description is on the garment's extraordinary size, following J.C. Greenfield, 'Ba'al's Throne and Isa 6:1', in A. Caquot, S. Légasse and M. Tardieu (eds.),

It has sometimes been suggested[3] that this description is intended in part as a deliberate contrast with the human king, since the chapter starts by noting the death of king Uzziah and is followed by a chapter most commentators regard as sharply critical of his next significant successor, Ahaz.[4] Whether or not this is so, the suggestion certainly alerts us to the possibility that it would be wise to examine the themes of divine and human kingship in tandem in the book of Isaiah. When we do so, certain observations arise from even the most cursory preliminary survey, which have the potential to establish some fundamental critical and theological guidelines to govern the remainder of our examination of king, Messiah and servant in the book as a whole.

By my reckoning the noun 'king (*melek*)' occurs 78 times in the book (of which 19 are plural), the related verb 'to rule as king (*mālak*)' five times, and words for 'kingdom

---

Mélanges bibliques et orientaux en l'honneur de M. Mathias Delcor (AOAT 215; Kevelaer, Butzon & Bercker/Neukirchen–Vluyn, Neukirchener Verlag 1985), pp. 193–8, and M.S. Smith, 'Divine Form and Size in Ugaritic and Pre–exilic Israelite Religion', *ZAW* 100 (1988), pp. 424–7; see too, more remotely, S.D. Moore, 'Gigantic God: Yahweh's Body', *JSOT* 70 (1996), pp. 87–115. All reference to clothing is dismissed by L. Eslinger, 'The Infinite in a Finite Organical Perception (Isaiah vi 1–5)', *VT* 45 (1995), pp. 145–73, building on the discussion in G.R. Driver, 'Isaiah 6:1 "his train filled the temple"', in H. Goedicke (ed.), *Near Eastern Studies in Honor of William Foxwell Albright* (Baltimore and London, Johns Hopkins 1971), pp. 87–96.
[3] See, for instance, J.N. Oswalt, *The Book of Isaiah* (NICOT; Grand Rapids, Eerdmans 1986), pp. 177 and 183.
[4] Among those who believe that Isaiah consistently supported Ahaz are J. Høgenhaven, *Gott und Volk bei Jesaja: Eine Untersuchung zur biblischen Theologie* (AThD 24; Leiden, E.J. Brill 1988), pp. 80–93, and S.A. Irvine, *Isaiah, Ahaz, and the Syro-Ephraimitic Crisis* (SBLDS 123; Atlanta, Scholars Press 1990), pp. 133–77.

(*mᵉlûkâ* and *mamlākâ*)' 16 times. A few of these are textually uncertain,[5] but the precise figures are not important; it is their distribution when combined with an
analysis of who is being referred to that is striking.

An overwhelming majority of the references to king in
Isaiah are completely neutral from our point of view. They
are simply a part of the title needed to identify the human
individuals referred to, such as the frequent 'king of
Assyria' in the narratives in chapters 36–7. In what follows
we shall concentrate on what emerge as the most significant uses.

The first point to observe is that in those parts of the
book agreed to come from the exilic period or later God's
kingship comes strongly to the fore, while conversely,
human kingship disappears completely from view, at least
so far as Israel is concerned.

In the earliest parts of the book, dating from the pre-
exilic period and included now in chapters 1–32, there is
no direct reference to God as king apart from the important chapter 6, already referred to. The passages we
shall examine in the next two chapters, including the
traditional messianic texts, all focus on the present or
future person of the human king.

From chapter 40 onwards, however, this picture is dramatically reversed. In 40–55 (often referred to as Deutero-
Isaiah) we find that God is called 'king of Jacob' (41:21),
'king of Israel' (44:6), and 'your [i.e. Israel's] king' (43:15).
In addition, the phrase 'your God reigns (*mālak'ᵉlōhāyik*)'
occurs at 52:7 in a passage which it is generally agreed

---

[5]   In particular, it is probable that one or two examples of *melek* in Isaiah are
references to the deity Molech; for discussion see G.C. Heider, *The Cult of
Molek: A Reassessment* (JSOTS 43; Sheffield, Sheffield Academic Press 1985),
and especially J. Day, *Molech: A God of Human Sacrifice in the Old Testament*
(UCOP 41; Cambridge, Cambridge University Press 1989).

marks a major climax in the structure of this part of the book.[6] In contrast, there is no direct reference to the king of Israel in these chapters, and the only mention of David is at 55:3, where it is made clear that the covenant God had formerly made with his house is now to be transferred to the people as a whole. Nothing whatsoever is said about a continuing role for the royal dynasty, and indeed, in line with the expectations of 55:3, the most overtly royal language in the so-called Servant Songs comes precisely at 42:1–4, where the servant seems most naturally in the context to refer to Israel as a whole. We shall consider these passages and their implications in more detail in chapter 4 below.

Finally, with regard to Deutero-Isaiah, it is well known that the title 'messiah' is ascribed to the Persian king Cyrus in 45:1. Although elaborate theological schemes have sometimes been spun out of this usage, it appears to me that not so much should be made of it. The word itself, of course, simply means 'anointed', and as such it could be applied to more offices than that of king alone. When it is remembered that nowhere in the Old Testament does the word 'messiah (*māšîaḥ*)' have the later technical sense of a future king,[7] and that at least one other foreign king was ordered by God to be anointed by a prophet (Hazael of

---

[6] Cf. J. Muilenburg, 'The Book of Isaiah, Chapters 40–66', (IB 5; New York and Nashville, Abingdon 1956) 5, p. 610; C. Westermann, *Das Buch Jesaja, Kapitel 40–66* (ATD 19; Göttingen, Vandenhoeck & Ruprecht 1981⁴), pp. 201–4 = ET, *Isaiah 40–66: A Commentary* (OTL; London, SCM Press 1969), pp. 249–253; A. Laato, 'The Composition of Isaiah 40–55', *JBL* 109 (1990), pp. 207–228; F. Matheus, *Singt dem Herrn ein neues Lied: Die Hymnen Deuterojesajas* (SBS 141; Stuttgart, Verlag Katholisches Bibelwerk 1990), pp. 56–9 *et passim*.

[7] Cf. J.J.M. Roberts, 'The Old Testament's Contribution to Messianic Expectations', in J.H. Charlesworth (ed.), *The Messiah: Developments in Earliest Judaism and Christianity* (Minneapolis, Fortress Press 1992), pp. 39–51. The figure of Daniel 9:25–6 is usually thought to be priestly.

Damascus, 1 Kings 19:15), it does not seem necessary to conclude further than that Cyrus is here said to be commissioned by God for a specific task. The king of Assyria had been so used according to Isaiah 10:5–15, as had the Babylonian Nebuchadnezzar, styled 'my servant' in Jeremiah 25:9, 27:6 and elsewhere. They, however, had been used as instruments of God's judgment against his people, whereas Cyrus is here his instrument for their deliverance. That in itself might be regarded as remarkable enough, of course, and this is borne out by the elaborate justification for his statement with which the prophet felt it necessary to preface his announcement (44:24–8).[8] Furthermore, there is no denying the astonishing way in which Cyrus' relationship with God is here described (e.g. 45:4–5; 41:25). None of this, however, amounts to an interpretation of 'messiah' in the way to which centuries of later usage have programmed us, and indeed the occurrence here suggests that the word did not yet have such a technical meaning. For our present concern perhaps the single most important conclusion to be drawn is the negative point that the agent of the anticipated restoration will not be an Israelite or Davidic king. But then, in Deutero-Isaiah we should not expect it to be, as we have already begun to see. So while we do not learn directly about a messianic hope from this passage, it serves the important point in our exploration of the book of Isaiah as a whole of underlining the contrasts already emerging between the various parts.

---

[8] Westermann, *Das Buch Jesaja*, pp. 125–126 = ET, p. 154. In my opinion, the denial of the integral connection between 44:24–8 and 45:1–7 is a weakness at the very start of the analysis of R.G. Kratz, *Kyros im Deuterojesaja-Buch: Redaktionsgeschichtliche Untersuchungen zu Entstehung und Theologie von Jes 40–55* (FAT 1; Tübingen, J.C.B. Mohr [Paul Siebeck] 1991), from which he goes on to develop an elaborate theory of redactional layers in Deutero-Isaiah as a whole.

In the third major part of the book, chapters 56–66 (often, but less satisfactorily, referred to as Trito-Isaiah), God is never expressly styled 'king (*melek*)',[9] but royal language is used in close association with him on a couple of occasions. The most striking such passage is 66:1, where he is said to have a throne and a footstool. The rhetorical use of this language, however, is not to stress his royal attributes as such. The emphasis of the passage is that he is not concerned with a physical temple, viewed as a divine throne room, but rather,

> *this is the one to whom I will look,*
> *to the humble and contrite in spirit,*
> *who trembles at my word. (66:2)*

A closely similar point is made at 57:15, where the title 'the high and lofty one (*rām weniśśā'*)' is an obvious allusion to the description of the divine king in 6:1. Here too, however, this language is only preparatory to the striking contrast that

> *I dwell in the high and holy place,*
> *and also with those who are contrite and humble in spirit.*[10]

It seems, therefore, that in this third part of the book of Isaiah the notion of divine kingship is so taken for granted that it can be used as an agreed basis for further development in terms of God's surprising condescension. We may note too that there is no reference in these chapters to a restoration of the Davidic monarchy or to a future king, whereas there is some evidence that there is an acceptance

---

[9]   On 57:9 see Day, *Molech*, pp. 50–2.
[10]   For fuller discussion of the rhetoric of this passage see my *The Book Called Isaiah: Deutero-Isaiah's Role in Composition and Redaction* (Oxford, Clarendon Press 1994), pp. 232–3.

and development of Deutero-Isaiah's notion of the democratization of the monarchy, as we shall see in chapter 5
below.[11]

Within Isaiah 1–39 itself there are several extended
passages which by common consent are to be dated to the
exilic or post-exilic periods. One such is the so-called
Isaiah Apocalypse in chapters 24–7. Here again we find an
explicit reference to the kingship of God in 24:23 ('for the
Lord of hosts will reign (*mālak*) on Mount Zion and in
Jerusalem'), perhaps in association with his divine council,[12] while 25:6–8, often characterized as a 'messianic
banquet', has been aptly described by Day as 'the banquet
in celebration of Yahweh's enthronement'.[13] A number of
other references in these chapters which recall the myth of
Ba'al's victory further suggest that the concept of divine
kingship may underlie even more of this material.

Finally, we should take note of Isaiah 33.[14] The date of
this chapter is disputed, though very few would place it
before the exilic period at the earliest.[15] It contains two

---

[11]   On the use of 'anointed (*māšah*)' at 61:1 see below, pp. 176–78.

[12]   As suggested by T.M. Willis, 'Yahweh's Elders (Isa 24,23): Senior Officials
of the Divine Court', *ZAW* 103 (1991), pp. 375–85.

[13]   J. Day, *God's Conflict with the Dragon and the Sea: Echoes of a Canaanite
Myth in the Old Testament* (UCOP 35; Cambridge, Cambridge University Press
1985), p. 148.

[14]   There are, of course, other passages in Isaiah 1–39 which date to the later
period, such as 34–5, but so far as I can see they do not contribute any
material of significance to our specific theme. The one exception, and that by
way of allusion rather than overt reference, might be 12:6 (again, exilic at the
earliest), on which see Brettler, *God is King*, p. 156.

[15]   I have surveyed the opinions and discussed the matter fully in *The Book
Called Isaiah*, pp. 221–39. My conclusion is that it served as the original
connecting passage between the pre–exilic form of the record of Isaiah's own
ministry and the bulk of the work of Deutero–Isaiah in chapters 40–55. Even
if this specific suggestion is wrong there are few today who would seriously

striking references to God as king – in verse 17,[16] where again there is a probable allusion by way of extension to chapter 6 ('your eyes shall see the king in his beauty'), and in verse 22 ('the Lord is our king'). Here too it is significant that, as in the case of the Isaiah Apocalypse, the considerable emphasis on the importance of Zion is not matched by any allusion whatsoever to the restoration or continuing role of the Davidic monarchy. If the argument from silence may be allowed, it would seem that the stress on God's kingship has completely supplanted that of the human king.

This brief preliminary survey of the treatment of kingship in the certainly non-Isaianic (that is to say, later) portions of the book of Isaiah shows a remarkable (though, so far as I am aware, hitherto unnoticed) consistency of approach. It shows first that the vision recorded in Isaiah 6 – the one early passage from Isaiah himself to refer to God as king – exerted a particular influence on these later writers, as indeed it has on other parts of the book as well.[17] Furthermore, despite the fact that their work spans the exilic and post-exilic periods, they show no interest in the Davidic monarchy beyond the one clear reference in 55:3 which indicates the transfer of

---

defend an earlier date. One exception to this is J.J.M. Roberts, 'Isaiah 33: An Isaianic Elaboration of the Zion Tradition', in C.L. Meyers and M. O'Connor (eds.), *The Word of the Lord Shall Go Forth: Essays in Honor of David Noel Freedman in Celebration of his Sixtieth Birthday* (Winona Lake, Ind., Eisenbrauns 1983), pp. 15–25.

[16] The view that this verse refers to God is rightly defended by Brettler, *God is King*, p. 173. Some other recent commentators have preferred a royal or even messianic interpretation; see, for instance, R.E. Clements, *Isaiah 1–39* (NCB; Grand Rapids, Eerdmans/London, Marshall, Morgan & Scott 1980), p. 269; Oswalt, *Isaiah*, pp. 602–3; J.A. Motyer, *The Prophecy of Isaiah* (Leicester, Inter-Varsity Press 1993), p. 267.

[17] Some of these will be examined below; see too *The Book Called Isaiah*, pp. 37–56.

its peculiarly privileged relationship with God to the people as a whole, while elsewhere a number of allusions to Davidic themes apply them in strikingly new ways, as we shall see. And this, it should be emphasized, is true not only of the second half of the book as a whole, but also of later material included in the first half (chapters 1–39) as well.

These observations fit very well, of course, with recent developments in the scholarly study of Isaiah. As more and more literary connections across the traditional boundaries of the book are recovered it becomes increasingly difficult to hold to the older view that the separate parts grew up in total isolation from one another. Of course, one might well expect that passages in the second half of the book would build on others in the first half; that is what normally happens in books. But the remarkable feature about Isaiah for our present purposes is that the same holds true even for material which, for whatever reasons, has not been added later at the end of the book, as might at first have been expected, but rather has been incorporated in the first part of the book, at chapters 24–7, 33, and so on. These editors, tradents, or whatever we want to call them, consistently work under the influence of the notion that God is king, and that there is no place, so far as can be seen, for a human, Davidic king.

Now we shall have more to say about this important observation later on, but at this stage of our investigation it seems worthwhile drawing attention to one potentially important consequence of a rather old-fashioned critical nature. There are in the first half of the book some four or five passages that deal in a sustained manner with the issue of the Davidic monarchy and its future. They are, of course, the traditional (and in three cases, at least, very familiar) messianic passages. Opinions about their date have varied widely over the years, and there is a strong body of opinion which would put all, or most, of them in the late post-exilic period.[18] At that time, when there was no king in Israel, their application as messianic in the narrow sense could seem plausible, so that a traditional interpretation is won at the cost of traditional authorship! In the light of what we have seen, however, a stronger *prima facie* case would seem to have been made for dating them in the pre-exilic period. Within the whole sweep of development we can trace with a reasonable degree of certainty in the growth of the book, an interest in human kingship gives way to divine kingship, so that to date these particular royal passages late would go very much against the grain of what we can recover of the ideological development of the Isaianic tradition as a whole. This is admittedly not a conclusive argument, nor does it point necessarily to an eighth- rather than a seventh- or even early sixth-century date. It does, however, indicate a firmly pre-exilic setting as the most plausible context within which to set about the task of interpretation, as the structure of the book suggests. Of course, we cannot rule out the possibility of an odd maverick addition here or there which stands apart from the main stream of Isaianic thought. To suggest, however, that all such passages must be post-exilic would seem not only to contradict the ideological flow of the book's development, but also to leave these presumed later writers with no trigger in the work as

---

[18]   See, for instance, O. Kaiser, *Das Buch des Propheten Jesaja, Kapitel 1–12* (ATD 17; Göttingen, Vandenhoeck & Ruprecht 1981[5]) = ET, *Isaiah 1–12: A Commentary* (OTL; London, SCM Press 1983); W. Werner, *Eschatologische Texte in Jesaja 1–39: Messias, Heiliger Rest, Völker* (FzB 46; Würzburg, Echter Verlag 1982), pp. 17–88; R. Kilian, *Jesaja 1–39* (EF 200; Darmstadt, Wissenschaftliche Buchgesellschaft 1983), pp. 5–26.

they knew it that could have caused them to take this radically different turn in the first place.

A second consequence of our preliminary survey derives from the probability that these later writers were not mistaken in regarding the vision of God in chapter 6 as of fundamental importance for the theology of Isaiah of Jerusalem himself, and that this had inevitable consequences for how both he and they approached the topic of human kingship.

The easiest point of access to this comes by way of the opening description of the Lord as 'high and lofty (*rām wᵉniśśā'*)', a phrase we have already found echoed by the later writer of 57:15. The uses of this phrase elsewhere in Isaiah's writings show clearly that any person or institution demonstrating pride, arrogance or hubris is effectively posing a challenge to God's supreme status, which leads immediately to their categorical condemnation. Nothing and nobody must seek to usurp or equal the isolated sovereignty of God, the exalted king.

In Isaiah 2:5–22, for instance (a passage which seems subsequently to have been extensively glossed or expanded), we read that

> the Lord of hosts has a day
>   against all that is proud and lofty (*rām*),
>   against all that is lifted up (*wᵉniśśā'*) and high.[19] (2:12)

This general statement is then illustrated by a list of features such as hills and mountains, some of which are qualified by the same adjectives, in verses 13–16. Framing

---

[19]   I have discussed the textual problems of this verse and the following one in *The Book Called Isaiah*, pp. 246–7. I agree with the emendation adopted by the NRSV of verse 12, as given above, and further believe that the words 'lofty and lifted up' in verse 13 are a later gloss, albeit accurately reflecting a correct understanding of the thought of the passage.

this introductory statement with its illustrative list are the virtually identical sayings in verses 11 and 17:

> *The haughty eyes of people shall be brought low,*
>   *and the pride of everyone shall be humbled;*
> *and the Lord alone will be exalted*
>   *in that day.* (2:11)[20]

From the wider context of the paragraph as a whole, in which the passage just analysed is central, we learn that material wealth, military power, and idols are also included under the rubric of human pride, and furthermore that in this particular regard Isaiah's invective is not, apparently, restricted to Israel and Judah.

This well-known feature of Isaianic theology is repeated in varying ways on many occasions. The bulk of chapter 5, for instance, is a series of woe-oracles directed mainly, it would seem, against the leisured and wealthy classes in Judean society of that time. The original series appears to have been expanded here and there with additional explanations and comments, and among these are verses 15–16:

> *People are bowed down,*
>   *everyone is brought low,*
> *and the eyes of the haughty are humbled.*
> *But the Lord of hosts is exalted by justice,*
>   *and the Holy God shows himself holy by righteousness.*

The connections of thought and vocabulary with the passage in chapter 2 we have just discussed are obvious, and it is partly this very fact that results in such wide differences of opinion among the commentators concerning date and authorship. How do we know whether this is a case of Isaiah emphasizing an aspect of his teaching of

---

[20] The only difference in verse 17 is that the opening two clauses invert the verbs used and omit the reference to 'eyes'. The general sense, however, is identical.

central importance to him, or of a later imitator seeking to capture the spirit of the master? And then there is a further complication! For some readers, these two verses seem to interrupt what they consider to have been an original connection between verses 14 and 17, so that 15–16 is judged to have been added later, while verses 14 and 17 are themselves thought to be part of a later expansion of the original series of woe-oracles because, as the sharp-eyed will see, both verses 13 and 14 begin with the word 'therefore',[21] while those who know Hebrew will further observe that there is an awkward shift from masculine to feminine suffixes between the two verses.[22] So on this extreme view, verses 15–16 are an addition to an addition! It is thus not difficult to find reputable scholars who think that the whole was written by Isaiah, or that verses 14–17 were added in the wake, perhaps, of the fall of Jerusalem to the Babylonians more than a century later, or that verses 15–16 come from much later still, in the post-exilic period.[23] Finally, there is the possibility that some genuine words of Isaiah have been moved from elsewhere to their present setting during the course of the

---

[21] For some perceptive comments on this feature here and elsewhere in Isaiah see B.W. Anderson, '"God with Us" – In Judgment and in Mercy: The Editorial Structure of Isaiah 5–10(11)', in G.M. Tucker, D.L. Petersen, and R.R. Wilson (eds.), *Canon, Theology, and Old Testament Interpretation: Essays in Honor of Brevard S. Childs* (Philadelphia, Fortress Press 1988), pp. 230–45.

[22] Cf. J.A. Emerton, 'The Textual Problems of Isaiah v 14', *VT* 17 (1967), pp. 135–42.

[23] For the first opinion see, for instance, M.A. Sweeney, *Isaiah 1–39, with an Introduction to Prophetic Literature* (FOTL 16; Grand Rapids, Eerdmans 1996), pp. 125, 128; for the second, Clements, *Isaiah 1–39*, pp. 61, 64; and for the third, J. Vermeylen, *Du prophète Isaïe à l'apocalyptique: Isaïe, i–xxxv, miroir d'un demi–millénaire d'expérience religieuse en Israël* 1 (Paris, Gabelda 1977), pp. 172–4; H. Barth, *Die Jesaja-Worte in der Josiazeit: Israel und Assur als Thema einer produktiven Neuinterpretation der Jesajaüberlieferung* (WMANT 48; Neukirchen–Vluyn, Neukirchener Verlag 1977), p. 192.

book's long composition history,[24] a procedure which seems to have happened in the case of some other passages.

Now, it is not my intention normally to go into these complex issues in such detail, nor to seek to discuss the merits of the various possibilities in this particular case. I have indulged myself on this one occasion merely to illustrate how many uncertainties confront us in trying to unravel the history of so complex a book as Isaiah and to serve as a reminder that dogmatism is itself a form of pride which Isaiah might well have condemned. In this case, at the risk of being accused of having our cake and eating it, we may conclude either that the theme under discussion was so central to Isaiah that he had no hesitation in repeating it, or that it was perceived to be so central to his message that later editors felt justified in imitating his expression of it. Either way, the important point of its centrality emerges as agreed, and the passage serves as an appropriate comment on the haughty pride of 'the nobility of Jerusalem' (verse 14).

So far we have examined this theme as Isaiah applied it generally. The same theology, however, seems to underlie his condemnation of specific groups within the population. For instance, at 3:16–17 it forms the basis of his invective against some of the women of Jerusalem: 'Because the daughters of Zion are haughty . . .'; in 9:7–11 (ET, 8–12) it explains the judgment on the inhabitants of the northern kingdom of Israel who spoke 'in pride and

---

H. Wildberger agrees with the literary conclusion of this third position, but does not specify a date; cf. *Jesaja, 1. Teilband: Jesaja, Kapitel 1–12* (BKAT 10/1; Neukirchen–Vluyn, Neukirchener Verlag 1980²), pp. 181–3, 189–92 = ET, *Isaiah 1–12: A Commentary* (Minneapolis, Fortress Press 1991), pp. 195–7, 204–7.

[24] See especially G.T. Sheppard, 'The Anti-Assyrian Redaction and the Canonical Context of Isaiah 1–39', *JBL* 104 (1985), pp. 193–216.

arrogance of heart'; and at 28:1–4 some of these same people are censured for similar reasons:

> *Ah, the proud garland of the drunkards of Ephraim,*
> *and the fading flower of its glorious beauty . . .*

As we have seen Isaiah did not, in principle, limit the application of this theology to Israel and Judah alone, and thus it is not surprising to find that it also underlies his attitude towards some of the foreign nations who came into contact with his own people. The best-known example of this concerns Assyria, whom Isaiah certainly regarded as God's chosen instrument to punish his people for their sin, but whose boasting revealed that she herself was guilty of the same pride which would eventually lead to her own downfall. This is most famously illustrated at 10:5–15, another passage that has been the subject of later elaboration intended to make the underlying theology clear. The paragraph opens by making clear that Assyria is indeed God's agent, 'Assyria, the rod of my anger' (10:5), but her boasting soon reaches further, indicating that she did not recognize the true source of her military victories: 'By the strength of my hand I have done it . . .' (10:13). Isaiah himself, who has already indicated by the use of the woe-form at verse 5 that Assyria is herself to be judged, explains the thinking behind this conclusion at the end of the passage with characteristically colourful imagery:

> *Shall the axe vaunt itself over the one who wields it,*
> *or the saw magnify itself against the one who handles it?*
> *As if a rod should raise the one who lifts it up,*
> *or as if a staff should lift the one who is not wood!*

A later prosaic editor has spelled out what this means in terms with which we are already familiar from the language of Isaiah himself elsewhere: 'When the Lord has finished all his work on Mount Zion and on Jerusalem, he will punish the arrogant boasting of the king of Assyria and his haughty pride (literally, 'the glory of the height of his eyes'; cf. 2:11)' (10:12).

It would be possible to continue at some length in this vein, but enough has been said to demonstrate that both for Isaiah and for those who built on his work[25] this theme of the essence of sin being human pride, which challenges the position of 'the high and lofty one', was central to their thinking. From so fundamental a theological tenet it is possible to go on to deduce that the prophet had a strong sense that everything should take its proper place within the divine ordering of things, whether natural, international, or social. His understanding of reality was distinctly hierarchical, and it is difficult not to believe that he would have agreed with the adage 'a place for everything, and everything in its place'.

It is for this reason, I suggest, that he regarded with horror, and indeed as an expression of God's judgment, the breakdown of the natural ordering of society as it slips into a state of anarchy. This first comes to extended expression in 3:1–12, which in its present setting elaborates on the judgment of 'that day' which we already studied in Isaiah 2. After God has removed from Jerusalem and Judah all those who were recognized as rulers and leaders (3:1–3), he 'will make boys their princes, and babes shall rule over them' (3:4). The expected hierarchy of respect will be broken down (3:5), and people will cast around for anyone, however unsuitable, to lead them (3:6), but it is not a position that anyone with any sense

---

[25] See, for instance, the comparable sentiments in the taunt against the unnamed king of Babylon in Isaiah 14:4–21, the interesting reversal of the theme, marked by the same vocabulary, at 30:25, and God's own stated intention at 33:10.

would wish to assume (3:7). The climax of the passage (politically incorrect, I fear) concludes:

> *My people – children are their oppressors,*
>   *and women rule over them.*
> *O my people, your leaders mislead you,*
>   *and confuse the course of your paths.*[26] (3:12)

The same sense of horror pervades the description of civil war, another unnatural condition, in 9:18–20 (ET, 19–21).

It is not only, however, in such dire circumstances that such notions come to expression. At a more humdrum level, the idea of children who disobey their parents is a violation of the same self-evident principle, and requires no further explanation (1:2–3; 30:8–9). Similarly, it is the place and task of leaders to lead, so that a society which either rejects their leadership, or where the leaders themselves are corrupt, is automatically doomed in Isaiah's eyes; see, for instance, 1:23; 3:14–15; 5:18–24; 9:15 (ET, 16); 10:1–4; 28:7–15; 30:10–11. It is clear from this lengthy list of passages (chosen at random without seeking to be exhaustive) that this too was a fundamental part of Isaiah's thinking.

For the last few pages, we have been considering some consequences of the fact that Isaiah saw the Lord as 'high and lofty' (6:1). We have seen what a deep impact this had on his thinking, and indeed on much of the subsequent Isaianic tradition, and how his whole understanding of the ordering of society seems to derive quite naturally from this fundamental starting point. It may seem that in our enthusiasm we have wandered rather far from our main subject of kingship, but in fact this is not so, for the last introductory topic that needs to be addressed in this

---

[26]   It is noteworthy that the last two lines of this passage are closely echoed at 9:15 (ET, 16), where they apparently refer to the northern kingdom, a further indication of the depth of Isaiah's revulsion at this state of affairs.

chapter derives directly from it and will bring us to the
heart of the matters which will govern much of the discussion of the more obviously royal passages in the next
chapter, and indeed of their development in the chapters
which follow. This topic can best be addressed by posing a
question: what are the foundational qualities, according to
Isaiah, of a society which, unlike that of his own day, is
properly ordered under God?

There are several key passages which help us to respond
to this question, and they each give a closely comparable
answer. From that remarkably secure position we shall be
able to go on to make some more general remarks.

First, in the paragraph starting at 1:21,[27] Isaiah contrasts the ideal past of Zion/Jerusalem with its present
doleful condition:

> *How the faithful city*
>   *has become a whore!*
> *She that was full of justice,*
> *righteousness lodged in her –*
>   *but now murderers!*

---

[27]   The repetition of language at verse 26 marks that verse as the obvious
conclusion of this paragraph in the present form of the text. In my opinion,
however, verse 26 was added to the original saying of Isaiah by the editor of
chapter 1 as a whole, an editor who, at a late stage in the growth of the book,
assembled a number of sayings of the prophet in this chapter in order to serve
as an introduction to the whole. In the process of so doing, he also added
some lines of his own, particularly at either the beginning or the end of
paragraphs. (I also think that he added the last sentence in verse 23, in order
to illustrate that the rebel princes were guilty of disobeying the injunctions of
verse 17: the language is the same, but expressd now in prose.) Since such
speculations are inevitably hypothetical, and not strictly relevant to the
present discussion, it would not be practical to set out the evidence in full
here. For some preliminary remarks on this chapter as a whole see my
'Synchronic and Diachronic in Isaian Perspective', in J.C. de Moor (ed.),
Synchronic or Diachronic? A Debate on Method in Old Testament Exegesis (*OTS*
34; Leiden, E.J. Brill 1995), pp. 211–26, and 'Relocating Isaiah 1:2–9', in C.C.
Broyles and C.A. Evans (eds.), *Writing and Reading the Scroll of Isaiah: Studies
of an Interpretive Tradition* (Leiden, E.J. Brill, forthcoming).

Three words characterize the golden age, apparently, 'faithful (*ne'emānâ*)', 'justice (*mišpāṭ*)', and 'righteousness (*ṣedeq*)'. These words occur a number of times in combination in the writing of Isaiah (and of those who most closely followed him), occasionally all three together, as here, but more often as a combination of just two of them. As we shall see, each can have a reasonably wide spread of meanings. It is the use of them together, however, as in this passage, which narrows the focus so as to make them into almost a catch-phrase that characterizes Isaiah's understanding of the ideal society.[28]

It is often the case that we learn most about the meaning of a word by noting that to which it is opposed. Here, for instance, we find first the notion of a whore. What specifically might this image tell us of Zion's unfaithfulness? There are two main possibilities. First, it could refer to religious unfaithfulness, such as idolatry or the pursuit of some god other than the God of Israel. That meaning is

---

[28]   These words also occur together frequently elsewhere in the Old Testament, as do their equivalents in other ancient Near Eastern literature. The material is magisterially reviewed, with reference to many other discussions, by M. Weinfeld, '"Justice and Righteousness" – משפט וצדקה – The Expression and its Meaning', in H.G. Reventlow and Y. Hoffman (eds.), *Justice and Righteousness: Biblical Themes and their Influence* (JSOTS 137; Sheffield, Sheffield Academic Press 1992), pp. 228–46; see too H. Cazelles, 'De l'idéologie royale', *JANES* 5 (1973), pp. 59–73; H. Niehr, *Herrschen und Richten: Die Wurzel špt im Alten Orient und im Alten Testament* (FzB 54; Würzburg, Echter Verlag 1986); H. Gossai, *Justice, Righteousness and the Social Critique of the Eighth-Century Prophets* (New York, Peter Lang 1993). Weinfeld is primarily concerned with what the usages have in common, and settles for 'social justice'. As we shall see, this is certainly a prominent aspect of Isaiah's use too, but our concern in the following discussion is his distinctive emphases and nuances within this commonality. The importance of these terms for messianism in Isaiah has, of course, been noted before, most recently by D. Schibler, 'Messianism and Messianic Prophecy in Isaiah 1–12 and 28–33', in P.E. Satterthwaite, R.S. Hess and G.J. Wenham (eds.), *The Lord's Anointed: Interpretation of Old Testament Messianic Texts* (Carlisle, Paternoster/Grand Rapids, Baker Books, 1995), pp. 87–104.

prominent in the work of the slightly earlier Hosea, and we have already seen that it was condemned in Isaiah 2. Secondly, however, it could be that Isaiah had a more political notion in mind: the development of alliances with foreign nations, such as Egypt, which he certainly condemned strongly in the later part of his ministry (chapters 30–31, for instance). In fact, the two possibilities are not entirely separate from one another, and both, of course, pose a severe challenge to the absolute sovereignty of God over his people.

Interestingly, neither possibility seems to bring us immediately into the realm of justice and righteousness (the second two words in our list) as normally understood, that is to say, the realm of the proper administration of the law. The continuation of the paragraph shows, however (again by way of a contrast), that this too is included:

> *Your princes are rebels*
>   *and companions of thieves.*
> *Everyone loves a bribe*
>   *and runs after gifts.* (1:23)

There need be little doubt that abuse of the legal system is included here,[29] but again it is not so clear that this is all that is intended. The culprits are identified by the more general term 'princes', who were not just members of the royal family, but 'men of authority who held high civil and military administrative posts'.[30] The possibilities for the abuse of power open to such administrators were extensive, as a number of the prophets demonstrate, so that it would be a mistake to impose some arbitrary limit on

---

[29] It was certainly so understood by the editor who probably (see note 26 above) added the last part of verse 23 and who also referred explicitly to 'judges' in his picture of the eventual restoration (verse 26).
[30] Clements, *Isaiah 1–39*, p. 36.

what Isaiah may have had in mind here. The same is true of the image of impurity which surfaces in verses 22 and 25.

Our brief look at the contrast in this passage between the past glories and present failures of Jerusalem society is thus instructive for our understanding of the three words by which Isaiah characterized his ideal, and it relates closely to what we might have expected following the previous analysis of his fundamental theology. We see once again his concern for the supremacy of the Lord, and at the same time, and by extension of this, his exposure of any abuse of human leadership. Leaders are essential, but they must lead with justice and righteousness in all areas of life.

If this is the kind of society to which Isaiah looked back with wistful eyes, what of the present? The well-known Song of the Vineyard in Isaiah 5:1–7 gives us a clear answer. As the image is made plain in the last verse, it becomes apparent that the reference is to the whole society of God's people, Israel and Judah together. This is therefore a suitable passage to ask about what God's expected ideal for them is:

> he expected justice (mišpāṭ),
>   but saw bloodshed;
> righteousness (ṣᵉdāqâ),
>   but heard a cry!

We see at once that the two characteristics looked for are the same as those which characterized the golden age in 1:21: justice and righteousness. It is not quite so easy to define the terms here by their opposites, because the choice of wording was clearly governed in part by the desire to achieve a very remarkable play on words (mišpāṭ and ṣᵉdāqâ). The second word refers to the cry of someone in distress, frequently because of political or social oppression.[31] This is by no means limited to the strictly legal sphere, however, so that we should allow that the contrast may relate to a wide range of social relationships. The first word is philologically less certain, though nothing more convincing than the NRSV's 'bloodshed' has been proposed. Assuming it to be correct, it would seem at first to refer to a general breakdown of law and order, for which all inhabitants of the land are partly responsible, but which may also be laid in particular at the door of those in authority charged with the enforcement of the law. At the same time, however, the possibility should also be considered that included within this is a specific condemnation of those who abuse the legal process for their own ends, no matter what the cost. Once again, therefore, we see that 'justice and righteousness' have a wide application, and this may be borne out by the varied targets of the series of woes which follow in verses 8–23.

From the past and present we turn finally to the future. Several passages use our terms in this connection (e.g. 1:26–8; 32:16,17; 33:5), but serious doubts have been raised as to whether any of these derive from Isaiah himself. Of course, even if they do not, they are still of great importance in demonstrating that, as we have already seen several times, those who developed Isaiah's writing in later times did so with a considerable degree of insight into his own way of thinking. The days when 'later addition' meant 'without value' have long since passed. However, the point can be made even more emphatically, because the same picture emerges from 28:16,17a, for

---

31 See Wildberger, *Jesaja 1*, p. 173 = ET, p. 185; G. Hasel, ' צעק ', *TDOT* 4, (Grand Rapids, Eerdmans 1974 –), pp. 112–22.

which a much stronger case for Isaianic authorship can be made out:

> *therefore thus says the Lord God,*
> *See, I am laying in Zion a foundation stone,*
>   *a tested stone,*
> *a precious cornerstone, a sure foundation:*
> *"One who trusts will not panic."*
> *And I will make justice (mišpāṭ) the line,*
>   *and righteousness (ṣᵉdāqâ) the plummet.*[32]

These words are addressed primarily to the leaders in Jerusalem (verse 14), who have flouted God's sovereignty either by entering into foreign alliances or, more probably, by relying upon the Canaanite underworld deity Molech.[33] The contrasted future in our verses, therefore, implies a judgment upon their whole programme.[34] In contrast with

---

[32] There are several difficulties of both text and translation in this passage which cannot be fully discussed here. We may note in particular that a good case can be made for the alternative rendering of the middle two lines as 'a precious cornerstone for a foundation, a foundation for the believer which will not shake'; cf. G.C.I. Wong, *The Nature of Faith in Isaiah of Jerusalem* (unpublished PhD thesis, Cambridge, 1994), pp. 41–51; J.J.M. Roberts, 'Yahweh's Foundation in Zion (Isa 28:16)', *JBL* 106 (1987), pp. 27–45.

[33] This latter suggestion has been forcefully argued by Day, *Molech*, pp. 58–64, to explain the meaning of the enigmatic 'covenant with death' and 'agreement with Sheol' in verses 15 and 18. (He also notes a number of less plausible interpretations.) It is certainly the case that other gods are frequently described as 'lies' and 'falsehood', and Day's view seems to offer a more natural explanation for the references to death and Sheol than the attempts to link these words with Egypt. A consequence of Day's argument is that the passage need no longer be dated to the reign of Hezekiah, but rather to the earlier time of Ahaz, which is the likely setting for the first part of this chapter as well.

[34] It might be better, therefore, to translate 'a testing stone' rather than 'a tested stone' in verse 16; cf. 8:14, 15. The matter is not helped by uncertainty over the correct etymology of *bōḥan*; see the difference of opinion between H. Wildberger, *Jesaja, 3. Teilband: Jesaja 28–39. Das Buch, der Prophet und seine Botschaft* (BKAT 10/3; Neukirchen–Vluyn, Neukirchener Verlag 1982), pp. 1066–7; M. Tsevat, 'בחן', *TDOT* 2 (Grand Rapids, Eerdmans 1974), pp. 69–72; and Roberts, 'Yahweh's Foundation in Zion', all with references to further literature. Wong, *The Nature of Faith in Isaiah*, pp. 42–4, argues that 'stone of testing' suits the plumb-line imagery in verse 17 best.

them, there is hope for the one who 'trusts (*ma' ᵃmîn*, from the same verb as 'faithful [*ne'ᵉmānâ*]' in 1:21)', just as there could have been for Ahaz in 7:9. If that way is taken, then there will be established a new Zion, in whose building the very walls will be aligned by the principles of justice and righteousness. The significance of these words is not further spelt out here. In the context, we may well suppose that they include negatively an absence of idolatry,[35] but in such a gnomic saying we should perhaps allow that the words are a consciously general summary of all that Isaiah thought lay at the foundation of a society properly ordered under God; the precise content would need to be filled in from his usage elsewhere, which we have seen is in any case considerably broad.

On the basis of these three passages, we clearly need to extend our inquiry into the use of these key words generally in the first part of the book of Isaiah. Taken on their own, they each have a variety of senses, as elsewhere in the Old Testament.[36] *Mišpāṭ*, 'justice', for instance, can refer to punitive judgment (4:4; 34:5), to the place of judgment (28:6), to the legal process in a narrow, forensic sense (3:14), to legal rights (10:2), and even simply to what is 'correct' (28:26) and right (32:7). Similarly, *ṣedeq*, *ṣᵉdāqâ*, 'righteousness', with the related verb and adjective, can refer to the opposite of those who are wicked or guilty (5:23; 26:10), and hence are innocent (3:10; 29:21), as well as to justified punishment (10:22).

---

[35] Or, if the traditional view of the background to the passage is favoured, of the panic measures (as Isaiah saw it) of entering into foolish foreign alliances.

[36] For a survey see Gossai, *Justice, Righteousness*. He includes a helpful summary of previous studies.

The single commonest use of these two words in Isaiah 1-39, however, is in close association with each other,[37] either in poetic parallelism (as in the three examples discussed above), or linked closely with one another, such as by the conjunction 'and'. Thus, of the 22 occurrences of *mišpāṭ*, 'justice', in these chapters, half fall into this category,[38] and, with only one exception (32:1), it is always the leading word of the pair. Conversely, the proportion of linked uses of *ṣedeq*, *ṣᵉdāqâ*, 'righteousness', is even higher, namely 13 out of 20,[39] and in a further two places it is associated with *ne'ᵉmānâ* or *'ᵉmûnâ* (1:26; 11:5). Finally, we may note that the third group of words – *ne'ᵉmānâ*, *ma'ᵃmîn*, *'ᵉmûnâ*, 'faithful(ness)', and related forms – is also often associated with one or other of these two other dominant words,[40] and that all three occur together or in proximity at 1:21, 26-7; 16:5 (*'ᵉmet*); 28:16–17; 33:5–6 (and cf. 11:4, 5).

While most of this material will be seen to fit closely into the pattern of uses already described in our three key passages, a few further comments are in order. First, it would seem to be confirmed that we are justified in regarding these words, when used in combination, as amounting to more than simply the sum of their parts.

---

[37] Isaiah is not alone in this, of course, though the proportions of usage itemized below remain striking; for the OT as a whole, see the works cited in note 22 above. Weinfeld, 'Justice and Righteousness', rightly insists that the pair appears as a hendiadys, the component parts of which may be distributed over adjacent lines in poetic parallelism.

[39] In parallel: 1:21, 27; 5:7,16; 16:5; 28:17; 32:1,16; joined by 'and': 9:6 (ET, 7); 33:5; in close association: 26:9, – 11 passages in all.

[39] This initially curious fact is to be explained by the facts that the two occurrences of the word at 32:17 amplify its use in verse 16, where it is in parallel with *mišpāṭ*, and that at 11:4 it is used in association with the related verb *šāpaṭ*, 'to judge'.

[40] So at: 1:21, 26; 11:5; 26:2; 28:16; 33:6; otherwise: 7:9; 8:2; 22:23, 25; 25:1; 30:21; 33:16.

Whereas on their own they reflect something of the spread of their semantic range as found elsewhere in the Old Testament, together they give expression to Isaiah's notion of 'the God-given norm to ensure a well-ordered society'.[41]

Secondly, although we have arrived at this conclusion by moving forward from an analysis of Isaiah's understanding of God to how that has influenced his presentation of the way in which God's people should reflect it in community, it is interesting to note also that these two points come together in a verse we have already cited and which may represent subsequent reflection on Isaiah's legacy:

> But the Lord of hosts is exalted by justice (mišpāṭ),
>   and the Holy God shows himself holy by righteousness
>   (ṣᵉdāqâ). (5:16)

If God's own exalted character, so fundamental for Isaiah, and his holiness, which comes to expression elsewhere in the book in the highly distinctive divine title 'the Holy One of Israel',[42] are revealed in justice and righteousness, then it is no wonder that a society which should order itself after the pattern of God's relationship with Israel should be based upon the same principles.

Thirdly, it should not be supposed that these characteristics are necessarily negative (as the English translations might imply). It is as 'a God of justice (mišpāṭ)' that 'the Lord waits to be gracious to you' and 'will rise up (yārûm) to show mercy to you' (30:18), and it is no doubt such a thought that also underlies the use of these terms in the portrayal of future restoration:

---

[41]   P. Uys, *NedGTT* 9 (1968), p. 185 (not available to me).
[42]   For an analysis of this title in the book as a whole see *The Book Called Isaiah*, pp. 41–6.

Zion shall be redeemed by justice,
   and those in her who repent, by righteousness. (1:27)

Then justice will dwell in the wilderness,
   and righteousness abide in the fruitful field.
The effect of righteousness will be peace,
   and the result of righteousness, quietness and trust for ever.
   (32:16-17)

The Lord is exalted, he dwells on high;
   he filled Zion with justice and righteousness;
he will be the stability of your times,
   abundance of salvation, wisdom and knowledge;
   the fear of the Lord is Zion's treasure. (33:5–6)

Although it is probable that all three of these passages come from writers later than Isaiah himself, it is clear that his understanding of God and his ways had penetrated deeply into their consciousness. There is also a close parallel with the manner in which in the second half of the book many of these concepts, which were originally used primarily to give expression to God's condemnation and punishment of his people, came to be seen also as tokens of his grace and compassion.

A final observation may serve to summarize and conclude this chapter. It is noteworthy that in all the passages referred to in this review of some of Isaiah's leading themes the person of the king receives little or no mention. As we shall see, some of these concerns, and especially those relating to justice and righteousness, do come to expression in the 'royal' passages which will be our concern in the next chapter. For the moment, however, it is particularly significant that (unlike, for instance, in Jeremiah) the king is not listed among the corrupt leaders, nor is the loss of kingship referred to as part of the breakdown of social order. The passages about kingship thus stand somewhat in isolation from the remainder of Isaiah's work.

On the one hand, this again suggests that there would not have been much of a trigger to cause later writers to add this material if they were responsible for these cardinal passages in their entirety. When this is coupled with our earlier comments on the ideological direction the development of the book of Isaiah as a whole took, it looks increasingly likely that something, at least, about human kingship must have been present in the work of Isaiah from the very start. On the other hand, the challenge which inevitably confronts us is to see whether (and which of) these passages can be integrated harmoniously into the picture of Isaiah's own theology that has just been sketched. It is with these questions in mind that we shall turn to a study of the so-called messianic passages in the next two chapters.

Two

First Variation: the Ideal King

There are five passages in the first part of the book of Isaiah which have traditionally been regarded as messianic, namely 7:14, 8:23*b*–9:6 (ET, 9:1*b*-7), 11:1–9, 16:4*b*–5, and 32:1–5, and it might seem logical to study them in that order. For two main reasons, however, 7:14 (the Immanuel saying) will be left for separate analysis in the next chapter; it will be necessary to devote rather more space to a consideration of its wider context than in the case of the other four passages, so that there would be a danger of the discussion becoming unbalanced, and, more importantly, we shall discover that in content it is somewhat different from the four which will be the subject of our attention in the present chapter. It is therefore best treated on its own.

1) Isaiah 9:1–7[1]

The range and complexity of the exegetical problems raised by this passage are far too formidable to be treated

---

[1] The verse numbers in this passage differ between the Hebrew text (8:23–9:6) and the English translations (9:1–7). Furthermore, the first sentence in the first verse of the passage ('But there will be no gloom for those who were in anguish') clearly serves as a link between the main part of the

here in full. I shall therefore limit myself rather severely to such points as can be established with some confidence about its understanding of the character and nature of kingship, with particular reference, of course, to those matters which relate to the discussion of the previous chapter.[2]

In the first place, human kingship comes explicitly to expression only in the last two verses of the passage. Its immediate context is set by the opening in verse 2,[3]

> *The people who walked in darkness*
> *have seen a great light;*
> *those who lived in a land of deep darkness –*
> *on them light has shined,*

with its explanation in verse 3 in terms of how 'you' (whom we must obviously assume to be God)[4] have made

---

passage and that which precedes it. For simplicity's sake I shall refer to the English verse numbers in the following and disregard the first sentence of 9:1. The only exception will be that I will add a reference to the Hebrew verse numbers in those cases where there is specific discussion of the Hebrew.

[2] For recent summaries of a wider range of topics arising from this passage, with fuller bibliographic surveys, see (in addition to the standard commentaries), for instance, Barth, *Die Jesaja-Worte*, pp. 141–77; Irvine, *Isaiah, Ahaz*, pp. 221-33; Kilian, *Jesaja 1–39*, pp. 5–10; A. Laato, *Who is Immanuel? The Rise and the Foundering of Isaiah's Messianic Expectations* (Åbo, Åbo Academy Press, 1988), pp. 173–96; Sweeney, *Isaiah 1–39*, pp. 175–88, and *idem*, 'A Philological and Form-Critical Reevaluation of Isaiah 8:16-9:6', *HAR* 14 (1994), pp. 215–31; M.E.W. Thompson, 'Isaiah's Ideal King', *JSOT* 24 (1982), pp. 79–88; Vermeylen, *Du prophète Isaïe*, pp. 232–45; P.D. Wegner, *An Examination of Kingship and Messianic Expectation in Isaiah 1–35* (Lewiston, NY, Mellen Biblical Press 1992), pp. 139–215, and *idem*, 'A Re-examination of Isaiah ix 1–6', *VT* 42 (1992), pp. 103–12.

[3] Not only is the translation of verse 1 uncertain. There are also a number of scholars who question its original connection with the verses which follow. While this latter position may go too far, it is clear that a new paragraph begins with verse 2 and that there is no real break thereafter until the end of verse 7.

[4] On changes in person in a thanksgiving hymn, see H. Gunkel–J. Begrich, *Einleitung in die Psalmen: Die Gattungen der religiösen Lyrik Israels* (Göttingen, Vandenhoeck & Ruprecht 1933), p. 47.

the people joyful.[5] In the form typical of thanksgiving psalms,[6] this is then substantiated with three reasons, each beginning 'for' (verses 4, 5, and 6–7).

The first reason (verse 4) is explicit in attributing the source of joy to the activity of God in the liberation of his people:

> *For the yoke of their burden,*
>   *and the bar across their shoulders,*
>   *the rod of their oppressor,*
>   *you have broken as on the day of Midian.*

---

[5] Quite inexplicably, the NRSV fails to adopt the obvious emendation of *hgwy l'* to *hgylh* at the start of verse 3 (Heb. verse 2). We should therefore certainly render the first line of the verse as 'You have multiplied (its) rejoicing' instead of 'You have multiplied the nation' (a translation which succeeds in rendering the first two words of the Hebrew text [9:2] only at the expense of completely ignoring the third, which, as it stands, is the negative particle 'not'). The emendation makes sense, whereas the present form of the Hebrew text does not; it is supported by the parallelism, and the structure of the rest of the verse builds upon it: the two words for 'joy' in the first line are resumed by their cognate verbs in the second two lines in chiastic order, so that our emended form relates to the verb rendered 'exult' in the NRSV. For further support, see *The Book Called Isaiah*, pp. 249–50.

[6] There is disagreement whether our passage is in fact such a psalm, or simply written in imitation of one. This has serious implications for certain aspects of the exegesis of the passage (it is not merely a scholarly quibble!), but not, perhaps, for us, on the minimal assumption that Isaiah would have agreed with the psalm if, in fact, he was quoting from one rather than being its first author. For some discussions of the form-critical analysis of the passage, see Barth, *Die Jesaja-Worte*, pp. 148–51, building explicitly on F. Crüsemann, *Studien zur Formgeschichte von Hymnus und Danklied in Israel* (WMANT 32; Neukirchen-Vluyn, Neukirchener Verlag 1969); Sweeney, *Isaiah 1–39*, pp. 179–83; Wildberger, *Jesaja 1*, pp. 365–7 (= ET, 387–8); Wegner, *An Examination of Kingship*, pp. 168–76. Wegner points to a number of weaknesses in the straightforward identification of the passage as a thanksgiving psalm, as with the main alternative view that it is an accession-oracle; he also notes that 9:6-7 closely follows the form of a birth-oracle (see below). If that is so, then we may, perhaps, provisionally conclude that the passage does not fit any one single form exactly, but that it has creatively drawn on several. This would argue strongly that it was written consciously for its present setting (whether by Isaiah or another), and not simply cited from the stock of Israelite psalmic liturgy.

It is therefore probable that we should understand his activity to lie behind the impersonally expressed second explanatory verse as well:

> *For all the boots of the trampling warriors*
> *and all the garments rolled in blood*
> *shall be burned[7] as fuel for the fire.* (9:5)

The third explanatory section, and the one which chiefly concerns us, continues this impersonal form of expression, but now with the use of verbs in the passive:

> *For a child has been born for us,*
> *a son given to us . . .* (9:6)

Both the overriding context as we have described it, and the obvious answer to the question as to who the 'logical subject' of these passive verbs is, make it clear that the birth of this child is due entirely to the activity of God. And if there were any doubt remaining it would be dispelled by the concluding assertion of the passage as a whole that 'The zeal of the Lord of hosts will do this' (9:7).[8]

The reason for stressing this rather obvious point is that it enables us to underline the fact that the birth of the king is not primarily to be seen as the arrival of a saviour-figure in his own right. Rather, it is part of the deliverance which God himself will effect for the people. The passive form of the verbs in verse 6 reinforces this impression, and the

---

[7] Literally, 'shall be for burning'. In other words, unlike in the English translation, there is no passive verb in the Hebrew (9:4). This contrasts with the construction in the next verse.

[8] It has sometimes been asserted that this line is a later addition; cf. B. Renaud, 'La Forme poétique d'Is 9, 1–6', in A. Caquot, S. Légasse and M. Tardieu (eds.), *Mélanges bibliques et orientaux en l'honneur de M. Mathias Delcor* (AOAT 215; Kevelaer, Butzon & Bercker/Neukirchen-Vluyn, Neukirchener Verlag 1985), pp. 331–48. This decidedly minority view is far from certain, however; the basis of some of the arguments mounted in its defence are explained differently below.

fact that the figure is not explicitly styled *melek*, 'king', may be related. The main focus of the passage, therefore, is on God's direct work on behalf of his people, and the provision of the royal figure is regarded as a part of this. He serves as a sign of its gracious nature, as well as being, of course, a primary agent through whom God will work.

In the second place, the purpose[9] behind God's provision of this character comes to expression in the second half of verse 7. All else in the passage, and especially the birth-oracle in 6–7*a*, on which so much scholarly attention has been focused, is structurally more in the nature of preparatory description. It is therefore severely misleading that the NRSV makes this into a separate and free-standing sentence, 'He will establish and uphold it with justice and with righteousness', for paradoxically this draws attention away from this statement as the goal of the whole section. It is far better to return to the older rendering of the original RSV

---

9   Wildberger, *Jesaja 1*, p. 384 (= ET, p. 405), followed by Irvine, *Isaiah, Ahaz*, p. 232, insists that the *l* + inf. construction in the third line of verse 7 (Heb. verse 6) must indicate concomitant action rather than purpose. Both are syntactically possible, but the latter is far more common. Wildberger's reason seems to be his concern to ensure that God, rather than the royal figure, is the subject of the verbs 'establish' and 'uphold', and he appeals in support to some passages in the Psalms concerning the foundation of God's throne. None of this seems to be sufficient cause not to take the construction in its commonest sense, however. As we have seen, God is certainly the dominant subject throughout, though that does not rule out the possibility of his acting through an agent, so that Wildberger is effectively introducing a distinction without a difference. Furthermore, the expression of purpose (ultimately *God's* purpose, as we may concede to Wildberger) in this clause may be regarded as an effective climax of the passage to which all else has been building up as a preparation (see especially Renaud, 'La Forme poétique'). Finally, the parallels in the Psalms and elsewhere are certainly apposite, but do not prove Wildberger's point. Apart from some differences in emphasis between those passages and the expression here (on which see further at 32:1–5 below) their application to 'the throne of David' inevitably draws the Davidic king into view alongside God.

> to establish it, and to uphold it
> with justice and with righteousness
> from this time forth and for evermore.

These lines bring us, of course, to the very heart of the concerns for the ordering of society which we saw in the last chapter were so central to Isaiah's thinking. Since verses 4–5 speak of God's work of deliverance of his people from foreign oppression without reference to any human agency, there is an indication here that the king's role relates in particular to the internal ordering of the life of the nation.

Ultimately, this conclusion needs to be modified in two ways. On the one hand, there need be little doubt that in the poetically expressed theology of the Old Testament talk of God's work for his people does not rule out human involvement, while on the other hand it is difficult to distinguish clearly who exactly is the subject of the verbs in this part of verse 7. Nevertheless, when all due allowance has been made for both these points, the fact remains that human agency comes explicitly to expression at this point in a way that is not the case earlier in the passage, and it would be a mistake not to take such a clear shift in emphasis into account. We may confidently conclude that this passage draws the person of the king into the centre of the task of inaugurating and maintaining God's ideal for the society of Israel, something we saw was lacking in the more generally expressed statements of this theme elsewhere in the book.

Thirdly, however, and having said that, there is another novel aspect to this passage which needs to be brought into the discussion. As most commentators point out, the wording of verses 6–7, and of the middle part of verse 7 in particular, seems to echo the promises made to the Davidic dynasty. Most obviously there are verbal echoes,

such as 'his kingdom, to establish it', with which we may
compare 2 Samuel 7:12, 'I will establish his kingdom' (the
same verb and noun are used in the Hebrew texts), while 2
Samuel 7:13, 'I will establish the throne of his kingdom for
ever', and 2 Samuel 7:16, 'your throne shall be established
for ever', seem also to be rephrased in our verse: 'for the
throne of David and his kingdom, to establish it . . . for
ever(more)'. In reviewing such echoes, it should be remembered that the Nathan oracle of 2 Samuel 7 shares its
significant wording with a considerable number of passages elsewhere in the Old Testament, including historical
writings, psalms and prophetic passages,[10] so that it would
be a mistake to expect precise citation of a single, specific
text. We are dealing here, rather, with a nexus of significant words and ideas which were clearly in wide circulation and which, when brought together in a
concentrated passage such as the present one, would have
been as instantly recognizable in antiquity as they are to
modern readers with their concordances and other aids.

As soon as that point is appreciated, it in fact becomes
attractive to read the whole of the wider context in this
light. The possibility that an individual king may need to
be disciplined 'with a rod such as mortals use' (2 Sam.
7:14) may be referred to in the earlier part of our passage
where foreign dominion is described as 'the rod of their
oppressor' (Isa. 9:4); nevertheless, the promise to the Davidic dynasty that its future would be secure 'for ever'[11] is

---

[10] See the survey in H. Kruse, 'David's Covenant', *VT* 35 (1985), pp. 139–64,
where over 40 passages are referred to.

[11] It should, perhaps, be remarked that 'for ever' in English has a rather
more 'eternal' sense than the Hebrew word which it translates, *lᵉʽôlām*. To go
no further, it is sufficient to observe that when the exact phrase which we have
here, 'from this time onward and for evermore', occurs at Psalms 115:18 and
121:8, it clearly means only for the rest of the speaker's or addressee's
lifetime.

reaffirmed in Isaiah 9:7. The names given to the child in verse 6 are reminiscent of God's words to David in the oracle, 'I will make for you a great name, like the name of the great ones of the earth' (2 Sam. 7:9). And finally, although the reference to a child/son in 9:6 is probably not an allusion to divine adoption of the king at his coronation (as at Psalm 2:7),[12] it is difficult to banish from our minds altogether the more general promise in 2 Samuel 7:14 that 'I will be a father to him, and he shall be a son to me'.

There is, therefore, a strong case to be made for the view that the promises to the Davidic dynasty underlie this passage, and if so, it is surely not without significance that the whole tradition of God's founding and establishing the dynasty is here made subservient, as it were, to the responsibilities of justice and righteousness. Of course, Isaiah is not the only writer either in Israel or beyond to draw these ideas into association. The opening of Psalm 72 especially moves in a similar circle of ideas:

---

[12] This has been a fiercely contested point ever since A. Alt published his famous essay 'Jesaja 8,23–9,6. Befreiungsnacht und Krönungstag', in *Festschrift Alfred Bertholet, zum 80. Geburtstag gewidmet* (Tübingen, J.C.B. Mohr 1950), pp. 29–49 = *Kleine Schriften zur Geschichte des Volkes Israel* 2 (Munich, C.H. Beck 1953), pp. 206–25, in partial development of G. von Rad, 'Das judäische Königsritual', *TLZ* 72 (1947), pp. 211–16 = ET, 'The Royal Ritual in Judah', in *The Problem of the Hexateuch and Other Essays* (Edinburgh and London, Oliver & Boyd 1966), pp. 222–31. Since the issue continues to divide the commentators down to the most recent, a full discussion would be out of place here, the issue not being central to our main concerns. The matter is further complicated by the possibility that we would not have an accession oracle *per se* here, but rather an independent reflection of one. Nevertheless, there are difficulties for this view, including (i) 'for us/to us' in verse 6 does not seem to fit an accession oracle, which is spoken directly by God to the king; (ii) there is no indication of divine adoption here, nor is the child identified as God's son; (iii) in the first line of verse 7, the leading word in the parallelism is 'child (*yeled*)', which never occurs in accession contexts; (iv) verses 6–7 take the form of a birth-announcement oracle. For further details on these arguments, as well as some other considerations, see especially Wegner, *An Examination of Kingship*, pp. 169–76.

Give the king your justice, O God,
  and your righteousness to a king's son.
May he judge your people with righteousness,
  and your poor with justice.
May the mountains yield prosperity (šālôm) for the people,
  and the hills, in righteousness.
May he defend the cause of the poor of the people,
  give deliverance to the needy,
  and crush the oppressor. (Ps. 72:1–4)

But what is here prayed for is promised in Isaiah. Whereas
the Psalm takes the dynastic promise for granted and
seeks to expand upon it by asking that the king may act in
righteousness, the prophet refuses to acknowledge such a
dichotomy. For him, the right ordering of society is the
very *raison d'être* of the dynasty. This shows, I suggest, that
Isaiah is adapting the well-known tradition of God's
choice of David to fit it into his wider perception of the
will of God for his people.

There has been much discussion about whether the
promise to David was originally conditional or unconditional, and passages aplenty can be found to support both
sides of this debate. Isaiah sees the matter rather differently. If I may put it in the form of a paradox – for Isaiah
the 'conditional' element is transformed into an inalienable part of the unconditional promise. The question is
not raised: what happens if the king fails in this duty?
Indeed, on this showing it cannot be raised, for such a
character would not be the occupant whom God has
promised for the Davidic throne. God's interest is ultimately not in the Davidic family as such, but rather in his
wider purpose of establishing justice and righteousness. It
is the task that matters, not the agent.[13]

---

[13]   It is worth pointing out again in this connection that the title 'king (*melek*)'
is not used of this figure, and some have argued that it is consciously avoided.

Fourthly, what are the conditions that need to prevail in order for rule of this nature to be inaugurated? The answer appears to be given at the start of verse 7 (Hebrew verse 6). Unfortunately, something has clearly gone wrong with the first word of the Hebrew text, so that there is an inevitable element of uncertainty about the reading. Some have used this as the basis for quite radical conjectures, but in my opinion these are not justified. Either we should translate 'There will be no end to the increase of the government and to peace',[14] or 'The government shall be great and there will be no end of peace'.[15] The difference between these two is slight, and not too serious for our present purposes.[16] 'Government' and 'peace' emerge as the necessary conditions for the proper establishment of Davidic rule.

'Government' in this context seems to be well defined by its use in the previous verse (and this fact is strengthened by the observation that the word occurs nowhere else in the Old Testament), where it is stated to be upon the

---

Harrelson's suggested explanation, followed by a number of others, would fit well with what has been seen above: 'The term *śar* [prince] is employed most frequently not of kings but of military or political leaders under the authority of a monarch. The words *miśrâ* ("dominion") and *śar* are derived from the same or related roots (*śārar* or *śārâ*). Isaiah's choice of the term *miśrâ*, which occurs only in this passage in the entire Old Testament, may be an instance of his deliberately avoiding the imagery of kingship; the coming ruler is to have an "office" under Yahweh's rule'; W. Harrelson, 'Nonroyal Motifs in the Royal Eschatology', in B.W. Anderson and W. Harrelson (eds.), *Israel's Prophetic Heritage: Essays in Honor of James Muilenburg* (London, SCM Press 1962), pp. 147–65 (151).

[14] I.e., reading with the *qere* and construing both nouns governed by *l* as dependent on 'there is no end'.

[15] I.e., deleting the first two letters of the first word (including the troublesome final *mem* in a medial position) as a dittograph of the ending of the previous word.

[16] Any 'tense' – past, present or future – would be grammatically permissible in either form of the line taken on its own; it can only be decided on the basis of the wider context, a topic taken up below.

shoulder of the child. This odd image (to which we have become immune only by dint of familiarity) must surely be related to the other 'shoulder' of verse 4. There, the people as a whole have suffered from a burdensome yoke, a bar on their shoulder and the rod of the oppressor, but this has now all been shattered by God. Thus, God has replaced an oppressive foreign rule with that of this child who is to sit on the throne of David. 'Government', therefore, seems to refer in this context to the security of the nation from external aggression.[17]

The word 'peace' is less straightforward. There are some passages closely associated with Davidic ideology, such as Psalm 72:3 cited above, which might initially lead us to suppose that it is 'prosperity' that is in view. If that is so, then we should have to suppose that 'government' refers to external affairs and 'peace' to internal; and this is by no means impossible. However, there seems to me to be evidence to support an alternative interpretation, namely that it was only under conditions of peace that the dynastic promise was issued in the first place; it would therefore be logical for the same to apply in the case of its reaffirmation, as here. In 2 Samuel 7 itself, this is differently expressed in terms of 'rest from all his enemies around him' (verses 1 and 11), and just this language is echoed by Solomon in 1 Kings 5:4. The reason for this choice of language in the Deuteronomic literature is related, of course, to the conditions as laid down by the book of Deuteronomy itself that it is only when God 'gives you rest from your enemies all around' (Deut. 12:10) that

---

[17] Whether this also includes renewed Davidic rule over the northern kingdom, as several commentators have suggested from the wider context, need not, perhaps, be answered here.

the central sanctuary is to be built in Israel.[18] Elsewhere, however, there are hints that this same general idea was expressed by use of the word 'peace'. This is most obviously the case in the Chronicler's representation of the oracle. In his parallel account to 2 Samuel 7 concerning Nathan's original delivery of the oracle, he either omits (verse 1) or changes (verse 10) the references to 'rest', doubtless because the stories of David's wars were about to fill his next three chapters.[19] When he later recaps on all this, however, he introduces alongside the 'rest' concept the idea of 'peace': 'See, a son shall be born to you; he shall be a man of 'rest'. I will give him 'rest' from all his enemies on every side; for his name shall be Solomon, and I will give peace and quiet to Israel in his days' (1 Chron. 22:9).[20] Whether or not this verse actually reflects knowledge of the wording of Isaiah 9:6–7,[21] it certainly makes clear that there were those who understood the Deuteronomic idea of 'rest' in connection with the dynastic promise in terms of 'peace'. A similar conclusion may be drawn from Micah 5:4 (ET, 5) and probably also from 1 Kings

---

[18]   The theme of the temple as a 'resting place' for the ark is undoubtedly related to this; cf. Psalm 132:8, 14. A number of other passages relating to this theme are discussed by G. von Rad, 'Es ist noch eine Ruhe vorhanden dem Volke Gottes: Eine biblische Begriffsuntersuchung', *Zwischen den Zeiten* 11 (1933), pp. 104–11 = ET, 'There Remains Still a Rest for the People of God: An Investigation of a Biblical Conception', in *The Problem of the Hexateuch and Other Essays* (Edinburgh and London, Oliver & Boyd 1966), pp. 94–102.

[19]   See my *1 and 2 Chronicles* (NCB; Grand Rapids, Eerdmans/London, Marshall, Morgan & Scott 1982), pp. 134–5.

[20]   The translation in the NRSV (as in the RSV before it) is badly misleading here, because it uses the word 'peace' throughout whereas the Hebrew uses two different words – and significant ones at that. I have restored 'rest' in the translation above to make the point clear. See further my *1 and 2 Chronicles*, pp. 154–5.

[21]   There are several potential points of contact, but it is hard to say whether they amount to anything more than the stereotyped use of formulaic language.

2:33; 5:4 (ET, 4:24); Ezekiel 34:25; 37:26. Finally, it should
not be forgotten that among David's sons not only Solomon but also Absalom (whom he had earlier anticipated
would succeed him) had names built on (or playing on)
this word.

It is thus reasonable to suppose that in a context heavily
influenced, as we have seen, by this tradition, a reference
to 'peace' would have been understood primarily in terms
of national security rather than internal prosperity or well-
being. In the line of Isaiah 9:7 which we have been
considering, therefore, it stands in more or less synon-
ymous parallelism with 'government' (NRSV, 'authority').
Once more, we see how well this part of the passage fits in
with Davidic ideology as preparation for the peculiarly
Isaianic twist later on in the verse. The opening line
effectively recaps the account given earlier in the passage
of God's deliverance from oppression, just as in the dynastic oracle it is when God has given rest/peace to his
people that he will then establish the dynastic family of
David.

At this point, however, a potential problem arises. It has
been stressed earlier that in the structure of the passage
God is solely responsible for the gift of these conditions
and that it is only at this point that the agency of the
Davidic figure comes into play in connection with establishing and upholding the throne and the kingdom with
justice and righteousness. The traditional rendering of the
child's names in verse 6, however, might suggest that, as
'Prince of Peace', he himself inaugurates these conditions,
and furthermore that as 'Mighty God' ('*ēl gibbôr*, which is
almost 'warrior God') he uses military power to achieve
this.

Without getting embroiled in the wider discussion of
these names, a recent alternative approach to them (which

seems to me to be worthy of at least very serious consideration) might be mentioned in response to this apparent difficulty. It has been usual to suppose that the child is
here given four[22] names, and their apparently exaggerated
statements with regard to a human being have been explained as conventional court language in connection with
an accession. If, however, as seems more likely, this is in
fact a birth-oracle, then the names pose a problem in any
case, quite apart from our particular difficulty just noted.
There is, therefore, merit in the suggestion[23] that we in
fact have here two theophoric names: 'a wonderful plan-
ner (is) the mighty God' and 'the Father of eternity (is) a
prince of peace'. Theophoric names, that is to say, names
that make a statement about God, were, of course, the
norm in ancient Israel, and there is good evidence that the
elements in this verse were understood as referring to
God, not a human being. In particular, *'ēl gibbôr*, 'Mighty
God', is expressly so used at 10:21. This approach, therefore, aligns these names with common practice, and cir-
cumvents the necessity to indulge in special pleading to
explain how divine titles could be ascribed to a human
king. At the same time it underlines once again that the
establishment of peace is the work of God, not the child.
Since this approach has only recently been worked out in

---

[22] Some scholars, noting that it was customary for the Egyptian king to be
given five throne names at his accession, have sought to find five here as well,
usually by reconstructing one out of the puzzling first word of verse 7
(Hebrew verse 6).

[23] See Wegner, *An Examination of Kingship*, pp. 183–201, and 'A Re-
examination', pp. 109–12, modifying and developing an earlier proposal of
W.L. Holladay, *Isaiah: Scroll of a Prophetic Heritage* (Grand Rapids, Eerdmans
1978), pp. 106–9. Wegner lists a number of additional arguments in favour of
his view to those noted above, as well as answering some potential objections.

detail it is too early to judge whether it will gain wide-spread acceptance, but for the moment there seems to be much to be said in its favour.

The final point we need to consider with regard to this passage is its time reference. The matter is confused because on the one hand most of the verbs are perfect, and might thus be thought to refer to the past, whereas the final verb, 'The zeal of the Lord of hosts will do this', is imperfect,[24] and this line could be held to dictate the intention of the whole, which has to be interpreted in terms of the so-called 'prophetic perfect'. In view of the well-known difficulties in understanding the force of 'tenses' in the Hebrew verbal system, and indeed the debate over whether they are 'tenses' at all, it seems unlikely that agreement will be reached by pursuing the discussion along those lines. Rather, it is more promising to suggest that the writer's standpoint comes to clearer expression in the phrase 'from this time onward and for evermore' (verse 7). This implies that the deliverance and new style of rule are on the point of inauguration, but that the outlook is towards the future. Such an understanding seems eminently appropriate at the time of a royal birth.[25] I have argued elsewhere that Isaiah's hopes for the future developed over the course of his long ministry[26] from an expectation of imminent change in his earlier years to a realization in his later years that this change would be delayed into the indefinite future. On the assumption that our passage comes from him its outlook would seem to fit

---

[24]　Perhaps see too the *wāw* + perfect in the last line of verse 5 (Hebrew verse 4).

[25]　Verse 6 certainly most naturally implies that the birth has taken place, as shown not only by the perfect verbs in the first line, but more tellingly by their continuation with *wāw*-consecutives.

[26]　See *The Book called Isaiah*, pp. 95–106.

in at the middle point of this development, closely in line with what we find at 8:16–18.[27]

There are many aspects of the interpretation of these opening verses of Isaiah 9 which we have not been able to explore here. Restricting ourselves to the topics closest to our central concern we may nevertheless conclude that the passage as a whole seems to announce that its readers are living at a turning point in the dynasty's fortunes and that the long hoped-for rule of justice and righteousness is about to begin. None of this implies a break in dynastic rule or a restoration of the monarchy. The predominant thought of the passage neither demands, nor is even particularly suitable to, a post-exilic date.[28] The hopes vested in the early Hezekiah or in the early Josiah would seem to be historically possible, and a case for both has been made by recent major studies. As was stressed earlier, however, this particular point is not the primary concern of the passage, and that may well be one of the reasons why it has proved so difficult to pin down its date more securely. For myself, I know of no compelling reason why Isaiah should not have written it (which is not quite the same as saying that he did!), and as I have sought to show there is much that fits well with other and broader aspects of his thought. To suggest an original setting within his ministry would be inevitably speculative, but its present redactional setting in the aftermath of the Syro-

---

[27] It is striking that in 8:18 Isaiah speaks of 'the children whom the Lord has given me', to which the first line of 9:6 is similar.

[28] For some further considerations see my 'First and Last in Isaiah', in H.A. McKay and D.J.A. Clines (eds.), *Of Prophets' Visions and the Wisdom of Sages: Essays in Honour of R. Norman Whybray on his Seventieth Birthday* (JSOTS 162; Sheffield, Sheffield Academic Press 1993), pp. 95–108. Some of the many other arguments which have been deployed in the debate are surveyed in the works cited in note 2 above.

Ephraimite crisis is by no means unreasonable. The question of how it is to be read in this wider setting (that is to say, the question whether a further layer of interpretation is implied by its present location in the book) cannot be addressed until after we have considered the Immanuel passage in our next chapter.

2) Isaiah 11:1–5

In discussions of this passage,[29] most attention has been focused on the first verse. Before we come to that, however, there are some more straightforward matters in verses 2–5 which are of direct relevance to our broader study. In order not to allow these to be overshadowed by what, from one point of view, is a secondary matter of 'authenticity', it will be convenient to treat these first.

First we are told that the spirit of the Lord will rest upon the figure who is being described. The phrase used here is not the usual idiom for the charismatic endowment of kings or of their predecessors in the so-called Judges period. The closest parallel is in Numbers 11:25–6, where God takes part of the spirit that was on Moses and transfers it to the 70 elders in order that they might help Moses in his administrative duties (though in fact the first thing that they do is prophesy). Similarly, in 2 Kings 2:15 the spirit of Elijah is said to rest upon his successor Elisha. In neither case is the 'spirit' in question explicitly termed the Spirit of the Lord, though it is probably implied in the first instance. An important element of Isaiah 11:2 is thus without parallel. Putting these two points

---

[29] There is little agreement over whether verses 6–9 form an original part of the unit or whether they have been added later. Since they are in any case of less significance for our present study, they will not be treated further here.

together, a clear picture emerges. On the one hand, the closest analogies in terms of phraseology indicate that the role in question is one of deputy, assistant or successor; while on the other hand the explicit qualification of the spirit as the Spirit of the Lord makes clear that the figure is here said to be endowed to act in that role in relation to God. Though expressed in a very different way, this is not far from the conclusions we reached with regard to the figure in chapter 9 and, interestingly enough, there is further support for the comparison in that 'the spirit of counsel and might (*'ēṣâ ûgᵉbûrâ*)' may well be a conscious echo of what was interpreted above as the first of the two theophoric names in 9:6.[30]

Secondly, the role for which this figure is so well suited is described in verses 3–5,[31] and it is without doubt primarily judicial. The repetition of verbs in verses 3 and 4*a* emphasizes that the poor and the meek will receive a fair hearing, unprejudiced by the corruption which more privileged members of society might seek to introduce into the judicial process:

> *He shall not judge by what his eyes see,*
> * or decide by what his ears hear;*
> *but with righteousness he shall judge the poor,*
> * and decide with equity for the meek of the earth.*

Such notions are fully in line with the wider Davidic traditions, as attested especially in Psalm 72, and beyond that they are shared to a considerable extent with wider ancient Near Eastern ideas of kingship.

---

[30] The attempt by Laato, *Who is Immanuel?*, pp. 204–5, to find further echoes of the names of 9:6 in 11:1–9 is not convincing, however.

[31] A strong case can be made out for the view that 3*a*, 'His delight shall be in the fear of the Lord', should be deleted as a corrupt dittograph of the preceding line.

At first, verse 4*b* might appear to introduce a new and wider application of this role than what we have seen hitherto:

> *he shall strike the earth with the rod of his mouth,*
> *and with the breath of his lips he shall kill the wicked.*

However, two factors encourage caution in drawing far-reaching conclusions from this. In the first place Wildberger points to similar ideas current in both Egypt and Mesopotamia, even though in the Hebrew Bible the notion of powerful word is more normally associated with prophecy than with kingship.[32] It is likely, therefore, that the function here would have been as instantly recognizable as was that of the previous lines. And, in the second place, we should not deduce that this function is here extended on a universal scale. (Contrast especially Psalm 2:8–9, which superficially has some points in common.) If the Hebrew text is sound, 'the earth' would have to take its meaning from the use of the same word in the previous line, where it clearly refers narrowly to 'the land' – home territory, so to speak. In fact, however, it is more probable that we should read 'the violent' instead of 'the earth' here,[33] in which case the restriction is even clearer. In short, verse 4*b* does little more than amplify on the judicial role of the previous lines.

Thirdly, does this all mean, then, that this passage has less to contribute to our overall theme than chapter 9 –

---

[32]   Wildberger, *Jesaja 1*, p. 454 = ET, p. 477.

[33]   *'āriṣ* instead of *'ereṣ*. This is admittedly conjectural, but it improves the parallelism, avoids an unattractive repetition, and removes the difficulty of an impersonal object of 'strike' in a context where all the other objects in a similar position are personal. There are, in fact, several passages in Isaiah where the occurrence of a word has caused assimilation to it of a similar-looking word shortly after, so that this may have been the failing of a particular scribe relatively early in the textual transmission of the book; see the notes on 1:7 and 6:11 in *The Book Called Isaiah*, pp. 245 and 249.

compatible with it, certainly, but ultimately more conventional because lacking a peculiarly Isaianic twist, such as we found in the earlier passage? Not necessarily! I should like to suggest that the somewhat conventional description of the king's role in verse 4 has been framed by material of a more peculiarly Isaianic stamp.

In verse 3, 'what his eyes see' and 'what his ears hear' is strikingly reminiscent of Isaiah 6:10, 'look with their eyes, and listen with their ears'. The similarities are, perhaps, closer than appears in the NRSV translation: the verbs of 6:10 have become their cognate nouns in 11:3; 'eyes' and 'ears' are in each case the same, of course. And the probability that we should associate these two verses is strengthened by the observation that the language of 11:3 is without parallel in the Old Testament.[34] Since the relevant paragraph in Isaiah 6 has exerted a pervasive influence on many parts of the book of Isaiah,[35] it seems probable that this is the explanation for the otherwise unparalleled language of 11:3 as well. The purpose, of course, will have been to draw a contrast between Isaiah's contemporaries as depicted in chapter 6 and the character of the coming ideal king, but applied now in particular to the judicial sphere.

The wording of verse 5, the other half of our 'frame', is also suggestive:

---

[34] *mišma' 'ōzen* occurs nowhere else; *mar'ēh 'ênayīm* does occur occasionally elsewhere, but not in legal or judicial contexts, nor in connection with hearing.

[35] See R.E. Clements, 'Beyond Tradition-History: Deutero-Isaianic Development of First Isaiah's Themes', *JSOT* 31 (1985), pp. 95-113 = *Old Testament Prophecy: from Oracles to Canon* (Louisville, Westminster John Knox Press 1996), pp. 78–92; *idem*, 'Patterns in the Prophetic Canon: Healing the Blind and the Lame', in G.M. Tucker, D.L. Petersen and R.R. Wilson (eds.), *Canon, Theology, and Old Testament Interpretation: Essays in Honor of Brevard S. Childs* (Philadelphia, Fortress Press 1988), pp. 189–200; see too my *The Book Called Isaiah*, pp. 46–51.

Righteousness (ṣedeq) shall be the belt around his waist,
and faithfulness (hā'ᵉmûnâ) the belt around his loins.

The language of righteousness and faithfulness brings us back to the centre of the vocabulary group we introduced in the previous chapter. The first word picks up explicitly on the judicial role in verse 4*a*, but by putting it now in parallel with the broader 'faithfulness' (cf. 1:21, 26), it suggests that that role is to be seen as an example, only, of the wider characteristics which mark the work of the ideal king. Indeed, this concern may explain why we do not find here the commoner 'justice and righteousness' so central to the passage in chapter 9. This king will 'judge (*šāpaṭ*)' in righteousness; had 'justice (*mišpāṭ*)' then appeared in verse 5 we should have been tempted to take the verse as merely a recapitulation of verse 4. As it is, however, the introduction of the alternative language of 'faithfulness' brings the passage as a whole into the wider sphere of the king as upholder of the ideal society.[36]

To sum up thus far, we may conclude that there is a close parallel between the king as depicted here and his role as teased out from chapter 9. In both cases, though in different ways, their function as (merely) an agent of God is emphasized[37] and, although the common ancient Near Eastern ideal of the king as supreme judge of his people is more marked in chapter 11, both passages ultimately testify to his important part in establishing the kind of

---

[36] Although the related word 'truth (*'ᵉmet*)' occurs elsewhere in combination with 'justice and righteousness' in royal contexts, this is not the case with *'ᵉmûnâ* as it occurs here; cf. Weinfeld, 'Justice and Righteousness'.

[37] This point is also emphasized by J.J.M. Roberts, 'The Divine King and the Human Community in Isaiah's Vision of the Future', in H.B. Huffmon, F.A. Spina and A.R.W. Green (eds.), *The Quest for the Kingdom of God: Studies in Honor of George E. Mendenhall* (Winona Lake, Ind., Eisenbrauns 1983), pp. 127–36.

society God desires for his people, a society which develops naturally from a correct understanding of God and his relationship with Israel.

We now turn to the first verse of the chapter:

> *A shoot shall come out from the stump of Jesse,*
> *and a branch shall grow out of his roots.*

It is on these lines that most attention in scholarly discussion has been focused. In particular, they have been thought to provide the main evidence for regarding the passage as a whole as post-exilic in date, as well as featuring in analyses of the passage's redactional setting within its wider context in the book.

We may start most conveniently by expressing agreement with those who, at least since the time of Herder,[38] have pointed out that the chapter division with which we are familiar is unfortunate at this point. Not only does the verse begin with the conjunction 'and/but' (passed over in the NRSV translation), but the imagery of a felled tree looks like a direct continuation of the last two verses of chapter 10:

> *Look, the Sovereign, the Lord of hosts,*
> *will lop the boughs with terrifying power;*
> *the tallest trees will be cut down,*
> *and the lofty will be brought low.*
> *He will hack down the thickets of the forest with an axe,*
> *and Lebanon with its majestic trees will fall.* (10:33–4)

---

[38] J.G. von Herder, *Vom Geist der Ebräischen Poesie*, 2: *Eine Anleitung für die Liebhaber derselben und der ältesten Geschichte des menschlichen Geistes* (Leipzig, J.R. Barth 1825³), pp. 406–8. The arguments either way in modern scholarship are summarized and documented by Wegner, *An Examination of Kingship*, pp. 246–9. Barth, *Die Jesaja-Worte*, pp. 57–76, also strongly affirms this connection, though he maintains that 10:33b–34 has been added later. Using the same arguments as those noted above he therefore sees an immediate connection between 10:33a and 11:1–5.

Establishing this link does not, however, immediately solve all our problems, because there is then the further dispute whether 10:33–4 refers to judgment on the Assyrians, or whether it refers to judgment on the people of Judah. A case can be made out for either interpretation.

In sorting out this ambiguity I find the discussion by Nielsen to be the most helpful.[39] In brief, she demonstrates that the first interpretation (i.e. that the reference is to the Assyrians) depends upon the passage's present redactional setting. Starting at 10:5, the whole passage is built up into two parallel panels of three sections each. Disregarding minor glosses and additions, we have 10:5–15 and 10:28–32 describing the Assyrian's pride, followed in each case by a judgment oracle (10:16–19 and 10:33–4), and then finally an indication that the fall of Assyria will lead to a positive future for Israel (10:20–7 and 11:1–9). We note further that the judgment oracle in each panel makes use of tree imagery: a forest fire in the first case and forest-felling in the second.

Few would doubt that material of varying origins has been brought together to assemble this tidy arrangement, and it follows, of course, that the earliest date for this interpretation would be the date of whatever is reckoned to be the latest section within the whole. Beyond that, however, it also frees us to inquire after the significance of each constituent section before it was assembled into its present wider context. If, then, we look at 10:33–4 on its own, we are at once struck by its close comparability with 2:9–17, a passage considered in some detail in the previous chapter. It shares a good deal of common vocabulary as well as similarity of general theme. There is thus a

---

[39] K. Nielsen, *There is Hope for a Tree: The Tree as Metaphor in Isaiah* (JSOTS 65; Sheffield, Sheffield Academic Press 1989), pp. 123–44.

strong probability that it originally represented a comparable threat against all that is proud in the land. If so, 11:1 would not refer so much to a restoration after foreign invasion as to the hope of a fresh beginning after God has purged his people by some unstated means.

On this basis it is possible to mount a reasonable case for the Isaianic authorship of the opening verses of chapter 11.[40] If our understanding of the redactional development of chapters 10–11 as a whole is sound, then our particular passage must predate the emphasis on the promised fall of Assyria. A strong body of current opinion would put that promise some time in the reign of king Josiah,[41] while others still maintain that it is Isaianic. Either way, our passage was first written before that, being originally intended for a different purpose. In further support of that conclusion, we may note with many other commentators that 10:33–4 is thoroughly Isaianic in both theme and wording, and that the role of a Davidic figure in the restoration of society after God's purging is closely parallel to what we have already seen in chapter 9. A

---

[40] An additional small argument is advanced by Cazelles, 'De l'idéologie royale', who observes that the parallelism of *ṣedeq* with *mîšôr* in verse 4 is close to early, especially Phoenician, usage, whereas, on the basis of the Psalms, it appears to have dropped out of use by the post–exilic period.

[41] Indeed, we may note that some scholars have argued that the king in 11:1–5(9) is himself Josiah; cf. Vermeylen, *Du prophète Isaïe*, pp. 269–75; Sweeney, *Isaiah 1–39*, pp. 204–5. The argument from the youth of the Davidic figure is strongest with regard to 11:6, which we take to be later in any case; that 11:1 refers to a young king is pure surmise. Furthermore, in terms of those who argue for a Josianic redaction of Isaiah's words on the ground that it was only then that an Assyrian withdrawal was a realistic possibility, such a situation will not have obtained as early as Josiah's accession; cf. N. Na'aman, 'The Kingdom of Judah under Josiah', *Tel Aviv* 18 (1991) pp. 3–71. Of course, it is more than likely that this passage would have been read with renewed hopes in Josiah's time, but that is not a sufficient argument for dating its composition then. It is noteworthy that neither of the two chief proponents of a Josianic redaction do so: Barth believes that the passage is authentically Isaianic, while Clements dates it to the post-exilic period.

further argument, which I have not seen noted elsewhere, derives from a consideration of 11:10. That verse clearly refers back to 11:1, but it interprets 'the root of Jesse' in terms of the 'signal for the nations' which follows in verse 12, where it is associated with the regathering of the dispersed exiles. This looks very much like the kind of development of the understanding of the ideas of kingship which we have seen is typical of the book of Isaiah as a whole, and suggests that 11:1, with its indication of a new individual Davidic ruler, is earlier than the interpretation given it in the exilic/post-exilic development which the second half of chapter 11 shares.

The only serious argument against this conclusion is the proposal that 'the stump of Jesse' in 11:1 presupposes the fall of the Davidic monarchy. If this verse be read as the direct continuation of 10:33–4, however, the stump imagery may be seen to derive directly from the picture of judgment there described and so does not necessarily presuppose any specific historical incident.[42] But what of Jesse? Does the fact that the writer goes back behind David imply that the house of David has fallen? If that were the intention, we might suppose rather that he would have referred to the stump of David, just as Amos 9:11

---

[42] Indeed, there are those who believe that the original anti-Judean aim of this saying (as opposed to its later anti-Assyrian redactional reuse) included a hidden reference to God's judgment on the currently reigning Davidic king, since 10:33a may refer to a single tree, and Lebanon also has royal overtones in several other contexts. If this is true, '10.33–11.9 forms a consciously created entity that interprets the *fall of the proud king of Judah* as resulting from Yahweh's righteous *punishment*, but then proclaims that the dynasty will nevertheless endure; a new king, a *new David* will appear . . . The connexion between tree-felling and new sprouting is as organic as it is possible to imagine: from the lineage of the old king is born the new king of Judah'; Nielsen, *There is Hope*, p. 136, following a detailed discussion.

speaks of 'the booth of David that is fallen'.[43] The point of referring to Jesse seems to be not so much negatively to dwell on the nature of the judgment which has fallen, as positively to make the point that the new ruler will be a second David.[44] Though the imagery is completely different, the underlying idea does not seem to be very far removed from that of 28:16–17, where the establishment of a new or renewed Zion speaks of a foundation stone without commentators necessarily drawing the conclusion that the old Zion has been physically razed to the ground. In both cases the need for such imagery certainly implies strong criticism of the prevailing *status quo*. In neither, however, is there any necessary implication that the institution in question is already a matter of the past. The most which might be deduced (and this is already a matter of some moment) is that Isaiah does not seem to be particularly concerned with a narrowly defined dynastic succession. His commitment is not so much to the next king in the biological line of descent, but more to the Davidic ideal of leadership as such. This, of course, is very much in line with the results of our discussion of 9:1–7 above.

I conclude, therefore, that 11:1–5 originally expressed a comparatively modest hope by Isaiah that the new society which he anticipated being established after the threatened judgment would be led both judicially and more broadly by a righteous Davidic-type figure. The shift in emphasis which came about with the redactional reuse of

---

[43] It is noteworthy in this connection that in the several references to this passage in the Qumran scrolls where a messianic interpretation seems to be advanced, 'the stump of Jesse' is said to be 'the branch of David'; for references and discussion, see conveniently K.E. Pomykala, *The Davidic Dynasty Tradition in Early Judaism: Its History and Significance for Messianism* (Atlanta, Scholars Press 1995), pp. 171–216.
[44] See Wegner, *An Examination of Kingship*, p. 233, with further references.

10:33–4 as referring to the downfall of Assyria entailed an accompanying movement towards a more 'messianic' application of 11:1–5,[45] even though the new David remains, apparently, within the historical continuum, and has not yet been cast as an eschatological figure.

3) Isaiah 16:4*b*–5

These verses appear to present us with a generally neglected royal or messianic prophecy.[46] They are rendered by the NRSV as follows:

> *When the oppressor is no more,*
> *and destruction has ceased,*
> *and marauders have vanished from the land,*
> *then a throne shall be established in steadfast love*
> *in the tent of David,*
> *and on it shall sit in faithfulness*
> *a ruler who seeks justice*
> *and is swift to do what is right.*

The points of contact with what we have already studied in some detail are obvious, and need not be elaborated again. It is, perhaps, sufficient to draw attention in particular to the points of comparison with 9:7, with which this passage has most in common: the language of establishing a throne, the language of 'justice' and 'righteousness' (here *ṣedeq*, 'what is right', rather than *ṣᵉdāqâ*), the reference to David while avoiding explicit use of the title 'king (*melek*)',

---

[45] If verses 6–9 are indeed a secondary addition to the passage (as I am inclined to think on other grounds), then they will have greatly contributed to this shift in interpretation.

[46] There is no discussion, for instance, in Wegner, *An Examination of Kingship*, nor in W.C. Kaiser, *The Messiah in the Old Testament* (Grand Rapids, Zondervan 1995), nor in the (admittedly selective) survey by Roberts, 'The Old Testament's Contribution'.

the fact that this will follow liberation from a time of oppression, and the fact that this figure is the recipient of these blessings, rather than their active initiator. To this list, we may add two other points: 'steadfast love' and 'faithfulness (here ' ^{e}*met* rather than " ^{e}*mûnâ*)' have both featured in our previous discussion, while the word translated 'ruler' in verse 5 is the same as that for 'judge' in, for instance, 11:3–4.

Beyond that, however, everything else about these verses in their wider context is fraught with uncertainty, making it extremely difficult to know whether it is safe to use this material as part of our portrayal of Isaiah's own expectation or whether we are dealing here with a later 'maverick' (see above, p. 11) interpolation.

The passage comes in the context of two chapters (Isaiah 15–16) which are headed 'An oracle concerning Moab' (15:1), one of the oracles against the nations which make up the bulk of chapters 13–23. One of the very few points of agreement among the commentators on this passage is that the last two verses of the oracle (16:13–14) indicate clearly that we are here dealing with more than one level of composition: 'This was the word that the Lord spoke concerning Moab in the past. But now the Lord says . . .'[47] That still leaves open two major questions, however, namely, whether the rest of the passage is a compositional unity, and what the chronological framework implied by 'the past' and 'now' of 16:13–14 refers to.

A further complicating factor is introduced by the observation that much of chapter 15 and of 16:6–11 has a parallel in Jeremiah 48, though the material does not all

---

[47] Compare the similar situation at 21:16–17.

appear in the same order.[48] By general consent, either Jeremiah is dependent upon Isaiah, or else both drew independently on a common original. Strikingly, however, 16:1–5, within which the passage that concerns us particularly falls, is the one extensive section to have no parallel in Jeremiah. Although it might initially be supposed that this is due to no more than the selection of material by the author of Jeremiah 48, Gray has added two supporting arguments for the more natural conclusion that these verses are an addition to the original composition. First, he observes that the shared material comprises what he calls an 'elegy' in three stanzas with a refrain-like element in 15:4*b*–5*a* , 16:7 and 11, and that there are roughly equal amounts of material between each occurrence of the refrain. Were 16:1–5 to be included, however, this balance would be seriously distorted. Secondly, the 'elegy' is descriptive, and when the first person singular occurs (e.g. at 15:5; 16:9, 11) it refers to the poet. On the other hand, the material in both Isaiah and Jeremiah which the two passages do not share in common is more 'prophetic' in character, and introduces God as the speaker (e.g. 15:9*b*).[49]

Finally, the further possibility has been frequently canvassed that even within 16:1–5 our particular verses are a still later element. The start of the chapter seems to be a petition by the Moabites or their leader for sanctuary in Jerusalem following the invasion of the land, described in chapter 15. It looks as though the invasion affects the

---

[48] See the tables in, for instance, H. Wildberger, *Jesaja, 2. Teilband: Jesaja 13–27* (BKAT 10/2; Neukirchen-Vluyn, Neukirchener Verlag 1978), pp. 607–9, and Vermeylen, *Du prophète Isaïe*, p. 304.

[49] G.B. Gray, *A Critical and Exegetical Commentary on the Book of Isaiah I–XXVII* (ICC; Edinburgh, T. & T. Clark 1912), pp. 271–2. Gray also stresses that the text of these chapters is difficult and apparently corrupt, so that reconstruction of its history is inevitably hampered by many uncertainties.

northern part of Moab, to judge by the place-names in
15:2–4, with the consequence that the refugees first flee to
the southern part of the country (15:5–7) and that they (or
some of them) then turn to Judah for sanctuary (16:1,
3–4a). For a considerable number of commentators,[50]
verse 6 represents the immediate reply of the Judeans to
this request, so that 16:4b–5 has to be regarded as a later
addition, attached by the catchword 'destroyer (*šôdēd*)'/
'destruction (*šōd*)'.[51] Against this, however, Wildberger argues that since verse 6 is part of the material which is
shared with Jeremiah 48 it can hardly serve as the response to material which was added only later; rather,
these opening verses of the chapter are a relatively self-
contained, and late, expression of a messianic hope. So far
as the one responsible for incorporating it is concerned, it
is not that the refugees are fleeing from some historical
catastrophe only to be told that they will be received when
oppression has ceased and a Davidic Messiah is established. Rather, the whole passage anticipates the day when
the nations, here typified by Moab, will come with tribute
to Zion, as envisaged in Isa. 2:2–4.[52]

It seems probable, therefore, that this oracle against
Moab has developed through time, but unfortunately this
still does not answer the question of when the process
started and finished. Several historical settings have been
proposed for each part of the passage, but the case seems
always to be circumstantial, so that it is difficult to arrive

---

[50] E.g. K. Marti, *Das Buch Jesaja* (KHAT 10; Tübingen, J.C.B. Mohr [Paul
Siebeck] 1900), p. 137; O. Kaiser, *Der Prophet Jesaja, Kapitel 13–39* (ATD 18;
Göttingen, Vandenhoeck & Ruprecht 1973), p. 61 = ET, *Isaiah 13–39: A
Commentary* (OTL; London, SCM Press 1974), p. 71.
[51] Cf. Vermeylen, *Du prophète Isaïe*, p.307.
[52] Wildberger, *Jesaja* 2, pp. 600–1, 619–24. Note that Wildberger brackets
verse 2 from his consideration as a misplaced fragment, probably from
chapter 15.

at anything approaching certainty.[53] The fact remains that the passage does not supply us with any clear historical references, and it would not be difficult to list objections to each of the proposals which have been advanced.

In the face of so many uncertainties it would clearly be unwise to allow this passage to influence our overall analysis too much. There is, however, one aspect of Wildberger's study to which it is worth drawing attention, namely the phraseology used in verse 5 to describe the figure of the ruler. We have already seen that it shows a considerable degree of similarity to that in chapters 9 and 11, even though some minor differences were also observed. Within that similarity, however, there are some minor distinctive features which may nevertheless be revealing. First, he is described as one who 'seeks justice (*dōrēš mišpāṭ*)'. This phrase is never used elsewhere of a royal figure, and while it does occur in the context of a general ethical exhortation (1:17), the parallelism here (see below), together with its application to a single individual, points rather in the direction of Ezra who set his heart 'to study (= seek, *lidrôš*) the law of the Lord' (Ezr. 7:10). Secondly, and in parallel, he is said to be 'swift to do what is right (*mᵉhîr ṣedeq*)'. The adjective here translated 'swift' occurs only four times in the Old Testament, of which one is again concerned with Ezra, 'a scribe skilled (*māhîr*) in the law of Moses' (Ezr. 7:6), and another occurs

---

[53] For a summary of earlier views, together with the addition of a new one, see T.G. Smothers, 'Isaiah 15–16', in J.W. Watts and P.R. House (eds.), *Forming Prophetic Literature: Essays on Isaiah and the Twelve in Honor of John D.W. Watts* (JSOTS 235; Sheffield, Sheffield Academic Press 1996), pp. 70-84. Most recently, Sweeney, *Isaiah 1–39*, pp. 240–51, has proposed that the bulk of the passage reflects Tiglath-Pileser III's invasion of Aram and Israel during the Syro-Ephraimite crisis, with 16:1-5 as an appeal by the king of Moab for temporary sanctuary in Jerusalem, followed by the re-establishment of Judean hegemony over Moab. The rereading in 16:13-14 reflects the later hopes of Josiah to extend his rule over Moabite territory.

in a comparable context – the 'ready scribe' of Psalm 45:1 (Hebrew verse 2).[54] There is therefore more than a hint here that this character is being presented in scribal guise. Thirdly, this may be related to the phrase 'the tent of David'.[55] This expression occurs nowhere else,[56] and it is initially unexpected in the present context, where one might, perhaps, have anticipated a reference to the palace or the like.[57] However, the sanctuary is not infrequently referred to as a tent. This applies not only to the desert sanctuary but also (no doubt by extension and in order to indicate continuity) to the temple, 'especially in connection with the idea of asylum (Ps. 27:5; 61:5[4]; cf. 15:1; 78:60; and Isa. 33:20f.)'.[58] Since the context of Isaiah 16 is precisely that of asylum-seeking, it is probable that this furnishes us with the clue to the coining of the phrase 'the tent of David'. Combined with the scribal allusions mentioned earlier, this seems to point us in the direction of a priestly context for our Davidic figure, something we have not encountered hitherto. In the absence of any other firm evidence to the contrary it is therefore probably best to see these verses as post-exilic, when such concerns began to come to the fore.

---

[54] The fourth occurrence is Proverbs 22:29.

[55] On metrical grounds Wildberger regards this phrase as a later gloss on the passage. This is not certain, of course, but if true it will merely indicate that the direction of interpretation which we have already begun to see was subsequently taken one step further.

[56] It should not, of course, be confused with the 'booth of David' of Amos 9:11.

[57] One might, perhaps, compare David's 'tent of my house' in Psalm 132:3, which Wildberger fails to mention.

[58] So K. Koch, *TDOT* 1, אהל p. 127. See too 1 Chronicles 9:23, and note that the introduction to the key dynastic text, 2 Samuel 7, begins by David contrasting the fact that 'I am living in a house of cedar, but the ark of God stays in a tent' (verse 2).

I therefore conclude that Isaiah 16:4*b*–5 is indeed a 'maverick' messianic passage within the book of Isaiah. It certainly draws on the broader stream of ideas which have already occupied us, but it turns them in an idiosyncratic direction, an unexpected variation on the major theme. Its puzzling incorporation in an oracle against Moab is a further indication of its uncharacteristic nature. If it is indeed post-exilic, however, then it is of particular note as comprising the most overtly 'messianic' text (in the technical sense) that we have yet encountered.

4) Isaiah 32:1–5

The opening verse of Isaiah 32 is rendered as follows in the NRSV:

> See, a king will reign in righteousness,
> and princes will rule with justice.

As is only to be expected, there have been many proposed identifications for the king referred to (such as Hezekiah, Josiah, or the Messiah) as well as disagreements over whether the passage was written by Isaiah himself, by one of his early (pre-exilic) editors, or by a late post-exilic redactor.[59]

On this occasion I believe it is possible to cut through much of the debate by proposing that the nature of this verse has been generally misunderstood. As we shall see immediately it has a number of features which distinguish it from those we have studied so far, features on which some commentators have seized to make the case that this passage cannot come from Isaiah. It would be a mistake,

---

[59] Once again, the various opinions are helpfully surveyed most recently by Wegner, *An Examination of Kingship*, pp. 275–301.

however, to move straight from this observation to a discussion of authenticity. Rather, it should lead us in the first instance to inquire more carefully about the form of this verse. In short, building on the insights of the minority of scholars[60] who regard this verse as hypothetical in form ('If . . .'), and so link it directly with the next verse ('then . . .'), I suggest that it takes the form of a proverb.

Among the reasons for this conclusion we may briefly note the following arguments: Unlike any of the passages we have studied so far this one refers explicitly to a king (*melek*), but it lacks the definite article and is set in parallel with 'princes'. Taken together, these points suggest that we are not here dealing with one specific king, but with any king – kings in general, even. The point is not to single out one king from others, but to refer to him as a leader of the people, just as princes are too. Next, the verbs in this verse are in the imperfect, and in each case the verb and the noun derive from the same root – *yimlok-melek* and *śārîm . . . yāśōrû*. Both these stylistic features are appropriate, each in its own way, to the proverbial form. Furthermore, against the run of what we have repeatedly seen to be the style both of Isaiah and of his later imitators, the key words 'justice' and 'righteousness (here *ṣedeq* rather than the usually preferred form *ṣᵉdāqâ*)' are given in reverse order. As we shall see, by putting *ṣedeq* first, and so giving it greater prominence, the thought of the verse is brought very much into line with the outlook of the wisdom writers. Significantly, when these key words are picked up

---

[60] See, for instance, E.J. Kissane, *The Book of Isaiah*, 1 (Dublin, The Richview Press 1941), pp. 357–63; R.B.Y Scott, 'The Book of Isaiah, Chapters 1–39', *IB* 5, pp. 342–3; Kaiser, *Jesaja 13–39*, pp. 254–6 = *Isaiah 13-39*, pp. 320–2; W.H. Irwin, *Isaiah 28–33: Translation with Philological Notes* (Biblica et Orientalia 30; Rome 1977), p. 120; J.D.W. Watts, *Isaiah 1–33* (WBC 24; Waco, Word Books, 1985) Biblical Institute Press pp. 411–12.

and developed later on in the chapter (verse 16) they are used in their usual form and order, giving the impression of an Isaianic interpretation of a non-Isaianic saying. And finally, several of the verses in the passage following this one are also proverbial in nature, as most commentators recognize (see certainly verses 6–8, but probably verses 4 and 5 as well), so that it would not be surprising to find verse 1 taking the same form too. We might therefore propose as an alternative translation: 'Behold, a king should reign in the interests of[61] righteousness, and princes rule for the furtherance of justice'.

As already mentioned, both the wording and the sentiment of this verse have some close parallels in the wisdom literature.[62] The most striking example of this is Proverbs 8:15–16, where in the first half of each verse we find precisely the same subjects and verbs as in our verse, as well as a generally similar outlook:

> *By me kings reign* (meˡākîm yimlōkû),
>   *and rulers decree what is just* (ṣedeq),
> *by me rulers rule* (śārîm yāśōrû),
>   *and nobles, all who govern rightly.*

The 'me' of this verse is, of course, wisdom, who here assumes a role very similar to that of the Egyptian goddess

---

[61] The translation of the preposition *l* has been variously discussed. The case for understanding it as an expression of purpose, as well as an exposure of the weaknesses in other views (widespread though they are) is carefully argued by J.W. Olley, 'Notes on Isaiah xxxii 1, xlv 19, 23 and lxiii 1', VT 33 (1983), pp. 446–53, and his position is adopted here.

[62] There has been a long history of discussion about the connections between Isaiah and the wisdom tradition. I have sought to summarize this, and to offer some guidelines for future work, in 'Isaiah and the Wise', in J. Day, R.P. Gordon and H.G.M. Williamson (eds.), *Wisdom in Ancient Israel: Essays in Honour of J.A. Emerton* (Cambridge, Cambridge University Press 1995), pp. 133–41.

ma'at, 'the foundation of right rule'.[63] Elsewhere in Proverbs the principles she embodies are frequently assumed by 'righteousness', as, for instance, at Proverbs 16:12, 'the throne is established by righteousness' (exactly the same thought is expressed at 25:5, and cf. 20:28).[64] Though it would therefore be tempting to look for such notions in Isaiah 32 as well, this would be a mistake. Righteousness and justice there are the purpose of rule, as elsewhere in Isaiah, not the more abstract principle on which such rule is founded. And that a king and rulers should govern in such a way as to establish justice is also a common thought in Proverbs, for example at 16:10, 13; 20:8, 26; 29:4, 14; 31:4–5.

We have here, then, two apparently separate lines of thought. The danger of confusing them comes about because the same range of vocabulary is used in Hebrew to express them both. In the one case 'righteousness' may be the foundation principle upon which rule is based, in the other 'righteousness' is the goal towards which proper rule should be directed. We should note finally, however, that this latter thought also leads to the establishment of the throne, according to Proverbs 29:14, and it is with this

---

[63] Cf. D.J. Reimer, 'צדק', in W.A. VanGemeren (ed.) *The New International Dictionary of Old Testament Theology and Exegesis*, 3 (Carlisle, Paternoster Press, 1997), p. 746. See further C. Kayatz, *Studien zu Proverbien 1–9: Eine form- und motivgeschichtliche Untersuchung unter Einbeziehung ägyptischen Vergleichsmaterials* (WMANT 22; Neukirchen-Vluyn, Neukirchener Verlag 1966), and for the broader idea within the ancient Near East as a whole H.H. Schmid, *Gerechtigkeit als Weltordnung: Hintergrund und Geschichte des alttestamentlichen Gerechtigkeitsbegriffes* (BhistTh 40; Tübingen, J.C.B. Mohr [Paul Siebeck] 1968).

[64] For righteousness and justice as the foundation of the divine throne see Psalms 89:15[14] and 97:2. This too is paralleled in other ancient Near Eastern texts; cf. H.-J. Kraus, *Psalmen, 2. Teilband: Psalmen 60–150* (BKAT 15/2; Neukirchen-Vluyn, Neukirchener Verlag 1978⁵), p. 788 = ET, *Psalms 60–150: A Commentary* (Minneapolis, Augsburg 1989), p. 207, and H. Brunner, 'Gerechtigkeit als Fundament des Thrones', *VT* 8 (1958), pp. 426–8.

that we may suppose that Isaiah would have agreed most heartily:

> *If a king judges the poor with equity* (be' ᵉmet),
>   *his throne will be established for ever.*

We have in Isaiah 32:1, therefore, a general saying about rulership. It is not possible to decide whether Isaiah coined it himself, or whether it was in general circulation for him to cite. (The slight differences we have noted from Isaiah's own usual formulations might incline us slightly towards the latter possibility.)

In the following verses consequences are drawn if such guidelines are followed. First, such rulers will be a protection for their people:

> *Each will be like a hiding place from the wind,*
>   *a covert from the tempest,*
> *like streams of water in a dry place,*
>   *like the shade of a great rock in a weary land.*

As Wildberger has shown,[65] the imagery used here was widespread in ancient Near Eastern royal ideology. However, with regard to the Hebrew Bible itself this is not the case; rather, the commonest use of these images by far is in association with the role of God towards his people.[66] From what we have seen previously, however, it would not be surprising if Isaiah had applied this to the consequence of righteous rule, since for him the rule of God and of his appointed king coincide so closely. Interestingly, the closest parallel to our verse occurs in the so-called Isaiah Apocalypse, at Isaiah 25:4–5, where the imagery is again applied to God:

---

[65] Wildberger, *Jesaja* 3, pp. 1255–6.
[66] See Roberts, 'The Divine King', pp. 133–4.

For you have been a refuge to the poor,
  a refuge to the needy in their distress,
a shelter from the rainstorm
  and a shade from the heat.
When the blast of the ruthless was like a winter rainstorm,
  the noise of aliens like heat in a dry place,
you subdued the heat with the shade of clouds . . .

The coincidences of vocabulary are so strong here that it seems clear we have a direct literary allusion. This is a subject which has been carefully analysed by Sweeney, who shows that it is characteristic of the Isaiah Apocalypse (Isaiah 24–27) to cite from elsewhere in the Isaiah tradition (as well as from elsewhere in the Hebrew Bible) in a consistently 'universalizing' direction, so that we should certainly hold that the same is the case here.[67] This is an important conclusion, because it demonstrates that this part of Isaiah 32 predates the Isaiah Apocalypse. That does not settle its date in an absolute sense, of course, but it is clearly in line with the direction in which we have been moving.

The next verse, 32:3, gives us further evidence to support the case:

Then the eyes of those who have sight will not be closed,
  and the ears of those who have hearing will listen.

It is obvious that this anticipated blessing is a reversal of the 'hardening' passage in 6:9-10. As was noted above in connection with chapter 11 the theme of this passage is one which has exerted a particularly strong influence on the whole of the Isaianic tradition. At this point, however, we need to note in slightly greater detail how that theme

---

[67] M.A. Sweeney, 'Textual Citations in Isaiah 24–27: Toward an Understanding of the Redactional Function of Chapters 24–27 in the Book of Isaiah', *JBL* 107 (1988), pp. 39–52. I have sought to build on Sweeney's insights in my *The Book Called Isaiah*, pp. 180–3.

was developed in order to be able to locate our present
verse within it. In brief, the main point to observe is that
in the second half of the book there is something of a shift,
in that the specific words 'blind' and 'deaf' are introduced
into the phraseology as though there is a movement from
the metaphorical to the literal,[68] and that this feature
becomes even more marked in passages relating to the
theme which, though included within the first half of the
book, are without doubt to be regarded as even later
additions – notably at 29:18 and 35:5–6.[69] In both passages
the healing, as it has now become, is put into the eschatological future. Our verse 32:3 is different in each respect
from this, however. There is no reference to the blind and
the deaf as such, and the overall context is not that of the
eschatological future. By contrast, the language is very
much closer to that of Isaiah himself. In addition to the
fact that 'the eyes of those who see' and 'the ears of those
who hear' is as similar as the context will allow to 'see with
their eyes' and 'hear with their ears' in 6:10, we should
note in particular that the rare verb *š"*, 'be smeared over,
closed', is used in both verses (at 6:10, NRSV translates 'and
shut their eyes'). This verb also occurs twice at 29:9 (NRSV:
'blind yourselves and be blind'), a verse generally agreed to
be by Isaiah himself. Indeed, these references may account for the sum total of uses of this verb in the Old
Testament, although it is difficult to be certain because of

---

[68]   This is noted especially by Clements in the works cited at note 35 above.
[69]   The same may well be the case at 33:23, though the matter is there
complicated by textual uncertainty. Contrast NRSV, 'Then prey and spoil in
abundance will be divided; even the lame will fall to plundering', and NEB,
'Then the blind man shall have a full share of the spoil and the lame shall take
part in the pillage', following the Targum; cf. G.R. Driver, 'Isaiah i–xxxix', *JSS*
13 (1968), pp. 36–57 (54), and Wildberger, *Jesaja* 3, pp. 1311–12.

possible confusion between it and the similar *š'h* else-where.[70] At any rate, it is not in doubt that the word is characteristic of Isaiah, and that it does not occur in the later writers who built on this theme elsewhere in the book. Finally, attention may be drawn to a characteristic juxtaposing of words in verse 4, 'The minds of the rash will have good judgment', which might be more literally rendered 'the heart of the hasty shall understand to know (*ûlᵉbab nimhārîm yābîn lāda'at)*'. Three of these four words also occur together in 6:9-10 in a way which, as I have tried to show elsewhere, was also influential on later tradition.[71]

From all this evidence I conclude that the formulation of 32:3 is certainly earlier than the major development in the Isaiah tradition which came about during the exile, and that in all probability it should be ascribed to Isaiah himself. *A fortiori*, the same will apply to 32:1, and I suggest that the appreciation that this verse is proverbial answers all the arguments which have been raised in order to suggest that it is post-exilic. The verse may have been quoted rather than written by Isaiah, but it should never-theless be included with the evidence for his view of kingship. Its setting near the end of what was probably the earliest form of his book is thus appropriate.

Indeed, we may conclude the lengthy discussion of this chapter as a whole by using 32:1 as a summary of our principal findings. Of the four main passages we have studied there seems to be a strong case for setting three in the pre-exilic period. While this is perhaps as far as we can go with real certainty, it is, further, probable that they

---

[70] Indeed, there is some confusion in the text about this issue in 32:3 itself, though the context leaves no doubt that the line adopted above is the correct one; for discussion see *The Book called Isaiah*, p. 254.

[71] See ibid., pp. 48–50.

were either written or used by Isaiah himself. Either way, however, we may conclude that they reflect his standpoint on the question of kingship.

Although two of these three (9:1–7; 11:1–5) show knowledge of the Davidic origins of the monarchy in Jerusalem and specifically some familiarity with the dynastic promise, this feature has not emerged as a central focus. The stress throughout has been on the role rather than on the person of the king. This was already the case to a limited extent in 9:1–7, and it is even more prominent in 11:1–5, where the reference to Jesse points back behind the immediate royal family to the hope for a second David – a fresh beginning, in other words. It comes most strongly to the fore, however, in 32:1, which comprises a general statement about the ideal ruler, without any particular reference to the current dynasty. No evidence has been found for the view that God was somehow inalienably wedded to the Davidic descendant: that God would protect him against his enemies regardless of his own conduct.

Secondly, this role is bound up as closely as it is possible to imagine with the maintenance of 'justice' and 'righteousness', terms which we saw in our previous chapter were far broader than simply the administration of the law courts. Rather, they stand as a sort of shorthand, for the ordering of society as a whole in accordance with God's will. And, although in the first two passages this is predicated solely in terms of the royal figure, 32:1 is again of importance in reminding us that other officials are also involved in this. This outlook, too, is what we should have expected on the basis of our analysis in chapter one of a godly society.

Thirdly, the language in which these ideas are couched is often familiar from elsewhere in the Old Testament, especially the Psalms and the Wisdom Literature, but it is given a particular twist in Isaiah. It is easy to overlook this point by moving straight from parallels of language to the assumption that precisely the same ideas are being expressed everywhere. A moment's thought will bring us to realize, however, that it is often the case in language of all sorts that a writer will use familiar phraseology in order to express his or her own particular applications of the ideas to which that language refers. As I have tried to show, that is certainly the case with Isaiah, who was nothing if not creative in so much of his writing. It is therefore not only the commonalities of his language, but especially the small, yet significant, variations he introduced on these themes which may be particularly revealing of what is most distinctive about his thought.

Fourthly, God's role in raising up such a king is emphasized in the first two of the three passages. Because of the form of the saying, 32:1 is silent on this particular topic, but it is noteworthy that in the development of the theme later on (32:15–20) the same thought inevitably rises to the surface.

Finally, although we have not devoted much attention to this topic, it needs to be recalled that these passages may not always have stood (and in some cases almost certainly did not stand) in connection with the same wider contexts as in the present form of the book. Quite apart from the inevitable influence upon our thinking of centuries of later reading traditions, there are instances where the messianic interpretation with which we are familiar is partly due to the present redactional placement of these passages. So far as the eighth-century prophet himself is concerned such a reading would, I believe, be seriously anachronistic. We have not found in any of the three passages a suggestion that a radical break or discontinuity in the historical continuum is envisaged. Naturally, these passages have a forward look, but only in the sense of 'from this time onward' (9:7). They are a blueprint for kingship (and it is impossible now to be sure whether they were intended for a specific individual, such as the young Hezekiah), not a prediction that such a one would inevitably arise at some unspecified future date. That the present order of society was corrupt and that it would be judged within the foreseeable future is one of the few things about Isaiah's ministry on which all scholars are agreed. I have also argued that his vision ranged further than just this, however, and that he did give some indications that he anticipated renewal after the crisis. At first, at the time of the Syro-Ephraimite invasion, it is likely that he thought of all this in fairly immediate terms. With the passage of time (see especially 30:8) he came to realize that the time-scale was longer than he had originally anticipated. No doubt, that fact in itself may have contributed to the later reinterpretation of his earlier words in a more messianic direction. Nevertheless, so far as Isaiah himself was concerned, he seems to have remained consistent in his presentation of the role of human kingship within the society focused upon Jerusalem.

Three

Second Variation: Immanuel

At the start of the previous chapter it was suggested that the famous Immanuel prophecy in Isaiah 7:14 would require separate treatment because it differs in two main respects from those we have studied so far, namely context and content. It is obvious that these two elements are likely to be closely related, and indeed a number of recent studies of the prophecy have built explicitly on the literary context in order to maintain, against the traditional view, that Immanuel was a child of the prophet himself. Equally, although others have continued to argue that this saying should be related in some way especially with the prophecy in chapter 9 (and perhaps further with that in chapter 11), they have taken little account of the fact that some of the common ideas we have been analysing do not come explicitly to expression in this passage. In order to find out why, we need first to understand, and then to examine in some detail, one of the fundamental assumptions about the prophecy's setting which has been determinative of so much of the modern scholarly discussion about it.

It is over a hundred years since the German Old Testament scholar Karl Budde first put forward in outline form his theory concerning this part of the book of Isaiah, which has come to be known as the Isaiah Memoir.[1] This theory, also found more or less in the classic commentary on Isaiah by Bernhard Duhm of 1892,[2] rapidly established itself as an assured result of critical biblical scholarship, and certainly since Budde returned to the subject in a full-scale monograph in 1928[3] it has been included as a given fact in virtually every commentary or other study on Isaiah to have appeared since.

Now, it so happens that I have long been uneasy about certain crucial aspects of this theory, and in recent years I have become bolder about saying so because of the fact that one or two other scholars have also begun to question its validity.[4] There can be few theories in Old Testament

---

[1] K. Budde, 'Ueber das siebente Capitel des Buches Jesaja', in *Études archéologiques, linguistiques et historiques dédiées à Mr. le Dr. C. Leemans, à l'occasion du cinquantième anniversaire de sa nomination aux fonctions de Directeur du Musée archéologique des Pays-Bas* (Leiden, E.J. Brill 1885), pp. 121–6. So far as I can determine he first used the actual term 'Denkschrift' = 'memoir', (without further introduction), in 'Zwei Beobachtungen zum alten Eingang des Buches Jesaja', *ZAW* 38 (1919–20), p. 58.

[2] B. Duhm, *Das Buch Jesaia* (HKAT; Göttingen, Vandenhoeck & Ruprecht 1892; it is usual nowadays to refer to the revised fourth edition, published in 1922). Again, Duhm did not himself use the term 'Denkschrift'.

[3] K. Budde, *Jesaja's Erleben: Eine gemeinverständliche Auslegung der Denkschrift des Propheten (Kap. 6,1–9,6)* (Gotha, Leopold Klotz Verlag 1928).

[4] These challenges take two forms. On the one hand, there are those who effectively reject the theory outright, such as H.G. Reventlow, 'Das Ende der sog. "Denkschrift" Jesajas', *BN* 38/39 (1987), pp. 62–7; S.A. Irvine, 'The Isaianic *Denkschrift*: Reconsidering an Old Hypothesis', *ZAW* 104 (1992), pp. 216–31. On the other hand, some still use the language of the Memoir, but effectively undermine its most powerful attraction by arguing that as it stands it does not represent an early independent 'book', but is the result of later redactional compilation, e.g. W. Dietrich, *Jesaja und die Politik* (BEvTh 74; Munich, Chr. Kaiser Verlag 1976), pp. 60–99; W. Werner, 'Vom Prophetenwort zur Prophetentheologie. Ein redaktionskritischer Versuch zu Jes 6,1–8,18', *BZ* N.F. 29 (1985), pp. 1–30; Kaiser, *Jesaja 1–12*, pp. 117–209 = ET, *Isaiah 1–12*, pp. 114–218; R. Kilian, *Jesaja 1–12* (DNEB 17; Würzburg, Echter Verlag 1986), pp. 47–69; more subtly, Sweeney, *Isaiah 1–39*, pp. 132–88.

scholarship which have had such a long unchallenged innings as this one, but the time seems now to have come to take a serious critical look at it. So, after explaining the theory more fully, I shall suggest a number of arguments which have tended to be shoved under the carpet, and suggest that we can no longer hold to the view in the form that Budde maintained.

Despite the familiarity of the theory to many students of the Old Testament, it is necessary to set it out reasonably fully for the simple reason that its most powerful attraction is the way in which it seems to hang together as a complete whole. The opening chapters of the book of Isaiah consist largely of prophetic sayings heavily critical of the people addressed, mainly, it would be agreed, the inhabitants of the southern kingdom of Judah, with its capital in eighth-century BCE Jerusalem. With chapter 6, however, there is a sudden and marked change. This is the famous chapter which begins 'In the year that king Uzziah died I saw the Lord sitting upon his throne, high and lifted up, and his train filled the temple'. We notice two things at once: from sayings of the prophet we move into a section of narrative description, and furthermore, that narrative is in the first-person singular, 'I'. In both respects, this is a complete change from what has gone before. The chapter continues with a scene in the heavenly court which leads to Isaiah volunteering to go to the people with the distinctly discouraging message that they are to have their hearts dulled and their ears and eyes closed until such time as they have been judged to the point of destruction and desolation.

Chapter 7 continues in this narrative vein with an account of Isaiah's dealings with king Ahaz, not long after, in the crisis events that have come to be known as the Syro-Ephraimite invasion. Perhaps, as part of their plan to frustrate the imperialistic expansion of Assyria,[5] the rulers of Syria/Damascus and of Israel/Ephraim had entered into an alliance which they wanted Ahaz to join. Ahaz appears initially to have been unwilling, but now the coalition has a plan to replace him by force with a puppet ruler of their own choosing, and Ahaz is possibly wavering. Isaiah, accompanied by his son Shear-Jashub, meets Ahaz to encourage him to stand firm against this threat. When he offers Ahaz a sign from God to reinforce his belief in the reality of divine protection, however, Ahaz equivocates, whereupon Isaiah declares that God himself will give him a sign: the famous Immanuel sign, whose precise interpretation is so disputed. Amidst much that is uncertain, however, it seems clear that Isaiah believes that one way or another the foreign threat will be lifted within a short space of time. The last part of the chapter comprises various prophetic sayings relating to the Assyrian threat. While some of these may indeed come from Isaiah, it is generally considered that they have been given their present setting at a later stage in the formation of the book, and I shall not deal with them further here. It is interesting to note, however, that some of these sayings pick up and develop striking phrases from earlier in the chapter and elsewhere in Isaiah, suggesting that they represent reflection on and interpretation of the earlier words of the prophet.

---

[5] This is the usual explanation for the 'invasion' of Judah by the northern coalition. It is by no means certain, however, as has been learnedly demonstrated by R. Tomes, 'The Reason for the Syro–Ephraimite War', *JSOT* 59 (1993), pp. 55–71. He points to several unacknowledged difficulties in the usual view, and tentatively suggests instead that the causes may have been no more than 'local'. See too B. Oded, 'The Historical Background of the Syro–Ephraimite War Reconsidered', *CBQ* 34 (1972), pp. 153–65, and, most radically of all, R. Bickert, 'König Ahas und der Prophet Jesaja. Ein Beitrag zum Problem des syrisch-ephraimitischen Krieges', ZAW 99 (1987), pp. 361–84.

With chapter 8 we return to our first-person narrative. The opening account of the birth of the unfortunately named son of the prophet, Maher-shalal-hash-baz, is again associated with the anticipated overthrow of the threatening coalition in the near future, so this passage clearly relates closely to the narrative in chapter 7, and could be thought to continue it. A difficult passage follows. The meaning of the Hebrew is far from clear, and there is disagreement about how much of it is from Isaiah, or how much might have been added later. In general, however, it seems to say that if Judah associates with the northern coalition in order to avert the immediate threat, the result will be a case of 'out of the frying pan and into the fire', because the Assyrians will still come and wreak even greater devastation. Isaiah then tells how he was encouraged to stand firm despite the opposition he encountered. Because of this opposition, he concludes: 'Bind up the testimony, seal the teaching among my disciples. I will wait for the Lord, who is hiding his face from the house of Jacob, and I will hope in him. See, I and the children whom the Lord has given me are signs and portents in Israel from the Lord of hosts, who dwells on Mount Zion' (8:16–18).

This paragraph seems rather clearly to mark the conclusion of a section in the book.[6] It is the end of the first-person narrative, and its apparent reference to writing down what has been said during the Syro-Ephraimite crisis, because the teaching has been rejected by the majority of the population, rounds the narrative off in a tidy fashion. It is as though Isaiah plans to withdraw from

---

[6] For a different opinion see recently Sweeney, *Isaiah 1–39*, pp. 175–88.

the public arena and to await developments in the future which he believes will ultimately vindicate his stand.

From this brief summary of chapters 6–8 of Isaiah it is but a short step to Budde's theory. As with most influential theories it has not been adopted into the scholarly mainstream in precisely the form Budde proposed, so it will be better here to concentrate on what has been accepted by nearly all commentators. Again, we should not suppose that everyone agrees about every single detail. What we confront here, rather, is an overriding idea accepted as a starting point, a given conclusion to which each interpreter may add his or her own individual variations. It is this idea, therefore, that we need to try to get hold of.

The idea is that the core of this extended passage is an account committed to writing by Isaiah himself shortly after the Syro-Ephraimite crisis, that it initially circulated as an independent document, and that its present position in the book as a whole is somewhat anomalous because it begins with Isaiah's call. It originally stood at the beginning of the book, according to Budde. He noted that the title of the book in 1:1, 'The vision of Isaiah son of Amoz, which he saw . . .', is unusual for a prophecy, and suggested that this led straight into the description of the great vision in chapter 6. It was moved to its present position *later* out of chronological considerations (because it relates primarily to Ahaz's reign, whereas 1:1 states that Isaiah also prophesied under Uzziah), and can be seen to be an insertion into its present setting by the fact that it interrupts the connection between the material which immediately precedes and follows it. As a consequence of this theory we have an extended passage of writing by a major prophet more or less contemporary with the events he is describing, and this has, therefore, to be the starting point for the study both of the composition history of the book and for an understanding of Isaiah's own thought and theology. The theory is neat and attractive, readily understood and congenial to our modern *penchant* for solid historical ground beneath our feet. It is really no wonder that the theory should have caught on so quickly and been more or less unchallenged for a century.

But is it true? It seems to me that there are several awkward facts about this material which suggest that the theory's enticing simplicity may have clouded our judgment somewhat. Let us look more closely at each of these points in turn.

First, contrary to what the theory would lead us to expect, the narrative in chapter 7 is not in the first person, but in the third. This fact comes as a surprise to some people when it is first pointed out to them, which is perhaps a testimony to the strength of the prevailing hypothesis which demands that the whole of chapters 6–8 must originally have been in the first person. Budde and many other commentators since have advanced the simple expedient of changing chapter 7 so that it is in the first person singular as well. Although this sounds extremely radical it in fact involves only slight changes to the Hebrew text of two verses (3 and 13), so that Budde was able to suggest that this was nothing more than a slip in the course of textual transmission. While this might, therefore, seem to be a plausible change, and no more extravagant than many which have to be proposed in order to make sense of other parts of the Hebrew Bible, it seems to me to be quite unwarranted in the present instance, and to be driven by no more than the demands of the theory in the first place, a clear case of circular reasoning. Not only is there no proper textual evidence whatsoever in favour of the change, but more positively there is good reason to resist it. If the text has correctly

preserved the first person in chapters 6 and 8 there would
have been every incentive for scribes to preserve it also in
chapter 7, had it ever been present. It is not, therefore, a
case of scribes assimilating a passage to what they might
have expected, but rather of their resisting precisely that
temptation. From a textual point of view this is a standard
case where one should prefer the more difficult reading,
which in this context is clearly the third person form.[7] The
fact that this has been accepted even by some who still
cling to the idea of an Isaiah Memoir[8] only reinforces the
point.

The consequences of this situation for the theory seem
to me, however, to be severely damaging. If chapter 7 is
indeed a third-person report it is most unlikely from the
first to have formed an integral part of a narrative by
Isaiah himself, comprising chapters 6–8. On a common
sense approach, which appears to be entirely justified in
the present instance, we should ascribe chapters 6 and 8
to Isaiah, and chapter 7 to someone else of as yet un-
determined date. This means that, on the one hand we can
no longer speak of the whole section as an Isaiah Memoir
at all, and on the other that an earlier Isaianic account has
been interrupted by new material at some later stage in
the composition of the book, for reasons and with consequences we have yet to explore. A first conclusion, therefore, is that we can no longer interpret every part of this
section with reference to every other part as reflecting the

---

[7] For some literary considerations which lead to the same conclusion see
P. Höffken, 'Notizen zum Textcharakter von Jesaja 7,1–17', *ThZ* 36 (1980),
pp. 321–37.
[8] E.g. Wildberger, *Jesaja 1*, pp. 265 and 269–70 = ET, pp. 284 and 288.

original intention of the prophet himself, as Budde proposed.

The second argument against Budde concerns his claim that the insertion of the Memoir has interrupted the original connection between the material which now precedes and follows it. He implied that this showed that the Memoir was a pre-existing booklet which had simply been inserted as a block into its present setting. On the face of it this is a reasonable, indeed a standard, way to proceed in trying to determine the pre-existing blocks of material out of which an Old Testament book might have been assembled, and arguments of this kind can be found in most critical commentaries. The question, of course, is whether the facts in this particular case fit the theory built upon them.

In brief, the bulk of chapter 5, which comes immediately before the Memoir, is a series of woe-sayings. Six times the prophet pronounces a threat against some section of the population by the use of this distinctive form: 'Ah (literally, woe to), you who join house to house', and so on. Similarly, in the section following the Memoir there is another extended passage with a repeated element, this time a sort of refrain, which occurs four times between 9:8 and 10:4, 'For all this his anger has not turned away; his hand is stretched out still'.

This tidy situation is apparently spoiled, however, by two factors. First, there is an example of the outstretched–hand refrain near the end of chapter 5, so that it seems to be separated from its partners by the Memoir. Secondly, there is an isolated woe-saying at the beginning of chapter 10, introducing the paragraph which concludes in verse 4 with the last occurrence of the refrain. Not surprisingly, many commentators believe that each of these two apparently misplaced items once belonged with the material with which in formal terms they seem to be related, so that for one reason or another there has been a sort of double crossover.

At this point things get extremely complicated, because there is no agreement as to exactly what has happened, or why. Each commentator has a different idea as to where exactly the misplaced material originally stood, and some think that the process was accidental, while others think it was deliberate.[9] Fortunately, we do not need to go into such detail for our present purposes. The only point we need to observe is that, even if we simply remove the Memoir, we are not left with a smooth join between the end of chapter 5 and either 8:19 or 9:8, which is what we should initially expect if Budde were correct. This can be most easily realized from the fact that the refrain, which in chapter 9 always stands at the end of its paragraph, does not come at the end of chapter 5. Rather, it seems to have been joined to the cycle of woe-sayings in verse 25 and then to be followed in verses 26–30 with a short paragraph which certainly sounds like the kind of material which, had it stood in chapter 9, would have come before the refrain.

---

[9] A selection of recent studies of this phenomenon includes (apart, of course, from the commentaries) C.E. L'Heureux, 'The Redactional History of Isaiah 5.1–10.4', in W.B. Barrick and J.R. Spencer (eds.), *In the Shelter of Elyon: Essays on Ancient Palestinian Life and Literature in Honor of G.W. Ahlström* (JSOTS 31; Sheffield, JSOT Press 1984), pp. 99–119; Sheppard, 'The Anti-Assyrian Redaction'; R.B. Chisholm, 'Structure, Style, and the Prophetic Message: An Analysis of Isaiah 5:8–30', *BibSac* 143 (1986), pp. 46–60; Anderson, '"God With Us"'; W.P. Brown, 'The So-Called Refrain in Isaiah 5:25–30 and 9:7–10:4', *CBQ* 52 (1990), pp. 432–43; Irvine, *Isaiah, Ahaz*, pp. 121–5; A.H. Bartelt, 'Isaiah 5 and 9: In- or Interdependence?', in A.B. Beck *et al.* (eds.), *Fortunate the Eyes That See: Essays in Honor of David Noel Freedman in Celebration of His Seventieth Birthday* (Grand Rapids, Eerdmans 1995), pp. 157–74.

Budde, of course, realized this, and so suggested rather vaguely that this apparent disorder was an accident, some-thing caused by mistake at the time the Memoir was inserted. But, needless to say, that appeals to the theory to support a pure conjecture in the interests of trying to establish the theory in the first place: another clear case of circular reasoning, just like the case of the supposed original first-person narrative in chapter 7 which we looked at before. So far, therefore, both arguments to establish the hypothesis in fact depend upon postulating it in the first place in order to work at all.

In fact, I believe that the curious situation at the end of chapter 5 is capable of a far more plausible explanation, which I have set out at length elsewhere,[10] and so shall not elaborate here. Suffice it to say that I agree that the end of chapter 5 probably belonged originally with 9:7–10:4, but that it was moved deliberately to its new position by a much later editor for perfectly intelligible reasons of his own. If this is right it obviously can tell us nothing at all about whether chapters 6–8 were inserted as a pre-existing block or not. This whole line of argument gets us nowhere as far as the question of a supposed original Memoir is concerned.

The third argument we need to discuss concerns the nature of chapter 6, the account of Isaiah's great vision of God. Budde assumed that this was a description of Isaiah's initial call, and that it therefore must originally have stood at the beginning of his account, rather like the call-visions of Jeremiah and Ezekiel at the beginning of their books. (Incidentally, this overlooks the fact that Isaiah's near

---

[10]   *The Book Called Isaiah*, pp. 125–43, and 'Isaiah xi 11–16 and the Redaction of Isaiah i–xii', in J.A. Emerton (ed.), *Congress Volume, Paris 1992* (SVT 61; Leiden, E.J. Brill 1995), pp. 343–57.

predecessor Amos seems to have his call-visions in chapters 7–8 of his book, not at the beginning, but we can let
that pass for the moment.) This shows, according to
Budde, that the Memoir must once have been an independent booklet, and that its present odd position is due
to the fact that it was only incorporated later into the
wider book of Isaiah as it was then developing.

Many readers of Isaiah have puzzled over the question
as to why Isaiah's call does not come first in the book,
regardless of whether they have ever heard of the Memoir
theory; so clearly on any showing there is a problem to be
faced here. At least, there is a problem if this describes
Isaiah's initial call, but I should like to query whether this
is necessarily so.[11] After all, the passage is very different
from the description of the call of Jeremiah or Amos, for
instance, but this does not mean that it is entirely without
precedent in the Old Testament. In fact, there is one other
account strikingly similar to it in some of its fundamental

---

[11] A few other scholars have also queried this common understanding of
Isaiah 6, e.g. M.M. Kaplan, 'Isaiah 6 1–11', *JBL* 45 (1926), pp. 251–9; Y.
Kaufmann, *The Religion of Israel from its Beginnings to the Babylonian Exile*
(New York, Schocken Books 1972), p. 388; O.H. Steck, 'Bemerkungen zu
Jesaja 6', *BZ* N.F. 16 (1972), pp. 188–206; J. Milgrom, 'Did Isaiah Prophesy
during the Reign of Uzziah?', *VT* 14 (1964), pp. 164–82; K. Koch, *Die
Propheten*, 1: *Assyrische Zeit* (Stuttgart, Kohlhammer 1978), p. 125 (3rd,
enlarged edition, 1995, p. 221) = ET, *The Prophets*, 1: *The Assyrian Period*
(London, SCM Press 1982), p. 113; H. Niehr, 'Zur Intention von Jes 6,1–9', *BN*
21 (1983), pp. 59–65; Watts, *Isaiah 1–33*, p. 70; J.H. Hayes and S.A. Irvine,
Isaiah, the Eighth-Century Prophet: his Times and his Preaching (Nashville,
Abingdon Press 1987), pp. 108–9; A. Hurowitz, 'Isaiah's Impure Lips and their
Purification in Light of Akkadian Sources', *HUCA* 60 (1989), pp. 39–89 (p. 41);
C.A. Evans, *To See and Not Perceive: Isaiah 6.9–10 in Early Jewish and
Christian Interpretation* (JSOTS 64; Sheffield, Sheffield Academic Press 1989),
pp. 22–3. Most recently, Sweeney, *Isaiah 1–39*, seems to want to have his cake
and eat it, arguing on the one hand that there are serious difficulties in terms
of both form and content in identifying the chapter as an example of a
prophetic call narrative (pp. 134–5), and yet on the other hand maintaining
that in the present form of the book 'it is meant to be understood as the
prophet's call or commission to his vocation' (p. 136).

aspects, and that is the story of a prophet called Micaiah, the son of Imlah, which is told in 1 Kings 22.[12] The situation is that Ahab and Jehoshaphat, the kings of Israel and Judah, are planning to go to war against Ramoth-gilead. Jehoshaphat wants divine sanction for this campaign, so Ahab obligingly provides 400 prophets to confirm that all will be well. Jehoshaphat is still not satisfied, however, and asks if there is not 'a prophet of the Lord' whom they can consult. Ahab admits that there is one, Micaiah, but he always says the opposite of what Ahab wants to hear. Nevertheless, he is summoned, and surprisingly he confirms the word of the other 400. Ahab 'smells a rat', however, and demands to hear the truth instead. Micaiah accordingly foretells defeat. 'See, I told you so', retorts Ahab, whereupon Micaiah, without further invitation, explains the contradiction as follows:

> I saw the Lord sitting on his throne, with all the host of heaven standing beside him to the right and to the left of him. And the Lord said, 'Who will entice Ahab, so that he may go up and fall at Ramoth-gilead?' Then one said one thing, and another said another, until a spirit came forward and stood before the Lord, saying, 'I will entice him.' 'How?' the Lord asked him. He replied, 'I will go out and be a lying spirit in the mouth of all his prophets.' Then the Lord said, 'You are to entice him, and you shall succeed; go out and do it' (1 Kgs. 22:19–22).

The close similarities with Isaiah 6 are obvious, and need no elaboration. The significant point for our present purposes, therefore, is to observe that this was clearly not Micaiah's initial call, but that it is an account of his presence in the divine court during the course of his

---

[12] Cf. W. Zimmerli, *Ezechiel, 1. Teilband: Ezechiel 1–24* (BKAT 13/1; Neukirchen-Vluyn, Neukirchener Verlag 1969), pp. 16–21 = ET, *Ezekiel 1: A Commentary on the Book of the Prophet Ezekiel, Chapters 1–24* (Hermeneia; Philadelphia, Fortress Press 1979), pp. 98–100.

ministry (as presupposed by some of the other prophets, though the details are not spelt out as fully as here) in order to receive a commission for some particular task. If there is validity to the argument from analogy then we may suggest that the same is true of Isaiah 6.[13] That does not, of course, mean that the book of Isaiah has been arranged on strictly chronological grounds (in fact, it certainly has not), but it does mean that we cannot argue from chapter 6 in support of the view that chapters 6–8 must once have formed an independent book. There are other possible ways of explaining the present position of chapter 6. For instance, an editor may have thought it appropriate that after collecting a series of woe-oracles against the people in chapter 5 he should follow this with the prophet's 'woe is me' (6:5), once he stands in the presence of the divine majesty.

So far we have allowed Budde's arguments in favour of the existence of an Isaiah Memoir to determine our agenda, and have found them wanting. I want now to turn to three points about this material which will reinforce this negative conclusion, but which will also begin to point us in a more positive direction.

First, it is well known that 7:1 is more or less the same as 2 Kings 16:5, where it fits smoothly into the history's account of the reign of Ahaz. Unless we are to indulge in the gratuitously speculative suggestion that it has been

---

[13]   Indeed, Micaiah's vision report, containing the account of his commission, is related only after that commission has been carried out. This raises the intriguing possibility that the same may be true of Isaiah, with important consequences for our understanding of the preceding chapters and of the 'hardening' saying in 6:9–10. For our immediate purposes the importance would be to strengthen the links of chapter 6 with chapter 5, and weaken the links with chapters 7–8, as presupposed by the Memoir hypothesis.

added later to an original Isaiah Memoir,[14] it makes us wonder whether the third-person narrative of Isaiah 7 which it introduces has not in fact been drawn in its entirety from somewhere else altogether, somewhere much closer to the circles that produced what we term the 'Deuteronomic History' – that great historical work comprising all the books from Joshua to 2 Kings, which probably came out in a first edition late in the period of the monarchy and which was worked over into its present form at some point during the exile.

The second point reinforces this impression, for a number of scholars in recent years have observed that there are some striking points of connection and contrast between this account in chapter 7 and the stories about the later king, Hezekiah, in chapters 36–39.[15] These points stretch

---

[14] This has frequently been maintained. For discussion, with abundant references to other literature, see J. Werlitz, *Studien zur literarkritischen Methode: Gericht und Heil in Jesaja 7,1–17 und 29,1–8* (BZAW 204; Berlin and New York, de Gruyter 1992), pp. 123–35.

[15] See, for instance, P.R. Ackroyd, 'Isaiah 36–39: Structure and Function', in W.C. Delsman *et al.* (eds.), *Von Kenaan bis Kerala: Festschrift für Prof. Mag. Dr. Dr. J.P.M. van der Ploeg O.P. zur Vollendung des siebzigsten Lebensjahres am 4. Juli 1979* (AOAT 211; Kevelaer, Butzon & Bercker/Neukirchen-Vluyn, Neukirchener Verlag 1982), pp. 3–21 = *Studies in the Religious Tradition of the Old Testament* (London, SCM Press 1987), pp. 105–20; J. Blenkinsopp, *A History of Prophecy in Israel from the Settlement in the Land to the Hellenistic Period* (London, SPCK 1984), pp. 109–10; K.A.D. Smelik, 'Distortion of Old Testament Prophecy. The Purpose of Isaiah xxxvi and xxxvii', in A.S. van der Woude (ed.), *Crises and Perspectives: Studies in Ancient Near Eastern Polytheism, Biblical Theology, Palestinian Archaeology and Intertestamental Literature* (*OTS* 24; Leiden, E.J. Brill 1986), pp. 70–93; M.A. Sweeney, *Isaiah 1–4 and the Post-Exilic Understanding of the Isaianic Tradition* (BZAW 171; Berlin and New York, de Gruyter 1988), pp. 12–13; E.W. Conrad, 'The Royal Narratives and the Structure of the Book of Isaiah', *JSOT* 41 (1988), pp. 67–81, substantially reproduced in *Reading Isaiah* (Minneapolis, Fortress Press 1991), pp. 34–51; C.R. Seitz, *Zion's Final Destiny: The Development of the Book of Isaiah. A Reassessment of Isaiah 36–39* (Minneapolis, Fortress Press 1991), pp. 89 and 195–6; *idem*, *Isaiah 1–39* (Louisville, John Knox Press 1993), p. 64.

all the way from the general and overarching to the specific and particular, and I cannot list them all here. Just to give a flavour, we may note that in both passages the king is confronted with an invading army which is threatening Jerusalem (7:1; 36:2), that he is reduced to near panic (7:2; 37:1), and that Isaiah offers him a reassuring 'fear not' oracle (7:4–9; 37:6–7), backed up in each case by the offer of a 'sign' (7:11; 37:30; see too 38:7 and 22). Although in both narratives the king and city are spared, this is followed by a prediction that a worse disaster will follow in the future (7:15–25; 39:6–7). A striking point of detail is the reference in both cases to the otherwise unknown 'conduit of the upper pool on the highway to the Fuller's Field' (7:3; 36:2), which can hardly be coincidental. Alongside these similarities, however, there are marked contrasts between the ways in which the kings react: Ahaz, as we have seen, rejects the way to deliverance offered by the prophet, while Hezekiah follows the way of faith and is spectacularly delivered. On the basis of these, and other such comparisons, we may agree with those who have concluded that there is a conscious attempt to contrast the responses of the two kings, one negative and the other positive.

Now, this contributes to our wider consideration when it is recalled that the longer narrative in chapters 36–39 is also recounted in virtually identical terms in 2 Kings 18–20. I think there can be little doubt that it has been taken over from Kings with generally only very slight changes and inserted in its present setting in the book of Isaiah by a later editor.[16] At the same time, however, there

---

[16] I have sought to defend this common view against some recently proposed alternatives in *The Book Called Isaiah*, pp. 189–211, and 'Hezekiah and the Temple', in M.V. Fox *et al.* (eds.), *Texts, Temples, and Traditions: A Tribute to Menahem Haran* (Winona Lake, Ind., Eisenbrauns 1996), pp. 47–52.

are a number of features of these chapters that distinguish them from most of the other material in Kings and associate them with what we may loosely call 'Isaianic circles'. Again, a mere sample of the evidence should suffice to substantiate this claim.[17] These chapters differ from the rest of the books of Kings in that, for instance, they are the only place in the Deuteronomic History where a prophet whose sayings are separately recorded in the books of the Latter Prophets is mentioned in the narrative, and, furthermore, in that they include poetic material. On the other hand, there are links with the rest of the Isaianic tradition which go beyond those already noted for chapter 7, for instance, (i) Shebna and Eliakim (36:3) are also the subject of 22:15–25; (ii) the use of the divine title 'the Holy One of Israel' (37:23) is peculiarly characteristic of the book of Isaiah; (iii) the emphasis on 'trust' in the Rabshakeh's speeches (36:4,5,6,7,9,15) recalls 30:15; (iv) the stress on the impotence of Egypt, for all her chariots and horses (36:6,9), is strongly reminiscent of Isaiah's anti-Egyptian oracles (30:1–5; 31:1–3); and (v) 37:30–32 has clear links with the Isaianic tradition, especially with regard to the remnant,[18] the structure of the first part of verse 32, which has a close parallel in 2:3*b*, and, most notable of, all the ending of verse 32, which is verbally identical with the ending of 9:7, 'The zeal of the Lord of

---

[17]   For fuller accounts see the works cited in note 14 above, together with J.W. Groves, *Actualization and Interpretation in the Old Testament* (SBLDS 86; Atlanta, Scholars Press 1987), pp. 191–201.
[18]   See R.E. Clements, ' "A Remnant Chosen by Grace" (Romans 11:5): The Old Testament Background and Origin of the Remnant Concept', in D.A. Hagner and M.J. Harris (eds.), *Pauline Studies: Essays Presented to Professor F.F. Bruce on his 70th Birthday* (Exeter, Paternoster/Grand Rapids, Eerdmans 1980), pp. 106–21.

hosts will do this'. In the light of this and other comparable evidence we need to envisage two stages in the development of this section of the book. Originally composed
by these Isaianic circles in a shape about which we can
only speculate, it was used as a source along with the
many others at his disposal by the author of Kings. It was
then further reused at a later date by an editor of the book
of Isaiah.

The thematic and stylistic similarities we have noted
between this material and Isaiah 7 lead us to conclude
that this latter chapter too was composed as part of the
same work sometime between the lifetime of Isaiah and
the composition of the book of Kings.[19] It is thus very
clearly to be distinguished from a first-person Memoir by
Isaiah himself, a conclusion our earlier discussion has
already made clear, and in a moment we shall have to
consider why it has therefore been placed where it is by
some later editor.

Before we come to that, however, there is one further
observation I should like to make about the material
Budde included in the Isaiah Memoir, and that concerns
the opening of chapter 9 – a passage we looked at closely
in the previous chapter. It may not have escaped notice
that although this was included in the Memoir by Budde
my introductory survey stopped short of it. I suggested,
rather, that there was a clear conclusion from a literary
point of view at 8:16–18, where the first-person account
comes to an end and where the reference to the writing
down of the prophet's teaching marks a natural break in
the text. We need not, perhaps, delay to consider the

---

[19]   By a different route, Bickert, 'König Ahas und der Prophet Jesaja', arrives
at a similar conclusion for what he takes to be the original form of Isaiah
7:1–9. His radical literary-critical surgery on these verses, however, raises
questions about how secure his results can be.

reasons Budde advanced for his anomalous proposal; the real reason is clear enough. Because the refrain-poem begins at 9:8 Budde had to include everything up to that point in order to maintain his opinion that the Isaiah Memoir had simply been stuck in between the end of chapter 5 and 9:8. Without that hypothesis we do not need to get into contortions to see that this is just another example of material having been put in its present position by the editor or compiler of the book of Isaiah, and there are clear traces of his having done so, which I have examined elsewhere and will not reiterate here.[20] The result of this and similar observations that we have been making along the way is that a rather different picture of how this part of Isaiah came into existence is beginning to emerge. Whereas Budde tried to demonstrate that the whole thing is as it is for the simple reason that Isaiah himself wrote every word as it stands, we are finding instead that we have material from a variety of dates, some of it certainly by Isaiah, some recording his words but committed to writing by others, some written by someone else but relating to Isaiah's activity, and yet more which may not originally have been by or about Isaiah at all, such as the last part of chapter 7, as is nowadays agreed even by most of those who otherwise still hold to the Memoir hypothesis.

At first this sounds as though it is perversely making everything as complicated as possible, whereas Budde's theory had the great advantage of simplicity. Well, that may be true, but it is only partially true. After all, his

---

[20]   *The Book Called Isaiah*, pp. 136–41.

theory too had complications, which might be provoca-
tively described as involving incompetent scribes and
copyists who messed up clear literary connections between passages, who thoughtlessly changed a first-person
narrative into the third person, who misunderstood the
nature of chapter 6 by not putting it at the start of the
book, and who simply proceeded by dumping in some
arbitrary place in the otherwise seamless book of Isaiah
an additional booklet they happened to have at their
disposal.

The conclusion towards which we seem to be driven
with regard to these particular chapters in Isaiah may be
linked with the considerable change which has come
about in the whole way that prophetic books are read
today, a change that can in fact be associated with a much
wider trend in the humanities and social sciences generally, and in particular such disciplines as history, literary
study, and archaeology. Before returning to the detailed
study of the Immanuel prophecy in the light of our findings it may be helpful first to reflect a little on this wider
phenomenon.

At the time when Budde was writing, and in fact for a
considerable period after that, the study of history was
dominated by a concern for great events of the past and
the leading personalities who were thought to have
brought them about. In line with this, in the Middle East
at least, archaeologists concentrated their attention on the
major administrative and military centres, with the hope
of unearthing evidence for these significant events, such as
a destruction brought about by war. Equally, a good deal
of ancient literature (and the prophets not least) was
studied for what it could tell us of these leading personalities and their impact on their times. The first duty of the
biblical scholar, therefore, was to strip away whatever

might have been added later in order to recover as accurately as possible the actual words and deeds of the person in question.

It is not difficult to see how smoothly Budde's theory fitted into this programme and indeed it seems likely, in retrospect, that it was driven by just such a concern in the first place. He seemed to have brought us in close touch with the very heartbeat of the great prophet himself.

More recently (and here of course I simplify to a considerable extent in the interests of clarity) two changes have come about. First, it has come to be appreciated that great people and movements are due to far wider considerations than the free exercise of will by particular leading individuals alone. The causes of particular events and the rise to prominence of specific individuals at such times are the outcome of many social, economic and environmental factors. Ideally these all need to be taken into consideration if we are to begin to understand the past, but much of our previous research strategy has not been designed to give us the kind of information we need for this. Secondly, and in line with this first point, it has increasingly come to be realized that it is a strange kind of history which focuses so exclusively on only up to 0.1 per cent of the people of the past. For the majority of the population of ancient Israel, for instance, life was for most of the time affected far less by who was king, or what battles he was fighting, than by the slow development of improved agricultural techniques, by changes in climate, by the imperceptible changes in economic circumstances as trade increased or declined, and so on. The impact of these considerations on archaeological goals and methods in the Middle East today has been extremely marked, as it has on the concerns of historians who work with the data archaeologists provide.

While such considerations might be thought to have taken us rather far from Isaiah and the Memoir, this is not really the case. We need this jolt to help us appreciate to what an extent our usual approach to the prophetic books has been shaped by these wider intellectual concerns of the past. The results of reading them primarily as an adjunct to the historical enterprise may be readily seen from the fact that some of the best-known works on individual prophets in fact rearrange the sequence of the material in the book in order to make it fit with the commentator's view of the life of the prophet.[21] Similarly, nearly all commentaries, as I have already said, strip away what they regard as material added later to the words of the prophet, and often give this so-called secondary material very little attention thereafter. These two procedures – rearranging and reducing – are clearly not study of the prophetic books themselves, but of something else thought to lie behind them: the prophet himself. Now, there need be no objection to this enterprise in itself, but it obviously must not be confused, as it so often has been, with a proper study of the books as artefacts in their own right, and neither must we allow a focus on the personalities of the prophets to lead us to downgrade the importance of those later writers, editors, and others who gave us these books as they actually exist and who rarely, if ever, were the prophets themselves. In short, if a king is only of relatively greater interest than a peasant, then the same may be said of a prophet and his editor.

Admittedly, most of those now engaged in the study of the prophetic books do not articulate their concern in

---

[21]   The best-known example of this is J. Skinner, *Prophecy and Religion: Studies in the Life of Jeremiah* (Cambridge, Cambridge University Press 1922). Of its kind, this is an exceptionally fine work of scholarship, fully deserving its 'classic' status.

quite this way, but nevertheless whether consciously or not it is what seems to be going on behind the scenes. On the stage itself, to continue the metaphor, what we find is a concern to study these books as they are and in their own right; and often this literary concern is pressed in a strident manner against history, whether that be the history of the prophet who stands behind the book, or the history of how the book reached its present shape. In my opinion, this can go too far, and with deleterious consequences. As many would still agree, if it is apparent that there is what we might call historical depth to the text, something we have begun to see in the case of our particular example in Isaiah, then the unravelling of such a text ought to help us to a better understanding of the finished product. To put it in another way, and one which sounds obvious as soon as it is said, if the book has grown up over a period of time, what we need to ask is what the later editor was doing when he added to or rearranged a passage, and what the effect of his activity is on the way that we now read even the older material. Earlier scholars, such as Budde, wanted to excavate back to the earliest form of the text and then go behind even that to the person of the prophet himself. Now, however, our interest moves in precisely the opposite direction, from the earliest material through the various stages in its growth to the point at which the present text emerges as the culminating point of the whole process, understanding of which is enhanced by such study over against a purely flat reading. For those who like labels this is what is known as 'redaction criticism'. Let us see, then, whether such an approach can help us with Isaiah 6–8, now that we may consider ourselves freed from the dominant Memoir hypothesis.

We may start by noticing that the general shape of Isaiah 6–8 is not unparalleled in the prophetic literature. A

number of years ago I wrote an article on Amos 7–8,[22] and
it was only much later, when I began to turn my attention
to Isaiah, that I realized how close the similarities with
Isaiah 6–8 are. In view of the fact that links of various
kinds between these two prophets have long been recognized,[23] it is somewhat surprising that this particular
connection has generally been overlooked by the commentators, a fact which probably has something to do
with the strength of the prevailing Memoir hypothesis.

In these chapters of Amos we again have the prophet's
own account of a series of visions, and again the narrative
is interrupted by a story about Amos in the third person.
The way in which Amos' four visions are written up, using
the same identical formulae, clearly shows that they once
all belonged together. The interruption comes between the
third and the fourth visions. The third vision indicates that
God is about to test his people in some way, while the
fourth states clearly that there is now no hope for
the future: 'the end has come upon my people Israel'
(Amos 8:2). The narrative which interrupts this sequence
of visions is the famous one about the confrontation of
Amos with Amaziah the priest at the sanctuary in Bethel,
in which Amaziah sends Amos packing back to his native
Judah. Amos protests by pronouncing that both Amaziah,
and indeed Israel as a whole, will themselves be sent
packing – into exile. The most probable explanation for

---

[22] 'The Prophet and the Plumb-Line: A Redaction-Critical Study of Amos vii',
in A.S. van der Woude (ed.), *In Quest of the Past: Studies on Israelite Religion,
Literature and Prophetism* (OTS 26; Leiden, E.J. Brill 1990), pp. 101–21,
reprinted in R.P. Gordon (ed.), *"The Place Is Too Small for Us": The Israelite
Prophets in Recent Scholarship* (Winona Lake, Ind., Eisenbrauns 1995), pp.
453–77.
[23] See especially R. Fey, *Amos und Jesaja: Abhängigkeit und Eigenständigkeit
des Jesaja* (WMANT 12; Neukirchen-Vluyn, Neukirchener Verlag 1963).

the inclusion here of this story, in my view, is to demonstrate that it is the rejection of the prophetic warning
which is the final straw that will lead to the inevitability of
final judgment, as announced by the fourth vision which
now follows. This was very much the viewpoint of the
historians responsible for the history in the books of
Kings, and it seems probable that circles closely associated with them placed this story in its present setting in
Amos, in order to explain his visions in line with their
theology.

Just before we look to see how close this is to the
situation in Isaiah we may note in passing that there is a
further, though more remote, parallel situation at the start
of the book of Hosea. Here, three different sorts of material have been brought together: a third-person account
about the birth of Hosea's three symbolically-named children following his surprising marriage in chapter 1, some
poetic oracles in chapter 2 which combine references to
the names of the children with a description of God's or
the prophet's pursuit of his faithless wife, and a first-
person account by Hosea about how he either marries or
takes back Gomer in chapter 3.[24] The shape of this extended passage is somewhat different from the two we are
mainly concerned with, but it is interesting because it too
combines first- and third-person narrative, and is generally agreed to be the result of an editor assembling
originally independent material in order to give an account of Hosea's troubled family life. It thus gives support
to the view that an important part of the editorial process

---

[24] The literary variety of the sources has allowed for a long debate, with no
assured results, about the course of Hosea's marriage. For a recent, introductory discussion of the issues involved, with an original solution of his
own, see G.I. Davies, *Hosea* (OTG; Sheffield, Sheffield Academic Press 1993),
pp. 79–92.

which has given rise to the prophetic books as we have them is the arrangement of earlier material. Even if every word of these passages is by the prophet in question, or is an accurate historical description of what he did, it is clear that a later interpretation can be put upon such material simply by means of the order in which the material is presented.

Returning now to Isaiah 6–8, the suggestion may be advanced that a similar process is responsible for what we have found here. If we look at the first-person material in chapters 6 and 8 on their own (and assume for the sake of the argument that Isaiah wrote them), we find a concern for the nation as a whole, characterized in each chapter by the title 'this people',[25] an expression that comes twice in the difficult hardening saying in chapter 6:

> *And he said, "Go and say to this people:*
> *'Keep listening, but do not comprehend;*
> *keep looking, but do not understand.'*
> *Make the mind of this people dull,*
>   *and stop their ears,*
>   *and shut their eyes,*
> *so that they may not look with their eyes,*
>   *and listen with their ears,*
> *and comprehend with their minds,*
>   *and turn and be healed."* (Isa. 6:9–10)

This phrase, which does not feature at all in chapter 7, comes three times in chapter 8 – in verses 5, 11 and 12 – so

---

25   It is true that there is a distinction between 'this people' and at least Isaiah and his disciples (cf. 8:11–15), and that some scholars have taken this further to argue that in fact 'this people' refers to only one party or faction in the nation; see, for instance, H. Klein, 'Freude an Rezin', *VT* 30 (1980), pp. 229–34. This latter point, however, involves reading conclusions from chapter 7 into chapter 8. Taking chapters 6 and 8 on their own, as proposed above, there seems to be little justification for not regarding 'this people' as a reference to the population at large, from whom Isaiah obviously distances himself to a considerable extent.

that we may naturally assume that Isaiah wrote that chapter in part to indicate how, despite the promise contained in the name Maher-shalal-hash-baz at the start of the chapter, 'this people' sealed their own fate because they preferred political intrigue to the way of God as indicated by the prophet; they heard, but did not understand. The judgment determined by God would fall, though it is clear from the way that Isaiah continues that he did not expect it to take the form of a total end of the nation, more a sort of purging.

This relatively straightforward situation has been elaborated at a later stage, however, by the addition of chapter 7. Here the focus is rather different, for it is no longer the people as a whole, but the king himself who is individually confronted by the prophet, and indeed, as we shall see later, a number of indications in the text make it clear that it is not the future of the nation, so much as that of the Davidic dynasty, which is at stake. The general shape of the events is certainly comparable with what we find in chapter 8, since here too Isaiah offers Ahaz a promised way of deliverance, which is clearly rejected by the king. In then delivering the Immanuel prophecy Isaiah seems to combine a rejection of the present ruling house with the expectation that hope may arise from a different quarter. So it is not the underlying theology which is different; rather, it is targeted on a different audience. Just as in the case of the story about Amos, so too here the fate of the nation is seen to be bound up much more in the decisions that its leaders take with regard to the prophetic word. And once again, this is very similar to the outlook of the historians responsible for the books of Kings. It is thus no surprise to find that, as we noted earlier, the opening of Isaiah 7 is more or less identical with a version of the same story in 2 Kings 16. In addition, we have already seen that Isaiah 7 has significant parallels with the stories about Hezekiah independently preserved both in Kings and later on in Isaiah, parallels which suggest that Hezekiah is presented as succeeding at the very points where Ahaz failed. Thus we may conclude that by his placing of Isaiah 7 where it now is our editor has used a much wider concern which developed later on in Isaiah's ministry – and for some considerable time thereafter – in order to add a further dimension to the interpretation of the difficult hardening saying of Isaiah.[26]

This does not, I should interject, necessarily mean that Isaiah 7 was invented from scratch by this editor. Indeed, there are a number of features in the text that strongly suggest they are based on elements which go back to the time of the Syro-Ephraimite invasion itself. But as we all know, it is possible for the same event to be written up in many different ways and with very differing emphases, and it seems that later editorial placement of material has resulted in two such emphases being juxtaposed now in Isaiah 7 and 8.

In this case I should certainly agree that Isaiah's, and his editor's, general outlook was rather more similar than in the case of Amos, so that Isaiah 7 does not strike us with such a jolt as does the story in Amos 7. Nevertheless, the literary structure and the shift in perspective are so similar in both cases that it is difficult to avoid the conclusion that similar processes have been at work in the formation of the two passages.

---

[26] A summary of the long history of interpretation of this difficult saying (including within the book of Isaiah itself) is offered by Evans, *To See and Not Perceive*. For the position adopted above, see the series of articles by O.H. Steck (despite his adherence to the Memoir hypothesis): 'Bemerkungen zu Jesaja 6'; 'Rettung und Verstockung: Exegetische Bemerkungen zu Jesaja 7.3–9', *EvTh* 33 (1973), pp. 77–90; 'Beiträge zum Verständnis von Jesaja 7,10–17 und 8,1–4', *ThZ* 29 (1973), pp. 161–78.

Although this discussion of the theory of an Isaiah Memoir has been somewhat lengthy, it has been necessary to help us break out of the endless circle of the debate surrounding the interpretation of the Immanuel prophecy itself, to which we may now turn.

There have been many suggestions over the course of the centuries concerning the identification of the 'young woman' of 7:14 and her child, but only two have ever commanded widespread support.[27] One, which was championed by Jerome as well as the medieval Jewish commentators Ibn Ezra and Rashi, has become especially popular in recent years, and that is the identification of the woman with the wife of the prophet, so making Immanuel one of the prophet's children.[28] This view rests on two primary observations: first, in 7:1–8:4 we have evenly-spaced references to three children who each carry symbolic names – Shear-jashub (7:3), Immanuel (7:14) and Maher-shalal-hash-baz (8:1) – and each may be said to be interpreted in a manner reassuring in the context of the

---

[27] There are available a number of surveys of the history of interpretation of this passage which include many minor opinions which it does not seem necessary to treat here; see, for instance, R. Kilian, *Die Verheissùng Immanuels Jes 7,14* (SBS 35; Stuttgart, Verlag Katholisches Bibelwerk 1968), pp. 59–94; Wildberger, *Jesaja 1*, pp. 288–95 = ET, pp. 306–14; Vermeylen, *Du prophète Isaïe*, pp. 216–21; Laato, *Who is Immanuel?*, pp. 136–54; Wegner, *An Examination of Kingship*, pp. 115–22. Probably the next most popular identification has been that the reference is to *any* young woman (whether present at the time or not): women now pregnant will call their sons Immanuel because by then the crisis will have passed 'and mothers will express the general feeling of relief at the favourable turn in public events . . . when they name their children' (Gray, *Isaiah i–xxvii*, p. 124, and see pp. 132–3 on the syntax of the definite article).
[28] See, for instance, J.J. Stamm, 'La prophétie d'Emmanuel', *RHPhR* 23 (1943), pp. 1–26, who mentions a number of earlier adherents to this view on p. 5; *idem*, 'Die Immanuel-Weissagung. Ein Gespräch mit E. Hammershaimb', *VT* 4 (1954), pp. 20–33; *idem*, 'Neuere Arbeiten zum Immanuel–Problem', *ZAW* 68 (1956), pp. 46–54; *idem*, 'Die Immanuel–Weissagung und die Eschatologie des Jesaja', *ThZ* 16 (1960), pp. 439–55; *idem*, 'Die Immanuel-Perikope im

threat to Judah at the time of the Syro-Ephraimite invasion. Secondly, at 8:18 we have Isaiah's reference to 'the children whom the Lord has given me' who are 'signs and portents in Israel from the Lord of hosts', and it is certainly striking that the Immanuel prophecy is introduced with the words 'Therefore the Lord himself will give you a sign'.

Our discussion of the history of composition of this part of Isaiah, however, puts a question mark over the strength of these arguments, because they both depend heavily on the view that chapters 7–8 originally formed a single literary composition.[29] The conclusion of our lengthy discussion about the hypothesis of an Isaiah Memoir, by contrast, was that 7:1–17 should be interpreted in the first instance somewhat in isolation from chapter 8, that it was likely to look back to chapter 6 rather than forward to chapter 8 for its primary point of reference, and that it was originally written considerably later than the surrounding first-person material. Without the support of the Memoir theory, there remains nothing in chapter 7 to

---

Lichte neuerer Veröffentlichungen', *ZDMG.S* 1 (1969), pp. 281–90; *idem*, 'Die Immanuel-Perikope. Eine Nachlese', *ThZ* 30 (1974), pp. 11–22; N.K. Gottwald, 'Immanuel as the Prophet's Son', *VT* 8 (1958), pp. 36–47; H. Donner, *Israel unter den Völkern: Die Stellung der klassischen Propheten des 8. Jahrhunderts v. Chr. zur Aussenpolitik der Könige von Israel und Juda* (SVT 11; Leiden, E.J. Brill 1964), pp. 16–18; H.M. Wolf, 'A Solution to the Immanuel Prophecy in Isaiah 7:14–8:22', *JBL* 91 (1972), pp. 449–56 (followed, at first sight surprisingly, by Oswalt, *The Book of Isaiah Chapters 1–39*, p. 213); J.J.M. Roberts, 'Isaiah and his Children', in A. Kort and S. Morschauser (eds.), *Biblical and Related Studies Presented to Samuel Iwry* (Winona Lake, Ind., Eisenbrauns 1985), pp. 193–203; R.E. Clements, 'The Immanuel Prophecy of Isa. 7:10–17 and Its Messianic Interpretation', in E. Blum *et al.* (eds.), *Die Hebräische Bibel und ihre zweifache Nachgeschichte: Festschrift für Rolf Rendtorff zum 65. Geburtstag* (Neukirchen-Vluyn, Neukirchener Verlag 1990), pp. 225–40 = *Old Testament Prophecy*, pp. 65–77.
[29] At least, the original parts of those chapters. As already noted, most scholars would regard 7:18–25 as a later addition, and possibly some other material as well.

suggest that the young woman was the wife of the prophet. Indeed, there must be a certain presumption against it, for the following reason: we already know that Isaiah has a child of his own (7:3), and yet Immanuel is to be born to an *'almâ*. We may agree, for the sake of the present argument, that this fiercely contested word does not (in its original context, at least) refer to a technical virgin, but equally it would be agreed by all that it cannot refer to a woman who has already borne a child some years before. Of course, it is possible to speculate that Isaiah had recently become a widower, and that the young woman was his new bride.[30] But, apart from the obviously speculative nature of this explanation, it imports an idea not mentioned in the text in order to explain that text. Had it been of importance to interpretation we may assume it would have been mentioned in order to prevent the misunderstanding that the presence of Shear-jashub would naturally arouse. The fact remains that the text itself contains no indication whatsoever either that the woman in question was the wife of the prophet, or that the child was to be his son – both of which could have easily been stated.

A further consequence of our earlier discussion is also relevant at this point. It was suggested that 7:1–17 was written (in the only form to which we now have access) considerably later than the time of Isaiah himself. By this stage (probably in the late pre-exilic or early exilic period) the early part of the book of Isaiah was already beginning to take shape, and this means that if we are to look to the wider context as a guideline for interpretation then that must include more than just the material of the so-called

---

30   Cf. Gottwald, 'Immanuel.' In fairness, it should be stated that, although he mentions these possibilities, Gottwald himself favours a different interpretation, one that sees in the young woman a female temple musician.

Isaiah Memoir. At this point the important observations of
Clements become relevant. Clements is one of the most
persistent and persuasive advocates of the view that Immanuel was a child of the prophet. Yet in a valuable
article[31] he argues carefully that over the course of time
this understanding was redactionally changed into a presentation of Immanuel as Hezekiah. He finds this attested
in two principal ways: the incorporation of the oracle at
the beginning of chapter 9, with its contrast of a faithful
Davidic king with the Ahaz of the previous narrative; and
the contrast which now exists between the faithless Ahaz
of chapter 7 and the faithful Hezekiah of chapters 36–39.
In the view for which I have argued above, however, what
Clements takes to be a later stage of redaction is in fact the
very period of composition of chapter 7 in the first place.
If such a view is broadly along the right lines then Clements' concession to what he regards as a later reinterpretation removes the prior need to appeal to the view of
Immanuel as the prophet's son.

This leads us naturally to a consideration of the other
major interpretation of this passage, namely that Immanuel is somehow to be related to the Davidic dynasty.
In taking up this approach, it should be noted that the
reader of 7:1–17 can hardly fail to be impressed by the
particular emphasis placed throughout on the present and
future of the dynasty. [32] First, both parts of the passage are
explicitly addressed to 'the house of David (*bêt dāwīd*)'

---

[31]   Clements, 'The Immanuel Prophecy'.

[32]   See especially E. Würthwein, 'Jesaja 7,1–9. Ein Beitrag zu dem Thema:
Prophetie und Politik', in *Theologie als Glaubenswagnis: Festschrift zum 80.
Geburtstag von Karl Heim* (Hamburg, Furche-Verlag 1954), pp. 47–63 = *Wort
und Existenz: Studien zum Alten Testament* (Göttingen, Vandenhoeck & Ruprecht 1970), pp. 127–43. Contrast B.C. Ollenburger, *Zion the City of the Great
King: A Theological Symbol of the Jerusalem Cult* (JSOTS 41; Sheffield, Sheffield Academic Press 1987), pp. 124–7.

(verses 2 and 13; see too verse 17). Secondly, in contrast with the account of the same events in 2 Kings 16, the main aim of the hostile coalition is specifically to replace the Davidic Ahaz with an apparently Aramean puppet (verse 6), while Ahaz's appeal to Assyria for help receives no mention. Thus the focus of the narrative is here restricted to its dynastic implications, in contrast with the different presentation in Kings.[33] Thirdly, the unexpressed, because obvious, conclusion to draw from Isaiah's emphasis on Rezin and the son of Remaliah as the 'head' of Damascus and Samaria respectively in verses 8*a* and 9*a*[34] is that Ahaz is the divinely appointed head of Judah and Jerusalem and he can therefore face the enemy in battle with confidence.[35] Fourthly, this confidence is reinforced by the recollection of the Nathan oracle in the (possibly proverbial) saying at verse 9*b*, 'If you do not stand firm in faith, you shall not stand at all' (see 2 Samuel 7:16, and cf. 1 Samuel 25:28; 1 Kings. 11:38; Psalm 89:28 and 37 [Hebrews 29 and 38]; Isaiah 55:3). The plural form of address in this saying suggests that the whole 'house of David' is in view, not just Ahaz as an individual. And

---

[33] As Tomes, 'The Reason for the Syro-Ephraimite War', has pointed out, several translations of Isaiah 7, especially verse 6, suffer by assuming that the purpose of the invasion was to force Ahaz into an anti-Assyrian coalition. Whether or not that was historically the case (and Tomes has demonstrated that it is by no means certain), it is important to realize that these wider international concerns play no part in Isaiah 7.

[34] Isa. 7:8*b* is certainly a later, intrusive gloss; see virtually any commentary.

[35] I take this also to be the purpose of verse 4, though the interpretation of that verse is disputed. It has often been thought to imply that Ahaz should do nothing, but simply trust in God for deliverance. Among 'war-oracles', however, the closest in wording to Isaiah 7:4 is Deuteronomy 20:3–4, a passage which shows that the promise of divine help is not opposed to human involvement; rather God's help is promised precisely in the forthcoming battle. The same thought provides a plausible background to Isaiah 7, despite the protestations of several commentators.

finally, the passage concludes in verse 17 with a reference to the division of the monarchy following the death of Solomon, an incident which also recalls the belief that, no matter how far an individual Davidic king might stray from God's appointed way, the promise that the dynasty itself would endure remained secure.

This last point, together with the prevailing dynastic context of the passage as a whole, seems to offer the most plausible background for the interpretation of the Immanuel oracle. Ahaz has been both challenged (verse 9*b*) and encouraged (verse 11) to exercise faith on the basis of the promises to David that his position is secure, but he has rejected the invitation (verse 12). At this point, Isaiah turns his back on the house of David: it is striking that address, 'hear (*šimʿû*)', personal suffix 'for you (*mikkem*)', and main verb 'weary (*taleʾû*)', are all plural, indicating clearly that what is to follow reaches beyond the individual Ahaz alone; this seems to link back to the comparable second-person plural formulation in verse 9*b*. Furthermore, as has often been remarked, Isaiah regards God as siding with him in his stance, rather than with those who are addressed, as the shift from 'your God' in verse 11 to 'my God' in verse 13 makes clear.

Some commentators have advocated the view that, despite the apparent impatience of Isaiah demonstrated by verse 13, the prophet continued to offer resolute support for Ahaz and his neutral political stance, and that the Immanuel oracle is an indication of such support.[36] The problem with this interpretation is that it fails to take seriously the conditional nature of verse 9*b*. Since Isaiah continued to stress that the enemy coalition would fail (cf.

---

[36] E. Hammershaimb, *Some Aspects of Old Testament Prophecy from Isaiah to Malachi* (Copenhagen, Rosenkilde og Bagger 1966), pp. 19–20; Høgenhaven, *Gott und Volk bei Jesaja*, pp. 87–93; Irvine, *Isaiah, Ahaz*, pp. 164–71.

verse 16), it cannot be the general safety of the land that is made conditional. Rather, it must be the continuity of the Davidic dynasty itself, as the allusion to the Nathan oracle in verse 9*b* further suggests.[37] It is this which Ahaz has apparently forfeited by his demonstrable lack of faith, and it will have further serious consequences in the form of Assyrian intervention in the affairs of Judah, as later passages indicate. Even within our restricted horizon of 7:1–17 this comes to expression in verse 17: 'The Lord will bring on you and on your people and on your ancestral house such days as have not come since the day that Ephraim departed from Judah – the king of Assyria.'

Taken on its own and without the reference to the king of Assyria, which is usually thought to be a later, historicizing gloss, this verse can be, and has been, taken as either a promise or a threat. Naturally, a decision either way depends to a large extent on how each commentator understands the difficult preceding verses, where similar ambiguities can be found. Without going into the problems of verses 15–16 here, however, it may be stated that in the light of our understanding of the passage as a whole, which is by now becoming clear, verse 17 seems best to be taken as a dire threat, not only against Ahaz personally, but also against his entire dynasty ('your ancestral house [*bêt 'ābîkā*]'), in contrast with the promise to Immanuel in the previous verses. In further support of this approach, it may be noted that 'bring on (*hēbî'* + *'al*)' is usually threatening in nature, and in addition that this interpretation has the advantage that the supposed gloss

---

[37] Irvine, pp. 158–9, recognizes the force of verse 9*b* in this sense ('the prophet warns the royal court that this divine promise will be forfeited'), but then fails to draw the obvious consequences.

at the end of the verse (which must be threatening) would not then be standing the intention of the remainder of the verse on its head, as has cavalierly to be assumed by those who find an original promise in this verse.

What, then, shall we say of Immanuel, in the light of this discussion? Two points would seem to follow. First, there is a clear suggestion that he represents a radical discontinuity with the present heirs of the Davidic family, who have collectively failed to live up to the hopes which might reasonably be expected of them. And secondly, since the sign element is predominantly to be sought in his name rather than in the circumstances of his birth,[38] he also represents continuity of a different sort, namely a continuity in terms of God's provision of effective leadership for his people. The name Immanuel itself contains an obvious allusion to the Zion tradition as attested especially in Psalm 46:7 and 11 (Heb. verses 8 and 12) and Micah 3:11, with which, of course, the royal dynasty was closely associated (see especially 2 Samuel 23:5). It therefore seems that God's commitment to his people overrides a specific concern for any particular historical dynasty.

All this implies that Isaiah 7:14 has somewhat more of a 'messianic' flavour than most recent commentators have been prepared to allow. That is to say, even among those who still accept a broadly royal interpretation of the

---

[38] This is not to deny, but only to put into proper perspective, the fact that the birth-oracle in 7:14 falls into a standard pattern attested both at Ugarit and elsewhere in the Old Testament. The parallels have been frequently set out by others, e.g. H.-P. Müller, 'Glauben und Bleiben: Zur Denkschrift Jesajas Kapitel vi 1–viii 18', in *Studies on Prophecy: a Collection of Twelve Papers* (SVT 26; Leiden, E.J. Brill 1974), pp. 25–54 (38–40); Wildberger, *Jesaja 1*, p. 289 = ET, p. 307; Høgenhaven, *Gott und Volk bei Jesaja*, pp. 88–90. Høgenhaven, *Gott und Volk bei Jesaja*, pp. 88–90

oracle, the tendency has been to regard the birth of Immanuel as the birth merely of Ahaz's successor: Ahaz is rejected, but the future of the dynasty is already secured. This reductionist interpretation does not do justice, however, to the element of discontinuity to which I have drawn attention. Nothing is said of the biologically Davidic nature of the child even while he takes the place that the ideal Davidide should hold. On the other hand, it needs hardly to be said that in the immediate context the prediction of his birth is securely tied to the prevailing historical circumstances of the reign of Ahaz, so that a long-range messianic prediction is ruled out, at least at the primary level. The passage seems to fall firmly between these two extremes.

It is now time to seek to draw together the threads of the argument of this chapter and to relate them to those of the previous chapters as well, in order to round off our discussion of kingship in the work of Isaiah himself and of his earliest tradents down to the time of the exile.

There are points both of contact and of difference between Isaiah 7 and the other royal passages in Isaiah 1–39. Even though the emphasis of the Immanuel sign is on the naming of the child, it is still noteworthy that nothing whatsoever is said about the character of his rule in the terms which we saw previously were fundamental to Isaiah's own understanding of human kingship, summarized above all by the twin concepts of justice and righteousness. At the same time, the passage evinces an interest in the specifically Davidic nature of kingship and its demise, something which was hardly of concern at all to Isaiah himself, so far as we can judge from his recorded sayings, but which coincides with one of the major interests of the Deuteronomists. In both of these respects, therefore, we find a certain confirmation of our conclusion

that there is a considerable distance between Isaiah the
historical prophet and the eventual author of Isaiah 7.

On the other hand, we may detect an element of continuity at a different level. We have seen repeatedly that
Isaiah was deeply committed to the fact of a divinely
appointed leader of the people within the broader context
of a framework of God's purposes for Zion. He could not
conceive of an ideal society without hierarchical leadership, and from everything that we know it would be
expected that such leaders would have implicit faith in
God. In chapter 7 every opportunity is given for that role
to be fulfilled by a member of the house of David, but
Davidic descent is not the sole, or even a necessary,
condition. We may therefore anticipate that Isaiah would
have agreed with the conclusion (cf. 11:1) that in the
broadest terms God is willing to guarantee the quality of
that leadership even at the expense of judging and, by
implication, removing the representatives of the present
dynastic family. And here it is worth reminding ourselves
that Immanuel is not, of course, explicitly designated as
king. As before, it is the role, not the individual or the
dynasty, which emerges as the most significant point.

With regard to Isaiah 7 on its own the suggestion has
already been made that it shows points of contact with the
Deuteronomistic school. If we might explore this possibility a little further, we should note that its attitude towards
the Davidic dynasty is similar to that found in Jeremiah
22-3. Here there is an equal openness to the possibility of
the end of the dynasty, especially in 22:24-30, which is
completely categorical in this regard:

> *Record this man as childless,*
> *a man who shall not succeed in his days;*
> *for none of his offspring shall succeed*

> *in sitting on the throne of Judah,*
> *and ruling again in Judas* (Jer. 22:30).

At the same time, however, we find shortly afterwards[39] an expectation that God will raise up another ruler 'for David', who will reign according to the ancient ideals of wisdom, justice and righteousness (23:5-6). I suggest, therefore, that whatever the prehistory of Isaiah 7 may have been (and my understanding of the history of its composition has already shown that it had such a prehistory), its incorporation into the book of Isaiah is most likely to have been as a reflection on the monarchy in the light of the fall of the house of David to the Babylonians.[40] Its concern was thus primarily to explain the judgment which had fallen in the light of the hardening passage in chapter 6.

In all this, of course, the importance of eventual redactional placement of these various passages should not be forgotten. We have seen, for instance, how important this was for chapter 11, with the shift from a concern for purely 'internal' considerations to a setting in association with the fall of Assyria, something which inevitably gave it a more future orientation. With regard to chapter 7, furthermore, we have seen how it was most likely written originally apart from the book of Isaiah, as we now have it, in close association with the material in chapters 36–9. Its present setting, however, could not have failed to have an influence on the reading of chapter 9, just as conversely it was itself affected by being included in a section of the

---

[39] Discussion of the complicated questions about the composition of this part of Jeremiah would take us too far from our present concern; my point is not whether the historical Jeremiah held this nexus of ideas, but focuses on their presentation in the text, which must be exilic at the earliest.

[40] For possible traces of such an exilic redaction elsewhere in Isaiah 1–39 (some more convincing than others), see R.E. Clements, 'The Prophecies of Isaiah and the Fall of Jerusalem in 587 B.C.', *VT* 30 (1980), pp. 421–36.

book which leads up to that oracle. For all these reasons it is not difficult to understand how both chapters could have come to be read in later Jewish tradition as referring to Hezekiah himself,[41] just as in Christian tradition they fed into a more overtly messianic interpretation. There are elements of truth to which both could legitimately appeal. It has been my contention, however, that what unites the Isaianic witness above all is not the identification of individuals or dynasties, nor the question of nearer or more distant hopes for fulfilment. Rather, it is that each passage contributes its own variation to the theme of the role of leadership in God's ideal society – a leadership characterized by faithfulness, justice and righteousness. Understood thus, Isaiah 32:1 indeed serves as a fitting epitome of the dominant thought of Isaiah on this subject:

> *A king should reign in the interests of righteousness,*
> *and princes rule for the furtherance of justice.*

---

[41] See especially Laato, *Who is Immanuel?*, and Clements, 'The Immanuel Prophecy'. This identification is ruled out by most modern scholars on the ground that the chronology is not possible. This is unlikely to have been appreciated by later readers in antiquity, however, and in view of the fact that the chronology of this period is certainly confused in the biblical record taken as a whole (as all those who have tried to sort it out are agreed), it would be unwise to rule it out categorically even for the earliest author himself of Isaiah 7.

Four

Third Variation: Israel, the Servant and the Nations

In this chapter we turn to the very different world of Isaiah 40–55, generally known as Deutero-Isaiah. With few dissenting voices, this section of the book is usually ascribed to an unnamed prophet of the exilic period who ministered to the community of Judean exiles in Babylon. It is true that in recent years a number of arguments have been raised in support of the view that these chapters have gone through a lengthy process of growth, to which several writers contributed,[1] and also that there have always been one or two scholars who have argued that the location of the writer should be sought in Judah rather than

---

[1] See, for instance, K. Kiesow, *Exodustexte im Jesajabuch: Literarkritische und motivgeschichtliche Analysen* (OBO 24; Freiburg, Universtätsverlag/Göttingen, Vandenhoeck & Ruprecht 1979); R.P. Merendino, *Der Erste und der Letzte: Eine Untersuchung von Jes 40–48* (SVT 31; Leiden, E.J. Brill 1981); J. Vermeylen, 'Le Motif de la création dans le Deutéro–Isaïe', in P. Beauchamp (ed.), *La Création dans l'Orient Ancien* (LecD 127; Paris, Cerf 1987), pp. 183–240; H.–J. Hermisson, 'Einheit und Komplexität Deuterojesajas: Probleme der Redaktionsgeschichte von Jes 40–55', in J. Vermeylen (ed.), *The Book of Isaiah* (BETL 81; Leuven, Leuven University Press and Peeters 1989); Kratz, *Kyros im Deuterojesaja-Buch*; O.H. Steck, *Gottesknecht und Zion: Gesammelte Aufsätze zu Deuterojesaja* (FAT 4; Tübingen, J.C.B. Mohr [Paul Siebeck] 1992).

Babylon.[2] This latter position is scarcely of relevance for our present concern, however, while the former remains difficult to evaluate, not least because its proponents differ so sharply among themselves. While acknowledging the uncertainty and consequent need for caution, I shall nevertheless adopt the usual view for the sake of the present discussion.

Of far greater interest and significance is the wealth of recent studies which have rediscovered the important connections between this and the other two major sections of the book of Isaiah as a whole. For a century or more the emphasis in scholarly work on the book was to treat each major part in complete isolation. This was, perhaps, an inevitable consequence of the well-nigh universal adoption of the hypothesis that different authors, writing at widely different times, were responsible for each main part; no one wished to be accused of fundamentalism by seeming to reintroduce any notion of the unity of the book! Thus it was that histories of prophecy and introductions to the literature of the Old Testament devoted different chapters to each part, separated from one another by other material which 'intervened' from a historical point of view, and commentaries on Isaiah were even published in separate volumes, often by different authors.

With a few earlier adumbrations, however, this totally dominating approach collapsed with astonishing speed in the 1980s, and its ramifications continue to be the subject

---

[2]   The best current representative of this position is H.M. Barstad. For a list of his predecessors, see his *A Way in the Wilderness: The "Second Exodus" in the Message of Second Isaiah* (*JSS* Monograph 12; Manchester, University of Manchester 1989), p. 6, note 9.

of lively discussion and research.[3] Lexical and thematic connections across the traditional boundaries continue to be unearthed, and this naturally leads on to the question whether there has been redactional work on the book as a whole, as well as within each discrete section. In all this, it should be emphasized that there is no going back on the strictly historical results our scholarly predecessors achieved; in my opinion unity of authorship is simply not a viable option. But if it may now be regarded as a reasonably secure hypothesis that at the literary level there are significant connections between the parts, then inevitably we shall read the work of these various authors in a fresh light.

As mentioned at the start of this book it is, perhaps, surprising that the topic of kingship does not appear to have been explored in this context. In traditional studies of messianism in the Old Testament, where each relevant passage was understood to contribute some facet to the portrayal of a single figure (usually, of course, understood retrospectively in the light of the person of Christ), this was not an issue. Passages from one Isaiah or many could be compounded with those of other Old Testament writers in the build-up of the photofit picture with little regard for matters of inner Old Testament literary history. But if, rather, we choose to move from the Old Testament for-wards, then, as we have already seen, it may not be a single portrait that emerges so much as a variety. And certainly within the context of the study of Isaiah, as it prevailed until recently, no one thought to relate the

---

[3] I sought to survey the course of all this in the first chapter of *The Book Called Isaiah* (pp. 1–18), and to add a contribution of my own in the remainder of the book. The flood of literature has not abated since, and it has now gone past the point where a full listing serves any useful purpose.

presentation of kingship in the first part of the book with anything in particular in the second.

In the context of more recent work, however, it might have been expected that the older paths would have been revisited, not simply to go back to outmoded exegesis, but to see whether there are literary connections embedded in this material as well. This, at any rate, is what the present chapter will seek to explore. In doing so, it should be made clear that the connections we shall look at are not in themselves of the sort that could establish that, say, Deutero-Isaiah was familiar with the written sayings of his great eighth-century predecessor. That is a conclusion which would have to be established on other, firmer grounds, and indeed I have previously sought to do just that. The present discussion, therefore, has necessarily to take that case for granted. *On the assumption* (which I take to be well-founded) that Deutero-Isaiah was familiar with an early form of the first part of the book, did he make any particular use of the material we examined in the previous two chapters?

An obvious place to begin our search is the one passage in Isaiah 40-55, namely 55:3–5, which refers explicitly to the person of David:

> *Incline your ear, and come to me;*
> *listen, so that you may live.*
> *I will make with you an everlasting covenant,*
> *my steadfast, sure love for David.*[4]
> *See, I made him a witness to the peoples,*
> *a leader and commander for the peoples.*
> *See, you shall call nations that you do not know,*
> *and nations that you do not know shall run to you,*

---

[4]   I have defended this traditional rendering against some who have challenged it in my '"The Sure Mercies of David": Subjective or Objective Genitive?', *JSS* 23 (1978), pp. 31–49; see too W.C. Kaiser, 'The Unfailing Kindnesses Promised to David: Isaiah 55.3', *JSOT* 45 (1989), pp. 91–8.

> because of the Lord your God, the Holy One of Israel,
> for he has glorified you.

The first point which has to be emphatically asserted about this passage is that it manifests radical innovation by comparison with what we have seen hitherto. The principal indication of this fact is that the covenant with David is here potentially transferred to the people as a whole.[5] The 'you' in the sentence 'I will make with you an everlasting covenant' is plural (*lākem*), as are the imperative verbs and pronominal suffixes which precede it.[6]

There are, of course, those who would construe this verse differently, suggesting that by reaffirming the covenant with David as an individual the people will be brought into the enjoyment of the blessings which accompany it for the nation as a whole. On this showing, the passage becomes more traditionally messianic.[7] But this minority approach seems unlikely for the following reasons, among others:

> (i) in the expression 'to make a covenant with', the person or people next referred to are those who enter into one side of the covenant relationship. It is true that in Hebrew there are various

---

[5] See, for instance, O. Eissfeldt, 'The Promises of Grace to David in Isaiah 55:1–5', in B.W. Anderson and W. Harrelson (eds.), *Israel's Prophetic Heritage: Essays in Honor of James Muilenburg* (London, SCM Press 1962), pp. 196–207 = 'Die Gnadenverheissungen an David in Jes 55, 1–5', in *Kleine Schriften* 4 (Tübingen, J.C.B. Mohr 1968), pp. 44–52; C.R. North, *The Second Isaiah: Introduction, Translation and Commentary to Chapters xl–lv* (Oxford, Clarendon Press 1964), pp. 256–8; Westermann, *Das Buch Jesaja*, pp. 227–8 = ET, pp. 283–4; R.N. Whybray, *Isaiah 40–66* (NCB; London, Oliphants 1975), pp. 191–2.

[6] In verse 5, there is a change to singular forms. Since it is difficult to see that any new subject has been introduced, these must be taken as collective, the situation having been made clear by what precedes.

[7] See recently, for instance, Kaiser, 'The Unfailing Kindnesses'; Motyer, *The Prophecy of Isaiah*, pp. 453–5; among older commentators, Duhm, pp. 385–6; J. Skinner, *The Book of the Prophet Isaiah Chapters xl–lxvi* (CBSC; Cambridge, Cambridge University Press 1917), pp. 159–60.

prepositions used in this expression, all of which tend to be translated 'with' in English. These, however, reflect the different nature of the covenant relationship, whether the two parties are equal or whether one is a superior, and so on.[8] In the present instance, the preposition l^e is used, appropriately reflecting God's superior status. I am not aware of any reason why it should here exceptionally have the sense 'make a covenant with someone else which will be of benefit to you'.[9]

(ii) Verses 4 and 5 support this understanding of the expression. In verse 4 the position of David ('him')[10] within the covenant is spelt out: he achieved a status of international leadership, and the verb is appropriately in the perfect. In parallel, verse 5 now says that Israel ('you')[11] will take this place, the verbs being imperfect. So there is a shift from David's role to Israel's, and this is to be understood as a consequence of God's transferring the Davidic covenant to the nation as a whole in verse 3*b*.

(iii) There is a close parallel to our verse at 61:8, 'and I will make an everlasting covenant with them', and there it is perfectly clear that 'they' are a party to the covenant. It seems probable, in view of the comparable wording, that this verse reflects knowledge of 55:3 and, although it obviously includes a further element of reinterpretation, it builds upon the understanding of 55:3 for which I have argued.

I conclude, therefore, that the usual understanding of this verse is correct. The covenant relationship David once

---

[8] See M. Weinfeld, 'ברית', *TDOT* 2 (Grand Rapids, Eerdmans 1974–), pp. 259–60.

[9] E.J. Young, *The Book of Isaiah*, 3 (Grand Rapids, Eerdmans 1972), p. 377, for instance, gives no reason or support for his dictum that '*For you* or *with you* is to be construed as an ethical dative of advantage, *for your benefit*'.

[10] Again, it is difficult to find other cause than special pleading for Young's opinion that the suffix refers 'to the seed of David, the Messiah' (p. 378).

[11] Motyer, *The Prophecy of Isaiah*, p. 455, maintains that this refers to David as well, and calls this 'a typical idiom of the prophets, introducing fresh emphasis by turning from description (4ab) to address (5ab)'. He gives no examples in support, however, and not even Kaiser, 'The Unfailing Kindnesses', takes verse 5 in this way (cf. p. 95). The conclusion of the verse, 'for he has glorified you', is close to what is said of Israel elsewhere in Deutero-Isaiah; cf. 44:23; 49:3; and for the the verse as a whole, cf. 49:7.

enjoyed with God is now to be enjoyed by the nation as a whole.

With that established, it is important next to notice, however, that 'the role of David that is transferred is quite limited'.[12] Based on the clear allusions to Psalm 18 (see especially verses 43-4 [Heb. verses 44–5]) and Psalm 89, together with the reference to David as a 'witness to the peoples', Clifford demonstrates what the context of verses 4–5 in any case suggests, namely that it is David's role towards the gentile nations which is uppermost in the author's mind. This is certainly the chief point in the Psalms in question, and the use of 'witness' in Deutero-Isaiah supports the same. This term is not used of David elsewhere,[13] so that influence from a wider royal tradition is unlikely. It is therefore reasonable to assume that it is here used with the same sense that Deutero-Isaiah gives it elsewhere, namely, Israel's witness to the sovereignty of God among the nations (cf. 43:9–10 and 44:8–9). 'Israel's prosperity, visible to the nations especially in its new exodus-conquest, witnesses Yahweh's superiority and hence Israel's primary place among the nations' (Clifford, p. 32). Here, then, is a second element of innovation in

---

[12]   R.J. Clifford, 'Isaiah 55: Invitation to a Feast', in C.L. Meyers and M. O'Connor (eds.), *The Word of the Lord Shall Go Forth: Essays in Honor of David Noel Freedman in Celebration of his Sixtieth Birthday* (Winona Lake, Ind., Eisenbrauns 1983), pp. 27–35; see too his *Fair Spoken and Persuading: An Interpretation of Second Isaiah* (New York, Paulist Press 1984), pp. 188–94. In both places, Clifford discusses helpfully the connection between the passage we are particularly examining and its wider context in the chapter as a whole.

[13]   Though see J.H. Eaton, 'The King as God's Witness', *ASTI* 7 (1970), pp. 25–40, and *Kingship and the Psalms* (SBT, 2nd series 32; London, SCM Press 1976; 2nd edition, Sheffield, Sheffield Academic Press 1986), pp. 182–95, who thinks it may be found at Ps. 89:37 [Heb. verse 38]. Usage elsewhere in Deutero-Isaiah (which Eaton also compares) seems a more likely source of elucidation than tasks described elsewhere in the Psalms which are not explicitly so designated.

Deutero-Isaiah by comparison with the first part of the book, for we saw there that the role of the Davidic king was restricted to inner-Israelite concerns.

Thirdly, the language of this passage also differs from that of Isaiah of Jerusalem. Although he refers to David (e.g. 9:7), he never refers to a 'covenant' with him in the manner of 55:3. We saw that he demonstrates awareness of some of the language and themes of such cardinal passages as 2 Samuel 7, or at least of the tradition which may lie behind them; but because his focus was on the Davidic role rather than on the survival of the dynasty as such, he did not make use of this technical terminology, perhaps precisely because it would have been open to misunderstanding, in terms of God's unconditional commitment to the Davidic family. Deutero-Isaiah shows no such inhibitions, however, but equally there is no danger of misunderstanding because in his case it is no longer the Davidic family, but rather the nation as a whole, which is in view. Nevertheless, this difference in usage makes it likely that the terminology which he does share with Isaiah of Jerusalem ('my steadfast, sure love for David [*ḥasdê dāwīd hanne'emānîm*]')[14] was not drawn from Isaiah, but rather directly from his knowledge of the broader Davidic tradition with its many literary reflexes, not least in the Psalms.

It is clear, therefore, that this passage should not be understood as building directly on the foundation of the so-called messianic passages in Isaiah 1–39. Thus far we do not seem to have so much a variation on a theme as a new theme, altogether. However, before we draw any such conclusion we shall need to set alongside this passage a

---

[14]   This phrase as such does not, of course, appear in Isaiah 1–39, but we have seen that each individual word within it plays an important part, one way or another, in his thinking.

good deal of the remainder of the teaching of this prophet in the light of our case that the promises to David, at least with regard to the nations, are now transferred to the people of Israel as a whole. It may be that that thought, so novel when we first meet it, will give us a clue to unravel the meaning of many other passages in this prophet which relate to the same circle of ideas. And if that should indeed prove to be the case, then it will be worth remembering that the verses we have been looking at come at the very end of this section of the book. We have come at them cold, so to speak. In reality, we ought to take them only after having read all that goes before. Perhaps, in that wider context, we shall find that they serve to bring a major line of thought to its climax rather than appearing as a bolt out of the blue, and that within that line of thought there will be material closer to, or at least relating to, the circle of ideas we explored in Isaiah 1–39.

Before turning to that, however, it should also be pointed out that there are a couple of details where echoes of the first part of Isaiah might be detected. We have been so caught up with drawing distinctions that we might be tempted to overlook them. First, the reference to 'listening' and the 'ear' at the start of verse 3 could point us in the direction of 6:10, especially in view of the obvious prominence of this theme in many other parts of the book, and this is strengthened in the present instance by the fact that it picks up in particular on the command in verse 2 to 'listen carefully'. This uses an unusual (though not unique) construction in the Hebrew, namely an imperative followed by the infinitive absolute, *šimʻû šāmôaʻ* (normally, these verbal elements appear in the reverse order, but cf. Job 13:17; 21:2; 37:2). It is therefore striking that exactly the same form is found at 6:9 (and nowhere else in the book), where the NRSV renders 'keep listening'.

Now secondly, if there is indeed a hint in this that Deutero-Isaiah's audience is being given a chance to undo (or at least not to repeat) the fateful inability of Isaiah's generation to listen, then it would fit very well with the fact that the promise about the Davidic covenant in verse 3*b* is clearly made conditional upon it. Once again this is unfortunately obscured in the NRSV, which starts a new sentence at this point: 'I will make with you . . .' In fact, however, this should certainly be connected with the preceding, either with an indication of purpose ('so that I may make with you . . .') or at least of consequence ('and then I will make with you . . .').[15] The implication that the people's assumption of their 'royal' role is dependent upon their faith and obedience fits very well with what we saw of Isaiah's own attitude with regard to the kings of his day, and indeed to the people as a whole. This was all found to come to particularly clear expression in the different levels of the redactional assemblage usually referred to as the Isaiah Memoir, so that the two points just mentioned, when taken together, suggest the possibility of reflection by Deutero-Isaiah on Isaiah 6 and its sequel.

In order to clarify, by way of summary, what we have chiefly learned from this passage in Isaiah 55, and by way of introduction to the following discussion, it may be helpful to set out the situation in diagrammatic form. In much of the literature which reflects the pre-exilic period the role of the king was pivotal in relation to the people and their God. As is clear from the frequent judgments

---

[15] The verb has a simple (not consecutive) *wāw* on a cohortative form of the imperfect: *weʾekretâ*. For the construction, see, for instance, B.K. Waltke and M. O'Connor, *An Introduction to Biblical Hebrew Syntax* (Winona Lake, Ind., Eisenbrauns 1990), p. 575; P. Joüon, *A Grammar of Biblical Hebrew* (translated and revised by T. Muraoka; Rome, Pontifical Biblical Institute 1993²), §116; J.C.L. Gibson, *Davidson's Introductory Hebrew Grammar: Syntax* (Edinburgh, T. & T. Clark 1994), §87.

expressed in the books of Kings, for instance, it was upon his obedience to God that the well-being of the nation depended. Similarly, in such psalms as Psalm 72, his faithfulness to God in the exercise of justice and righteousness is the key to the prosperity of the people Israel. If he was faithless or disobedient, the people suffered. Equally, of course, it was necessary for the people to obey the king if the whole system was to function effectively. This may be set out simply as follows:

Each link in the diagram works on a two-way basis: of faithful obedience from bottom to top, and of consequent 'blessing', broadly conceived, moving from top to bottom. Both sets of relationship needed to be ordered properly if blessing was ultimately to flow from God to the people.[16]

If we now translate this in the terms of Isaiah 55 we find that the people have moved up into the position occupied previously by the king, and further it is clear from verses 4–5 that it is the nations who move into the slot vacated by the people, thus:

---

[16] Cf. J.P.M. Walsh, *The Mighty from their Thrones: Power in the Biblical Tradition* (Philadelphia, Fortress Press 1987).

In respect to the nature of the relationships nothing else
has changed.

It seems to me that this rather simple way of looking at
things helps to clarify several matters with regard to
Deutero-Isaiah as a whole. I shall very briefly give an
outline of these before moving on to consider in more
detail a few key passages which relate to our central theme
in particular.

In the first place it becomes easier to appreciate why
Deutero-Isaiah expends so much effort seeking to build up
the faith of his audience. After many years in exile it is
clear that they have become totally discouraged, feeling
either that God has abandoned and forgotten them or
that, if he has not, he is powerless to do anything practical
to help them. The fragments quoted from their laments
reflect this point of view, e.g. 40:27; 42:22; 50:1–2;
51:12–13. To counter this point of view Deutero-Isaiah
advances a long series of arguments, which may broadly
be broken down into three groups:[17] God is the creator,
and thus has the power to change things (e.g. 40:12–31);
he controls history even now with the early rise of Cyrus,
so that it is not idle to believe that he will move to restore
Israel (e.g. 41:1–20); and he has told the truth through his

17   Cf. D.R. Jones, 'Isaiah – II and III', in M. Black and H.H. Rowley (eds.),
Peake's Commentary on the Bible (London, Nelson 1962), pp. 517–18.

prophets in the past, so that it is reasonable now to believe his new message of liberation and restoration which Deutero-Isaiah is commissioned to deliver (e.g. 41:21-9). What is more, Deutero-Isaiah skilfully uses methods of argumentation, such as the disputation and the trial speech, which function persuasively in rhetorical terms to press home his message of comfort, assurance and encouragement.[18] Clearly, if the relationships set out schematically in our diagram were to be effective, it was a prerequisite that Israel should stand in a position of faith and obedience towards her God; otherwise there was no hope that the prophet's larger vision would even get off the ground.

Secondly, I believe that this way of looking at things helps resolve one of the long-standing disagreements among students of Deutero-Isaiah regarding his attitude to the gentile nations. During rather more than the first half of this century, and perhaps under the influence of the prevailing liberal theology of those times, Deutero-Isaiah was understood as the great universalist of the Old Testament. Much emphasis was placed on those passages which speak of 'a light to the nations' (42:6; 49:6; cf. 51:4), of 'all the ends of the earth' turning to God to be saved (45:22), and of salvation reaching to the ends of the earth (49:6). This was linked logically with what was seen as the prophet's uncompromising monotheism: if there is only one God, then he must be the God of all the nations, and Israel's role, not least as servant, was to witness to him on a universal scale. Such a view comes to classic expression in a commentary such as that of C.R. North (1964).

---

[18] See, for instance, A. Schoors, *I am God your Saviour: A Form–Critical Study of the Main Genres in Is. xl–lv* (SVT 24; Leiden, E.J. Brill 1973); Y. Gitay, *Prophecy and Persuasion: A Study of Isaiah 40–48* (FThL 14; Bonn, Linguistica Biblica 1981).

This prevailing opinion was sharply challenged, however, from the 1950s onwards,[19] as scholars began to draw attention to another set of passages which speak rather of the nations' subservient role to Israel (45:24–5; 49:22), of them coming over to her in chains and bowing down to her (45:14; 49:7) and licking the dust on her feet (49:23). On this view Deutero-Isaiah's vision was restricted to the redemption of Israel, and he had little or no interest in the fate of the nations who had formerly oppressed her. He was, in short, a thoroughgoing nationalist. The first commentary, so far as I know, to seek to work out this view in such a format was that of R.N. Whybray (1975).

At first sight it seems difficult to reconcile these two points of view, and indeed there are some who have adopted various devices to get round the problem: perhaps we are dealing with more than one author, or a single author changed his mind over time, or he did not appreciate the full significance of the more universalistic parts of his message, or the terms which he used should be redefined.[20] And the problem becomes more intractable when the commentaries written from one perspective are

---

[19] See, for instance, N.H. Snaith, 'The Servant of the Lord in Deutero-Isaiah', in H.H. Rowley (ed.), *Studies in Old Testament Prophecy Presented to Professor Theodore H. Robinson* (Edinburgh, T. & T. Clark 1950), pp. 187–200; and, more fully, 'Isaiah 40–66: A Study of the Teaching of the Second Isaiah and its Consequences', in H.M. Orlinsky and N.H. Snaith, *Studies on the Second Part of the Book of Isaiah* (SVT 14; Leiden, E.J. Brill 1967), pp. 135–264; P.A.H. de Boer, *Second-Isaiah's Message* (OTS 11; Leiden, E.J. Brill 1956); R. Martin–Achard, *Israël et les nations: la perspective missionnaire de l'Ancien Testament* (Neuchâtel and Paris, Delachaux & Nestlé 1959), esp. pp. 13–30 = ET, *A Light to the Nations: A Study of the Old Testament Conception of Israel's Mission to the World* (Edinburgh and London, Oliver and Boyd 1962), pp. 8–31.

[20] For documentation of all these possibilities see the opening pages of D.W. Van Winkle, 'The Relationship of the Nations to Yahweh and to Israel in Isaiah xl–lv', *VT* 35 (1985), pp. 446–58. A balanced approach to the topic may also be found in J. Blenkinsopp, 'Second Isaiah – Prophet of Universalism', *JSOT* 41 (1988), pp. 83–103, though he approaches the issue in a very different way from that adopted above.

consulted in relation to the passages which those of the opposite persuasion trumpet as their major proof texts. To be blunt, there appears to be a good deal of wriggling and special pleading going on, which suggests that neither side can proclaim an outright victory.

It may be suggested that our presentation offered above on the basis of Isaiah 55:3–5 may point to a way forward.[21] We have seen that, like the king in the pre-exilic period, Israel now stands in a mediating position between God and the nations, and that this involves a two-way nature to the relationship between each adjacent pair in the diagram. The purpose of the whole is that God's blessing (or 'salvation', to use Deutero-Isaiah's preferred term) should reach from himself to the wider circle represented by the bottom line of the diagram – in this case the nations. This, however, is mediated through the central figure, who thus from one point of view enjoys a peculiarly privileged relationship with God, and from the other is in a position of particular and sometimes costly responsibility. Equally, however, there are privileges and responsibilities by those on the bottom line: responsibilities of obedience and submission to God's chosen mediator on the one hand, and the potential to enjoy as a result all the blessing which God has in store for them. It seems to me that on this understanding we can hold together the apparent tension between those groups of passages which seem to favour universalism on the one hand, and nationalism on the other. Both are true, and the emphasis on one side or the

---

21 For a fuller discussion than is possible here see the article of Van Winkle just cited, to which I am much indebted. Van Winkle does not, however, start from (or even refer to) Isaiah 55; his concern, rather, is for exegesis of some of the key passages which have featured in the universalist/nationalist debate. He points out that his approach was advanced, only, apparently, to be completely forgotten, by G.F. Oehler, *Theologie des Alten Testaments*, 2 (Stuttgart, J.F. Steinkopf 1882²), pp. 205–8.

other of the relationship in any given passage will depend upon the prophet's rhetorical purpose at that particular point.

I am aware that this seems at first to be a rather crude and oversimplified way of looking at what is certainly a complex situation, but I believe that the basic pattern is well founded, and we shall be returning to it when we consider some cardinal passages in more detail to see how it works out on the ground of specific texts.

The third and final general reflection that arises from our presentation of Isaiah 55 brings us even closer to the heart of our main topic, for it concerns the issue of kingship directly. It will be recalled that in chapter one considerable weight was placed upon the observation that in Deutero-Isaiah only God was termed 'king', and that somewhat emphatically.[22] As a reminder, the specific texts are 41:21, 43:15, 44:6, and 52:7. Now, since the human king has dropped out of Deutero-Isaiah's scheme altogether, this creates no difficulty or confusion, and of course the two points are no doubt closely related. At the same time, however, we have seen that Israel as a whole now assumes the role which the human king once played, and therefore we might expect that language formerly used of the king will now be applied to Israel. And this we find, not only explicitly in 55:4–5, but elsewhere too. For instance, Conrad has stressed that earlier in the book (as

---

[22] J. Blenkinsopp, *Prophecy in Israel*, sees this as part of a wider polemic, 'intended to counter the allure of Babylonian religion and the Marduk cult in particular' (p. 213). He draws attention to a number of features of this cult, as celebrated notably in the New Year *akitu* festival, to which aspects of Deutero-Isaiah's message seem intended to respond as a kind of mirror image. Behind all this will have been the issue of where real power (including political power) resides. There is no need to question this in principle; my concern is to go on to the further question of the implications of God's kingship for Israel and the nations in Deutero–Isaiah's thought. The two approaches are not mutually exclusive.

well as elsewhere) the 'fear not' oracles, which he regards as war-oracles, are directed towards the individual kings Ahaz and Hezekiah (7:4-9; 37:6); now, in Deutero-Isaiah, these are addressed regularly and exclusively to Israel as a whole (e.g. 41:8-13; 41:14-16; 43:1-7; 44:2-5).[23] 'The fact that Second Isaiah uses a royal form to address the chosen community is further evidence that Second Isaiah is applying royal traditions to the community' (p. 109). Similarly, Wildberger has argued that the election of Israel, which is so prominent a feature in Deutero-Isaiah, is to be traced to the traditions associated particularly with the election of the Davidic king.[24] And finally, Eissfeldt has demonstrated that there is an extraordinarily high incidence of common language between Psalm 89 and Deutero-Isaiah, so much so that the prophet almost certainly knew this Psalm.[25] If so, it not only reinforces the point that the language of election probably alludes to the royal traditions (cf. Psalm 89:4 [3]), but also suggests that the regular designation of Israel as God's servant in Deutero-Isaiah is also a deliberate transfer to the people of a title once ascribed especially (though of course not exclusively) to the person of the king (cf. Psalm 89:4,21,40 [3,20,39]; Isaiah 41:8,9; 43:10; 44:1,2; 44:21; 45:4; 48:20[26]).

---

[23]   E.W. Conrad, 'The Community as King in Second Isaiah', in J.T. Butler, E.W. Conrad and B.C. Ollenburger (eds.), *Understanding the Word: Essays in Honor of Bernhard W. Anderson* (JSOTS 37; Sheffield, Sheffield Academic 1985), pp. 99–111.

[24]   H. Wildberger, 'Die Neuinterpretation des Erwählungsglaubens Israels in der Krise der Exilzeit', in H.J. Stoebe (ed.), *Wort–Gebot–Glaube: Beiträge zur Theologie des Alten Testaments: Walter Eichrodt zum 80. Geburtstag* (ATANT 59; Zürich, Zwingli 1970), pp. 307–24.

[25]   Eissfeldt, 'The Promises of Grace to David'.

[26]   In these passages, it is either stated explicitly or at least clearly implied that Israel (or Jacob) is God's servant; we shall return shortly to some of the other passages where there is reference to a servant but where there is no such overt identification.

With this background in mind, we turn now to consider a few specific passages in Deutero-Isaiah which seem to be particularly relevant to our main theme. First, Isaiah 42:1–4:

> Here is my servant, whom I uphold,
>   my chosen, in whom my soul delights;
> I have put my spirit upon him;
>   he will bring forth justice to the nations.
> He will not cry or lift up his voice,
>   or make it heard in the street;
> a bruised reed he will not break,
>   and a dimly burning wick he will not quench;
>   he will faithfully bring forth justice.
> He will not grow faint or be crushed
>   until he has established justice in the earth;
>   and the coastlands wait for his teaching.

This is, of course, the first of those four passages which, since the time of Duhm, have been known as the Servant Songs. In consequence, they have often been treated in isolation from their wider context in Isaiah and exclusively in relationship with one another, and this has allowed a wide variety of identifications of the servant to be proposed.[27] Commentators have become increasingly dissatisfied with this approach, however,[28] so that even though there remain features which distinguish these

---

[27] For an exhaustive survey of older views see C.R. North, *The Suffering Servant in Deutero-Isaiah: An Historical and Critical Study* (Oxford, Oxford University Press 1956²). For more recent discussions see H. Haag, *Der Gottesknecht bei Deuterojesaja* (EF 233; Darmstadt, Wissenschaftliche Buchgesellschaft 1985).

[28] See especially T.N.D. Mettinger, *A Farewell to the Servant Songs: A Critical Examination of an Exegetical Axiom* (Lund, CWK Gleerup 1983), and H.M. Barstad, 'The Future of the "Servant Songs": Some Reflections on the Relationship of Biblical Scholarship to its own Tradition', in S.E. Balentine and J. Barton (eds.), *Language, Theology, and the Bible: Essays in Honour of James Barr* (Oxford, Clarendon Press 1994), pp. 261–70.

passages from others in Deutero-Isaiah[29] it is no longer considered appropriate to extract them, so to speak, from their present context and to treat them as some kind of separate book. In support of this it is perhaps not sufficiently realized how much they differ among themselves. Form-critically they are diverse, just as they are in terms of speaker and addressee: the present passage is spoken by God to an unspecified audience (which the content of the passage shows cannot, at least, be identified with the nations), 49:1–6 is addressed by the servant himself to the nations, 50:4–9 is a soliloquy by someone who is not identified at all in the passage (so that one naturally thinks in the first instance of the prophet himself[30]), but which the interpretative verses 10–11 following suggest was early understood to be the servant, and 52:13–53:12 is again spoken by God (cf. 52:13, 53:12), but incorporates a lengthy report in the first-person plural (53:1–10), which the context suggests is spoken by the kings of 52:15. In view of such differences at the formal level, to go no further, it would be difficult to see how these passages could be read together and in isolation as if they formed a separate book.

---

[29] See, for instance, J.A. Emerton's review of Mettinger's monograph in 'Review of Mettinger, *A Farewell to the Servant Songs*', *BiOr* 48 (1991), cols. 626–32.

[30] It is noteworthy in this connection that 50:4–9 has fewer parallels of language and phraseology with the first two passages than they share between themselves, and that it is linked on the same basis with a wider circle of other Deutero–Isaianic passages than they are; cf. A. Laato, *The Servant of YHWH and Cyrus: A Reinterpretation of the Exilic Messianic Programme in Isaiah 40–55* (ConB, OT series 35; Stockholm, Almqvist & Wiksell International 1992), pp. 29–46.

There is a considerable degree of agreement nowadays that, whatever else is to be said about the servant in Isaiah 42:1–4, he is presented to us in royal guise.[31] This conclusion is based both on inner Old Testament parallels and on connections with certain Babylonian sources. Although individual points mentioned about the servant in verse 1 can be paralleled with other groups within ancient Israel, such as prophets or priests, the king is the only figure of whom they can all be postulated. The combination of all these points therefore gives the strongest possible support to the view that the servant here is a royal figure.

Without any attempt to be exhaustive, the following list gives a flavour of the evidence on which such a conclusion is based:

> (i) 'The first words plainly describe a designation. This means that someone with the right to do so designates or appoints someone else to perform a task or to hold an office.'[32] This was the form adopted for the presentation of the first kings of Israel, Saul (1 Samuel 9:17; 12:13; cf. 10:24, which additionally introduces the language of God's choice; see below), and David (with slightly different language, 1 Samuel 16:12; the language of election is again present in verses 8 and 10, while endowment with the Spirit follows in verse 13 – again, see below); see too Zechariah 9:9 for a later example of the same formula in connection with a king.

---

[31] In addition to the commentaries see especially O. Kaiser, *Der Königliche Knecht: Eine traditionsgeschichtlich-exegetische Studie über die Ebed-Jahwe-Lieder bei Deuterojesaja* (FRLANT 70; Göttingen, Vandenhoeck & Ruprecht 1959), pp. 14–31; H. Ringgren, *The Messiah in the Old Testament* (SBT 18; London, SCM Press 1956); J.H. Eaton, *Festal Drama in Deutero-Isaiah* (London, SPCK 1979), pp. 47–9 (this, however, as part of a wider thesis which I am unable to follow); Laato, *The Servant of YHWH and Cyrus*, pp. 74–87.

[32] Westermann, *Isaiah 40–66*, p. 93 (= German original, p. 78).

(ii) 'My servant': although this is a widespread title for those in the service of God in the Old Testament,[33] the king (and especially David) is certainly included prominently among them, as we saw from Psalm 89.[34]

(iii) 'Whom I uphold (*tmk*)': the verb with this sense is not very common in the Old Testament, but is used with reference to the king in Psalm 63:9 [8] (verse 12 [11] shows that the king is in view). It has long been recognized, however, that the expression here needs to be understood in connection with its use elsewhere in Deutero-Isaiah and against its background in some close parallels in Akkadian inscriptions.[35] At 41:10 God says of his servant Israel that 'I will uphold you with my victorious right hand', while elsewhere he uses a similar expression, though with a different verb, both of Israel again ('I . . . hold your right hand', 41:13; 'I have taken you by the hand and kept you', 42:6) and of Cyrus ('whose right hand I have grasped', 45:1). Many examples of this motif have been found in Akkadian sources which are close in time to Deutero-Isaiah, and in which Marduk grasps the hand of the king (often in ritual contexts) in order to support him. It is likely that the prophet's use of the terms is part of his anti-Babylonian polemic.

(iv) 'My chosen': the situation here is somewhat similar to that in the case of 'servant', in that (with God as subject) a number of different types of people are chosen for office, among them again the first kings of Israel (e.g. 1 Samuel 10:24; 16:1–13; 2 Samuel 6:21; 1 Kings 8:16; 11:34; cf. Deuteronomy 17:15), and we saw how this belief was also reflected in Psalm 89. Indeed, it is striking that Psalm 89:4 [3] is the only place outside the second half of the book of Isaiah where the specific form 'my chosen one

---

[33] Cf. H. Ringgren, U. Rüterswörden and H. Simian–Yofre, 'עבד', *ThWAT* 5, (Stuttgart, Kohlhammer 1970-), cols. 982–1012.

[34] Among other references, cf. 2 Sam. 3:18; 7:5, 8, 19–21, 25–9; 1 Kgs. 11:13, 32, 34; 14:8; 2 Kgs. 19:34; 20:6; Jer. 33:21–2, 26; Ps. 78:70; 132:10, 2 Chron. 6:42; for the use of the equivalent term, used of the king in Akkadian inscriptions, see M.-J. Seux, *Épithètes royales akkadiennes et sumériennes* (Paris, Letouzey et Ane 1967), pp. 360–3.

[35] See, for example, Kaiser, *Der Königliche Knecht*, pp. 20–1; S.M. Paul, 'Deutero-Isaiah and Cuneiform Royal Inscriptions', *JAOS* 88 (1968), pp. 180–6; Laato, *The Servant of YHWH*, p. 57; for the texts, see Seux, *Épithètes*, pp. 345–6.

($b^eh\hat{\imath}r\hat{\imath}$)' stands in parallel with 'servant'.[36] There is, however, an additional point to be made here, and that is that, unlike in the case of 'servant', the language of divine election is not used of the prophets. Seebass follows Quell[37] in explaining this as due to the fact that the prophetic word is characterized by the unexpected and unforeseen, and continues, 'Therefore, it does not seem very likely to me that Isa. 42:1 means God's servant is chosen as a prophet is chosen. With Westermann,[38] it is much better to think of a *homo politicus*, whose politics, of course, are fundamentally different from politics as it is usually understood'.[39]

(v) 'I have put my spirit upon him':[40] this phrase too is (perhaps deliberately) reminiscent of the election of David as king; cf. 1 Samuel 16:13, and inasmuch as anointing is associated symbolically with the gift of the Spirit (see further Isaiah 61:1), there will always have been a reminder of this endowment at the accession of each new king. But of course, beyond this general association of the Spirit with kingship, we have already met the specific instance of Isaiah 11:2, which many commentators also assume to be in the back of the writer's mind at this point, particularly because in both cases the gift of the Spirit seems to be preparatory for a judicial role.

---

[36] The plural form occurs once in a comparable parallelism at Psalm 105:6 (= 1 Chronicles 16:13), where the servant is Abraham (in Chronicles: Israel) and 'his chosen ones' are the 'children of Jacob'.

[37] G. Quell, 'ἐκλέγομαι, B. Election in the Old Testament', *TDNT* 4, (Grand Rapids, Eerdmans 1964–74), pp. 153–4.

[38] In fact, Westermann, *Isaiah 40–66*, p. 94 (= German original, p. 78) reaches this conclusion by a different route: 'One feature makes a clear distinction between the designation of the Servant here and that of a prophet – the very nature of the latter means that there can be no witnesses to it. All the passages which describe a prophet's call leave this in no doubt. On the other hand, . . . at a king's designation the presence of witnesses to whom it is said, 'Behold this is . . .' is essential.'

[39] H. Seebass, 'בחר', *TDOT* 2 (Grand Rapids, Eerdmans 1974-), p. 76.

[40] I have deliberately passed over the phrase 'in whom my soul delights' as being insufficiently precise for our purposes; so far as I can see, the verb is used in relation to the king only in the later 1 Chronicles 28:4. For the general sentiment (though with a different verb) see, for instance, Psalm 18:20 [19], and for ancient Near Eastern parallels see Laato, *The Servant of YHWH*, pp. 51–3.

At the risk of repeating myself, while most of these five points could individually be explained in connection with some other role for the servant, such as that of a prophet, the only one which allows us to hold them all together is that of a royal figure.

It has been necessary to justify this conclusion carefully, even though it is widely accepted nowadays, because two important consequences for our study follow directly from it. In the first place, it gives us a clear context within which to interpret the one phrase in the first verse to which we have not yet given attention, 'he will bring forth justice to the nations'. This role seems to be the goal of all the preparatory designation which has gone before it, and that it is the main theme of the passage as a whole is confirmed by the observation that it is virtually repeated twice more in the following verses: 'he will faithfully bring forth justice' in verse 3, and '. . . until he has established justice in the earth' in verse 4. It is this role, rather than discussion of the identity of the servant, which ought to be at the centre of exegesis of this passage.[41]

'Justice (*mišpāṭ*)' here has been understood in an astonishing variety of ways.[42] These range from the very general, such as 'religion',[43] 'truth'[44], 'the principles of true religion',[45] or 'revealed law',[46] through to so specific an interpretation as that it refers to the judgment or verdict

---

[41]   So correctly North, *The Second Isaiah*, p. 107: 'These words must be the key to the understanding of the passage'.

[42]   In addition to the commentaries see especially W.A.M. Beuken, '*Mišpāṭ*. The First Servant Song and its Context', *VT* 22 (1972), pp. 1–30; and J. Jeremias, 'מִשְׁפָּט', im ersten Gottesknechtlied', *VT* 22 (1972), pp. 31–42.

[43]   H. Wheeler Robinson, *The Cross in the Old Testament* (London, SCM Press 1955), p. 61.

[44]   P. Volz, *Jesaja II* (KAT 9; Leipzig, A. Deichertsche Verlagsbuchhandlung D. Werner Scholl 1932), p. 153.

[45]   Skinner, *Isaiah Chapters xl–lxvi*, p. 30.

[46]   North, *The Second Isaiah*, p. 108.

of the law court in the trial scenes (e.g. 41:1–5, 21–9) that the gods of the nations are nothing and that the Lord alone is God.[47] It is difficult to see, however, how this latter suggestion of the proclamation of the court's verdict can be related to the patient activity of the servant in verses 2–3, while the former, general proposals seem to go considerably beyond what *mišpāṭ*, without further qualification, can bear.

In the context of the introduction of one who is so clearly a royal figure, it seems to me that we should not look for any such unusual meaning for *mišpāṭ* here. As we have seen, both in the Old Testament and in the wider world of the ancient Near East, justice was consistently regarded as one of the primary responsibilities of the king. Furthermore, in the exercise of that duty, he was to have particular regard for those least able to defend themselves, such as the orphan and widow, and the 'bruised reed' and 'dimly burning wick' of verse 2 are an admirable poetic description of such people. And finally, we have already noted that the endowment with the Spirit, which immediately precedes our phrase, points us clearly in the direction of 11:1–5, where its purpose was precisely for the exercise of this same function.[48]

This last point suggests that our passage may have been written in conscious development of the work of Isaiah of Jerusalem. I have already indicated that this is almost certainly the case in terms of Deutero-Isaiah as a whole, so

---

[47] Westermann, *Isaiah 40–66*, p. 95 (= German original, pp. 79–80); so too Motyer, *The Prophecy of Isaiah*, p. 319, though he endeavours to include some of the broader meanings within it as well. It is interesting in this connection to note that the announcement of this verdict in the previous verse (41:29) also starts 'behold'.

[48] In my discussion of that passage in chapter two I explained why the specific word *mišpāṭ* was not used. Nevertheless, the verb *šāpaṭ* introduces the task in verse 4.

that if we come across one of Isaiah's key terms, the likelihood that the same consideration applies is high, even though in the case of such a common word as 'justice' that alone could not establish the case. Furthermore, I have argued that Isaiah had a rather wider conception of 'justice' than legal administration alone; he seems to have thought rather of the total ordering of the well-being of society. Consequently, I propose that the same is true here.[49] Of course, there is a major difference in this verse, namely that whereas Isaiah himself related this circle of ideas exclusively to the Judean king and his own society, here it is extended to the nations as a whole. We shall return shortly to think through the implications of that extension.

Before coming to that, however, we need to take account of verse 4, where 'justice' stands in close parallelism with 'his law (*tôrâ*)'. Since this has sometimes been used to justify the more general meanings of *mišpāṭ* which we noted earlier, we need to ask whether it presents a problem for our view, or whether in fact it can support it. I believe that the latter is the case. There are some echoes[50] in this passage, of which this is a prominent one, of the famous oracle at the start of Isaiah 2 (verses 2–4):

> *In days to come*
> *the mountain of the Lord's house*
> *shall be established as the highest of the mountains,*
> *and shall be raised above the hills;*
> *all the nations shall stream to it.*
> *Many peoples shall come and say,*

---

[49] It may be noted that at 28:17, a passage to which particular reference was made in chapter one in trying to determine the specific way in which Isaiah uses this term, it occurs as the object of *śym*, 'to put, place', exactly as at 42:4. This combination is rare elsewhere in the Hebrew Bible.

[50] See in general and most recently Laato, *The Servant of YHWH*, pp. 80–81.

"Come, let us go up to the mountain of the Lord,
    to the house of the God of Jacob;
that he may teach us his ways
    and that we may walk in his paths."
For out of Zion shall go forth instruction (tôrâ),
    and the word of the Lord from Jerusalem.
He shall judge between the nations,
    and shall arbitrate for many peoples;
they shall beat their swords into plowshares,
    and their spears into pruning hooks;
nation shall not lift up sword against nation,
    neither shall they learn war any more.

In common with several other scholars I agree that a strong case can be made for the view that Deutero-Isaiah was familiar with this passage and drew upon it several times elsewhere in his work. In addition, I have argued specifically that it was in fact he who set this passage where it now stands in the form of the book of Isaiah for which he was responsible, with the heading in 2:1 as its introduction.[51] It served, so to speak, as his ideal vision of how things should be, and much of the rest of the book as it then existed tells first of how Israel fell far short of this vision, and then of how Deutero-Isaiah envisaged that it could ultimately be realized. Even without that specific suggestion, however, there is sufficient evidence to justify Clifford's assertion that Isaiah 2:1–5 is 'a text mined more than once by Second Isaiah'.[52]

In 2:2-4, it is clear that *tôrâ* cannot have the technical sense of the Mosaic law. In a careful and detailed study,

---

[51]   See *The Book Called Isaiah*, pp. 144–54. Isaiah 1 is then to be regarded as an even later redactional assemblage, introducing the final and complete form of the book of Isaiah. Isaiah 2:2–4 was almost certainly written later than Isaiah himself, shortly before the time of Deutero-Isaiah.
[52]   Clifford, *Fair Spoken and Persuading*, p. 46.

Jensen[53] has demonstrated first that the Lord is here conceived as the divine king, and that it is in this connection that he judges between the nations. More controversially, he then tries to establish that the reference to *tôrâ* is to be understood from within a specifically wisdom context (with which, of course, the king was also traditionally associated), so that the passage as a whole speaks of 'the King who imparts instruction in the proper way of life and who renders just and saving judgment for those subject to him' (p. 95). Whether or not we follow Jensen all the way in this, it is clear that he has drawn attention to an important facet of the passage – one which helps explain 42:4. Instruction and judgment with arbitration are two parts of the role of the divine king in 2:2–4 in his dealings with the nations, and the same is true of the servant in 42:4. On my particular understanding of the important position of 2:2-4 within the book as edited by Deutero-Isaiah, it is entirely appropriate that his initial vision should be echoed here where the ideal servant is first introduced, but even without that we have sufficient ground for associating the *tôrâ* with the royal task of administering, upholding and even initiating justice among the nations.

This brings us to the second consequence of regarding the servant in 42:1–4 as primarily a royal figure, namely whether this can help us resolve the question of his identity. It will probably already be apparent from all that has been said so far that we are heading towards the view that he should be identified with Israel. To spell out the indications pointing to this conclusion I should observe

---

[53]   J. Jensen, *The Use of* tôrâ *by Isaiah: His Debate with the Wisdom Tradition* (CBQMS 3; Washington, D.C., The Catholic Biblical Association of America 1973), pp. 89–95.

that first, we have already seen that Deutero-Isaiah consistently (and in 55:3–5 explicitly) presents Israel as a royal figure. The title 'king' is reserved for God himself, but Israel takes over the status and functions regarding the nations that in pre-exilic times the king had with regard to Israel. Therefore, when we come across an unnamed royal figure in his writings our first thought will be that it is Israel which is in mind. Secondly, in the previous chapter, Israel has already been introduced more than once as the servant (41:8 and 9). Furthermore, the same language is used there to describe the nature of God's relationship to him as is used in 42:1 of the servant: as well as being a servant, Israel too is 'chosen' (41:8 and 9) and 'upheld' by God's hand (41:10, and cf. 41:13).[54] In view of these close similarities we should certainly suppose that the two passages refer to the same character unless there are strong reasons to the contrary. Thirdly, it does not, I think, need spelling out in detail that the role of the servant *vis-à-vis* the nations in 42:1–4 fits closely with what we have seen (and illustrated in simplified form in the diagrams above) of how Deutero-Isaiah conceives of Israel's relationship with the nations. The servant here undertakes a role that on the basis of other passages we should expect Israel to undertake. It is worth adding at this point, in partial confirmation of the view of 'justice' and 'teaching' adopted above, that the verb 'wait for (*yhl*, pi'el)' in verse 4 is always used of expectant, hopeful

---

[54]   See further J. Goldingay, 'The Arrangement of Isaiah xli–xlv', *VT* 29 (1979), pp. 289–99; and U. Lindblad, 'A Note on the Nameless Servant in Isaiah xlii 1–4', *VT* 43 (1993), pp. 115–19. Goldingay draws slightly different, but not, I think, incompatible consequences for the identity of the servant from these parallels. More extreme is N.L. Tidwell, 'My Servant Jacob, Is. xlii 1: A Suggestion', in *Studies on Old Testament Prophecy* (SVT 26; Leiden, E.J. Brill 1974), pp. 84–91.

waiting.[55] It is not at all that the nations dread some coming judgment, but that they eagerly look forward to the establishment of a new social order.

Some of the major alternatives to this view, such as that the servant is a prophet (or even Deutero-Isaiah himself), have already been discussed in the course of our investigation. Furthermore, I should emphasize once again that it would be a mistake to isolate the four Servant Songs and seek to interpret them exclusively in relation to one another and as all having an identical referent. Even if the servant later assumes a more individual character (though see further below), this should not override our conclusions regarding 42:1–4 based on both close and more remote contextual grounds; there are other possible ways of explaining the differences with the later servant passages.

Two major potential objections to our view remain to be discussed, however. It is frequently observed that there is a difference between this servant and the servant Israel elsewhere (such as in chapter 41). This servant is clearly an ideal character, one in whom God delights and who himself clearly delights to do God's will. Israel in chapter 41 and elsewhere, however, is very far from ideal. She seems to lack all the qualities of faithfulness, responsiveness to God's word and obedience which the servant of chapter 42 displays. In support of this it is pointed out that in 41:8, and frequently elsewhere, Israel stands in parallel with Jacob. Jacob/Israel, then, is the term Deutero-Isaiah uses for what we may call empirical Israel, that is to say, the circle of people whom he was addressing, the dispirited exiles who had such difficulty believing that God

---

[55]   Cf. C. Barth, 'יחל', *TDOT* 6 (Grand Rapids, Eerdmans 1974–), pp. 49–55.

wanted anything more to do with them (cf. 40:27). Conversely, there is no passage where Deutero-Isaiah clearly refers to empirical Israel as servant without further qualification, as would be the case in 42:1. Therefore, the two servants cannot be the same.

In response to this argument, it should first be agreed that there is a good deal of truth in these observations, and we shall have more to say shortly about the importance specifically of the term Jacob/Israel. Furthermore, I should agree with those scholars who, seeing the force of both the connections and differences we have observed, suggest that 42:1–4 describes an 'ideal Israel' from a certain point of view.[56] However, for reasons already explained, I should stop short of defining this as an ideal group of prophets whose mission is to lead Israel back to the Lord. Rather, the figure of 42:1–4 is quite simply the Israel whom God wants his chosen people to be. He is 'ideal', not in the sense that he exists as a small and perfect group which may be contrasted with the remainder of the (far from ideal) people, but in the sense of an ideal held out before them as vision and aspiration. He is Israel as Deutero-Isaiah hopes (and perhaps at this stage still expects) his people to become. Thus in my opinion it is a mistake to speak of a loyal Israel and a disloyal Israel as though there were two such groups which existed at the time of Deutero-Isaiah, and which he could therefore address separately and in turn. Rather, there was one Israel – Jacob/Israel – which the prophet hoped would be transformed under his ministry into the ideal servant-

---

[56] See, for instance, H.-J. Hermisson, 'Israel und der Gottesknecht bei Deuterojesaja', *ZThK* 79 (1982), pp. 1–24, closely followed by Laato, *The Servant of YHWH*, pp. 34–6.

Israel. In 42:1–4 the servant is thus a vision of what he hopes Israel will soon be.[57]

The other objection to the approach adopted here is one that I anticipate coming from within the specifically Christian community. Writing as a Christian believer myself, I address that objection in the following paragraphs in what I hope are explicitly Christian terms. It will be pointed out that in Matthew 12:18–21 this passage is cited almost complete to support the view that Jesus' withdrawal from confrontation with the Pharisees was 'to fulfil what had been spoken through the prophet Isaiah' (12:17), and further that there are other probable allusions to this passage in the New Testament which connect it with Jesus. Therefore, the question of the identity of the servant is closed: it refers to Jesus, and the passage should consequently be interpreted exclusively in terms of predictive prophecy.

In response, I should like to suggest that this infers more from the meaning of the word 'fulfilment' than it can legitimately bear. The method of interpretation implied is that any 'messianic' passage in the Old Testament refers exclusively, in a one-to-one equivalence, to Jesus, so that once he has fulfilled it, it has nothing more to say to us. But there is an alternative way of looking at the situation, namely to say that Jesus fulfils, but does not thereby exhaust, the prophecy. A foolish example in the reverse direction may help to clarify my meaning. In 1 Corinthians 13 we find Paul's great 'hymn' on the virtue of love. I have sometimes heard devotional sermons on this passage, pointing out how perfectly Jesus 'fulfilled' it, how he

---

[57] For a similar conclusion, with some other considerations to support it as well, see P. Wilcox and D. Paton–Williams, 'The Servant Songs in Deutero–Isaiah', *JSOT* 42 (1988), pp. 79–102.

was 'patient', 'kind', 'not envious or boastful or arrogant' (verse 4), and so on. All of which is perfectly true. But no one would suppose for a moment that this is not therefore also addressed to all Christians as a pattern which they should follow. We may, if we wish, say that Jesus 'fulfilled' 1 Corinthians 13 (even though he lived before it was written), but he does not thereby exhaust it; it still comes to us as vision and aspiration for Christian living. Precisely the same may be said of Isaiah 42:1–4 if the servant is understood as Israel. As we have seen, it was written as a vision and aspiration for the community of Israel in Deutero-Isaiah's day regarding their role within God's purposes for the nations, building on and developing the pre-exilic role of the individual king. I have no difficulty in envisaging Jesus as fulfilling that role while at the same time maintaining that it was a role first given for Israel before his time and remains open as a role to be fulfilled after his time. With some reservations it would even be possible to add two further variations to our diagrams given above, the first giving one possible view of Jesus as the 'fulfilment' of the servant:

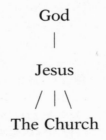

God

|

Jesus

/ | \

The Church

The second suggests one model for how the same pattern of relationships might still be considered operative for the Christian church even after the time of Jesus:

God

|

Church

/ | \

The World

I am acutely conscious of the possible misunderstandings to which this approach might be subject. In particular, it would be necessary to fill out in much greater detail than is possible here the patient, suffering role the servant has to adopt in order to fulfil his vocation. It is surely no accident that the prophet chose the role of servant – and suffering servant at that – to flesh out the substance of what it means to adopt a royal persona. It would therefore be equally mistaken for modern-day Israel and for the modern-day church to draw comfort from their position within these diagrams. All talk of power, and still more of violence, are explicitly ruled out by the content of the passages on which the models are based (and for the Christian, of course, from the example of Jesus from whom the church's role derives). It is not through such worldly means that God's blessing and salvation can flow through them into the world of the nations. But with that strong caveat, I leave it to those who find any of this helpful to work through in their own thinking the implications of what has been said for their own situation, and return to the exegesis of the texts under consideration.

To conclude on Isaiah 42:1–4: we have found both connections with, and variations on, the major themes which occupied us in Isaiah 1–39. The connections come by way of the fact that the servant is presented as a royal figure and that emphasis is placed on his role of proclaiming and establishing justice, which the verb 'wait for' in verse 4 confirms is to be construed positively. We have also found that the focus of attention is on this task, and that there is considerably less interest in the particular identity of the person who is to undertake it. The variations, which cannot be too strongly emphasized, are that this role is now to be transposed to Israel (if she will but respond), and that the sphere within which she is to exercise that role is universalized. Thus there is an underlying theology which remains constant here (it is not by chance that God remains at the top of each diagram), even while its outworking varies dramatically according to its new context. Putting the two parts of Isaiah together, so far as we have traced them, we should conclude that God's purpose, which is directed always to those at the bottom of the diagrams, is not beholden to any particular individual, family or people. His intentions are consistent, but he chooses in a conditional manner the instruments he will use for their realization, the condition being, of course, the level of responsiveness of the mediator in each particular case.

I have suggested that 42:1–4 represents Deutero-Isaiah's vision of the ideal for his people, so that the question naturally arises next as to how that worked out in practice. This leads us to a consideration of 49:1–6, where we shall find a further variation on the theme we have been considering. It is the second of the four so-called Servant Songs, so that some of our introductory remarks on 42:1–4 apply here also. In particular, we have learnt that we do not necessarily have to attempt to interpret each one of them on the same level; the possibility of change or development should be borne in mind.

That possibility becomes stronger when we take note first of the position of this passage within the book. So far, we have spoken of the work of Deutero-Isaiah as a single whole, without drawing any particular internal distinctions between its sections. In fact, however, as many have observed before, there is quite a sharp break which occurs at the end of chapter 48.[58] Among the main indications of this are that it is only in chapters 40–48 that we read of Cyrus, of the imminent downfall of Babylon, of anti-idol polemic, of trial scenes, and of the contrast between 'the former things' and 'the new (or coming) things'. Conversely, there is a new tone in chapters 49–55, with less interest in these external political matters and a greater concern for what may be termed the inner life of the exilic community.

It goes closely along with this that there is also a shift in the terms by which the prophet addresses the people. In 40–48, as we have already seen to a limited extent, a particularly common form of address is 'Jacob' in parallel with 'Israel'. It occurs 15 times, and with only one exception Jacob always stands first. (In addition, both terms of address are occasionally used on their own.) Discounting 49:1–6 for the moment this designation never occurs in

---

[58] See, for instance, M. Haran, 'The Literary Structure and Chronological Framework of the Prophecies in Is. xl–xlviii', in *Congress Volume, Bonn 1962* (SVT 9; Leiden, E.J. Brill 1963), pp. 127–55; E. Nielsen, 'Deuterojesaja: Erwägungen zur Formkritik, Traditions– und Redaktionsgeschichte', *VT* 20 (1970), pp. 190–205; P.-E. Bonnard, *Le Second Isaïe, son disciple et leurs éditeurs: Isaïe 40–66* (EB; Paris, Gabalda 1972), pp. 210–11; Blenkinsopp, *A History of Prophecy in Israel*, pp. 207–18; *idem*, 'Second Isaiah – Prophet of Universalism'; Wilcox and Paton-Williams, 'The Servant Songs in Deutero-Isaiah'.

49–55.[59] On the other side of the watershed, we find the community addressed several times as 'Zion' and 'Jerusalem', terms which occur only once as an object of address in 40-48, and that in the prologue (40:9).[60]

The shift in emphasis between the two halves of his work in Deutero-Isaiah's message thus seems to be accompanied by a change in the way he relates to the people, and in this context it is no accident, I believe, that 49:1–6, which stands as a hinge between the two parts, is itself a passage which plainly talks of a transition in the ministry of the servant:

> Listen to me, O coastlands,
>   pay attention, you peoples from far away!
> The Lord called me before I was born,
>   while I was in my mother's womb he named me.
> He made my mouth like a sharp sword,
>   in the shadow of his hand he hid me;
>   he made me a polished arrow,
>   in his quiver he hid me away.
> And he said to me, "You are my servant,
>   Israel, in whom I will be glorified."
> But I said, "I have labored in vain,
>   I have spent my strength for nothing and vanity;
> yet surely my cause is with the Lord,
>   and my reward with my God."
>
> And now the Lord says,
>   who formed me in the womb to be his servant,

---

[59] For further details on this see, in addition to the article of Wilcox and Paton-Williams, my 'The Concept of Israel in Transition', in R.E. Clements (ed.), *The World of Ancient Israel: Sociological, Anthropological and Political Perspectives* (Cambridge, Cambridge University Press 1989), pp. 141–61 (esp. 144–7).

[60] Some translations would eliminate even this example by rendering 'O thou that tellest good tidings to Zion', etc, but I believe that the NRSV is correct to render rather as 'O Zion, herald of good tidings', etc. This best explains the feminine forms used in the Hebrew. The image is of Zion/Jerusalem proclaiming the advent of her God to her dependent villages, 'the cities of Judah'.

> to bring Jacob back to him,
>   and that Israel might be gathered to him,
> for I am honored in the sight of the Lord,
>   and my God has become my strength[61] –
> he says,
> "It is too light a thing that you should be my servant
>   to raise up the tribes of Jacob
>   and to restore the survivors of Israel;
> I will give you as a light to the nations,
>   that my salvation may reach to the end of the earth."

In order to understand this passage we need to note carefully that the speaker here is explicitly addressing the nations (verse 1), and that by the end all he has told them is how he comes to have a mission to them in the first place (verse 6). He is announcing to them that he has been commissioned by God to be a light to them, and that God's intention in this is that his salvation should reach to them. This, of course, is precisely the task which in the earlier chapters we thought was the role of the servant Israel (see especially 42:6), so we are led to ask whether there has been a change of plan. The previous verses show that indeed there has.

As the speaker explains what has led up to his role he first describes how he was carefully prepared for the task by God from the start (verses 1b–2) and then presented publicly (verse 3). Despite this, the first part of his ministry was frustrating and appeared to achieve nothing, in spite of the fact that he was prepared to leave his reputation in God's hands (verse 4). Finally, and initially somewhat surprisingly, God tells him that his mission to Jacob/Israel (which we must therefore assume is the part

---

[61] This and the previous line seem somewhat out of place here; many commentators think that they have been accidentally misplaced in the course of the transmission of the text from their original position at the end of verse 3, where they would fit very well.

of his work which has been an apparent failure up to date)
is 'too light a thing'; he is to be given the even greater task
of serving as a light to the nations.

Here, then, is someone who started out with a mission
to Jacob/Israel, but one whose mission was not particularly successful; it sounds like the prophet himself, or at
most (since the poetic language can probably be stretched
this far, as we shall see) the prophet together with those
who may have supported him. The importance of his
mission to Jacob/Israel was stressed earlier in connection
with God's wider purpose of bringing salvation to the
nations, since it was only if Israel was prepared to respond
to God in faith and obedience that she could serve as the
royal mediator. But from all that we know from the earlier
chapters Jacob/Israel did not respond in that way. So, as
verse 6 clearly indicates, God did indeed initiate a change
of plan by transferring that role to the one who is speaking
here. His ultimate purpose was of primary importance,
and he was prepared to change the person of the mediator
if his initial choice proved not to be up to the job.

The reason why commentators have had such difficulty
in coming to terms with this explanation is because of a
perceived contradiction between verses 3 and 5–6. If the
servant in verse 3 is Israel, they endlessly ask, how can he
have a mission *to* Israel in verses 5–6? One device to which
resort has frequently been made to get round this is to
delete 'Israel' from verse 3.[62] This, however, is textually

---

[62] This 'solution' has a very long scholarly history; it has been kept alive in
recent decades by H.M. Orlinsky, 'The So-Called "Servant of the Lord" and
"Suffering Servant" in Second Isaiah', in H.M. Orlinsky and N.H. Snaith,
Studies in the Second Part of the Book of Isaiah (SVT 14; Leiden, E.J. Brill
1967), pp. 79–89; Westermann, *Isaiah 40–66*, p. 209 (= German original
p. 169); and Whybray, *Isaiah 40–66*, pp. 137–8.

completely unjustified[63] (one might even go so far as to call it special pleading), and in fact rests, in my opinion, on a misunderstanding of verse 3 in the first place. The solution lies in observing that verse 3 is not a *description* of Israel as the servant (as though Israel were a vocative) but is rather a *designation* of the one addressed as both servant and as Israel. After all, if the servant has been consistently named Israel in the preceding chapters, then to call the one addressed here 'servant' is in fact as much a problem as it would be to call him Israel. To make clear what I mean let me paraphrase prosaically the terse parallelism of the verse: 'He [God] said to me, "I now designate you as my servant; I now designate you 'Israel', in whom I will be glorified'." If this understanding of verse 3 is correct, then, of course, the apparent clash with verses 5–6 disappears. The addressee's designation as servant and Israel in no way confuses him with Jacob/Israel to whom he has a ministry of restoration. He is here given a new identity with a new name – or rather, an old name redefined.

Isaiah 49:5–6 is, in fact, the last time that we hear of Jacob/Israel in chapters 40–55. What was initially envisaged as a vision for the role that they should play is now

---

[63] The suggestion has been emphatically rejected by N. Lohfink, '"Israel" in Jes. 49, 3', in J. Schreiner (ed.), *Wort, Lied und Gottesspruch: Beiträge zu Psalmen und Propheten. Festschrift für Joseph Ziegler* (FzB 2; Würzburg, Echter Verlag 1972), pp. 217–29. For the fragile nature of any case based upon the unique omission of 'Israel' from the Hebrew manuscript known as Kennicott 96, see A. Gelston, 'Isaiah 52:13–53:12: An Eclectic Text and a Supplementary Note on the Hebrew Manuscript Kennicott 96', *JSS* 35 (1990), pp. 187–211, supporting the main conclusion, while correcting some of the details, of J.A. Bewer, 'Two notes on Isaiah 49.1–6. 1. The text critical value of the Hebrew MS. Ken. 96 for Isaiah 49.3', in S.W. Baron and A. Marx (eds.), *Jewish Studies in Memory of George A. Kohut 1874–1933* (New York, The Alexander Kohut Memorial Foundation 1935), pp. 86–8.

transferred to another, and although they are still undoubtedly in view in some of the passages which follow,
our initial impression that we are at a point of transition
in the work seems to be confirmed by the fact that 49:1–6
itself speaks of a transition.

It is further of interest to note that some aspects of the
servant's person and task here clearly pick up and reapply
to him things that were earlier said of the people as a
whole. For example, the fact that this servant was called
before he was born and named while he was still in his
mother's womb (49:1) echoes the similar description of
Jacob/Israel, who was similarly 'formed in the womb'
according to 44:2 (cf. 43:1; 46:3). This, incidentally, shows
that in principle the servant of chapter 49 could also be a
group, perhaps of those who responded to the prophet's
teaching; the seemingly individualistic language of 49:1
can evidently be used as a poetic collective. We have no
way of telling, so far as I can see, whether the servant of
49:1–6 is an individual or a group. Again, in addition to
the titles of servant and Israel being transferred to the
speaker in verse 3, this verse also says that it is now in this
'new' Israel that God will be glorified. This too was something originally envisaged for Jacob/Israel in 44:23. In
49:4, the servant affirms that, despite the setbacks he has
faced, 'my cause (*mišpāṭî*) is with the Lord'. This looks like
a deliberate contrast with Jacob/Israel, who had earlier
complained that 'my right (*mišpāṭî*) is disregarded by my
God' (40:27). And finally, as has already been mentioned,
the task of being 'a light to the nations' is exactly that
originally entrusted to the servant in 42:6.

In view of these parallels, we are led naturally to ask
whether the servant of chapter 49 is presented as a royal
figure. We saw that this was certainly the case in 42:1–4, so
that if the same task is here being entrusted to another, or

to only a selection of those who were in view on the earlier occasion, we might expect that he or they would now be viewed in similar terms. There are certainly those who have thought so.[64] It is pointed out, for instance, that the passage as a whole, in which a speaker addresses the nations, may be intended as an example of the self-vaunting speech of a king at the time of his coronation, such as seems to be envisaged by Psalm 2, while it is possible to find parallels for some of the details of the passage with other Psalms where the king is possibly in view. This latter point is, of course, problematic, in that there is little agreement over how many of the Psalms are in fact 'royal'. Eaton's attempt to relate virtually every aspect of the passage to the king undoubtedly rests on what most scholars would regard as an overly generous allocation in this regard. Despite this reservation, one may nevertheless compare verse 2 with Isaiah 11:4, while the form of verse 3 is similar to Psalm 2:7, and the apparently political aspect of the task of restoring the Israelite tribes in verses 5–6 may well be based on pre-exilic royal aspirations. We may therefore conclude that there are royal aspects to the person and work of the servant in 49:1–6.

The case is distinct from that in 42:1–4, however, in that the situation is neither so clear in this instance, nor does it adequately account for all aspects of the passage. In particular, there are other features of the description which inevitably remind the reader primarily of some of

---

[64] See especially Kaiser, *Der Königliche Knecht*, pp. 53–65; Eaton, *Festal Drama*, pp. 61–5.

the prophets. The call from the mother's womb in verse 1, for instance, while it may be possible to harmonize with royalty, is on the surface far closer to the account of the call of Jeremiah (cf. Jeremiah 1:5), where interestingly the language is used explicitly in connection with a call to be 'a prophet to the nations'. Reminiscent also of Jeremiah's experience is the servant's complaint that 'I have spent my strength for nothing and vanity' (verse 4; cf. Jeremiah 15:15–18; 17:14–17; 20:7–18), while the reference to the effective word in verse 2 also seems more appropriate for a prophet.

It looks, therefore, as though we have something of a mixture here, leading to the conclusion that the servant as portrayed in 49:1–6 is *sui generis*.[65] This conclusion, it may be suggested, also bespeaks the transitional nature of this passage, even as a primarily prophetic figure takes over a role that was previously deemed to be suitable for royalty. It is perhaps for this reason that nothing is said explicitly about the royal administration of justice, which we have seen to be so important everywhere else.

We may draw the main threads of this discussion of 49:1–6 together by pointing out once again that there are elements of both continuity and innovation with what has gone before. The main element of continuity is that God's

---

[65] See, for instance, Westermann, *Isaiah 40–66*, pp. 206–12 (= German original, pp. 166–72); Laato, *The Servant of YHWH*, pp. 106–22 (Laato ultimately concludes that the passage draws primarily on the royal ideology, but he accepts that much of the evidence is ambiguous and that many of the royal motifs in evidence here are ones which had themselves already been adopted into prophetic ideology).

ultimate purpose with regard to the nations remains constant. As in the case of the servant of chapter 42 he is to bring them 'light' (further explained here as 'salvation'). This, in Deutero-Isaiah, is already a development of the royal role in the first part of the book, a role restricted to dealings within Israel alone. The underlying theology of a divine mediator is the same, however, so that it is better to talk here of development, or variation, than to think in terms of a completely separate theme. To put the same in another way, the focus here as elsewhere is on the task to be performed, not the identity of the person who is to undertake it. On the other hand, there is greater innovation to be observed in the fact that there is less emphasis on the royal status of the mediator by comparison with the introduction of prophetic elements. And, as we have seen, this fits with other aspects of the passage which mark it out as transitional in the thought of the prophet, so that it occurs appropriately at the 'hinge' between the two main parts of Isaiah 40–55 as a whole. Finally, it should not be overlooked that there is nothing to suggest that this servant's role to Jacob/Israel is to be abandoned, only that a new and additional task is also entrusted to him. It is therefore perfectly feasible to assume that the passage in 55:3–5, from which we started out in this chapter, still stands as a 'last chance appeal' to Israel to assume her intended role. What the present passage clearly demonstrates is that the road to that still hoped-for destination is rather longer than the prophet perhaps realized when he first set it out in chapter 42.

Throughout this discussion of Isaiah 40–55 we have continually found ourselves referring to the tension between God's desire to bring light and salvation to the nations by way of a 'royal' mediator and the unpreparedness of his preferred servant, empirical Israel, to fulfil that task. For the final passage from these chapters which we shall consider, therefore, it seems appropriate to turn to 51:1–8, where these two elements are brought together.[66]

These verses comprise, in my understanding, the first half of a longer passage in two main parts which stretches right through to the beginning of chapter 52. It is then followed by what we have already seen are the climactic verses in 52:7–12. If this analysis is correct, then the verses we are concerned with here stand at the start of the sustained build-up to what is in many respects the high point of Deutero-Isaiah's proclamation to the people in exile.

This literary structure is to be seen principally in two ways: one formal and the other based on a parallel development in thought. The formal structure is straightforward. The three units which make up 51:1–8 each begin with an imperative, which the NRSV translates identically on each occasion: 'Listen to me' (verses 1, 4 and 7). In the Hebrew text, the first and third are indeed identical (*šim'û 'ēlay*), but the middle one is different (*haqšîbû 'ēlay*). A parallel pattern emerges in the second part of this extended composition, with the (repeated) imperative 'Awake, awake (*'ûrî 'ûrî*)' at 51:9 and 52:1, and in between the reflexive (hithpólel) form of the same verb, 'Rouse yourself, rouse yourself (*hit'ôr^erî hit'ôr^erî*)'; in fact, some older English versions, such as the RV, translated 'Awake, awake' here as well. So here we seem to have two parallel panels, each in three parts, in which the first and third

---

66 In view of the closely interconnected nature of Deutero-Isaiah's discourse there is a great deal of other material which might equally be studied in relation to our theme. An exegesis of the whole of his work is out of the question here, however, so that it has been necessary to be severely selective. It is hoped that, by focusing in some detail on the central passages which have been chosen here, there will be sufficient guidelines established to enable readers to see for themselves how they are reflected elsewhere in his work.

parts are introduced in each case with identical wording and with a closely related variant form to introduce the second, middle part, thus: a:a^{var}:a/b:b^{var}:b. This seems hardly likely to be accidental.[67]

The development of thought in each panel is also parallel. While this clearly cannot be expounded in detail here, the whole may be characterized as a process of 'internalization'. Thus the addressees in 51:1 are defined as those who 'pursue righteousness', but by the start of the third part they have become 'you who know righteousness, the people who have my teaching in your hearts'. In a closely similar manner, the second panel begins with an appeal (apparently by Zion) for external help: 'Awake, awake, put on strength, O arm of the Lord!', but by the time the third section begins this too has been internalized: 'Awake, awake, put on your (own) strength, O Zion!'

If we return now to 51:1–8 in the light of these observations it will be clear that the third section, verses 7–8, is the climax of the development of thought through this first panel:

> Listen to me, you who know righteousness (sedeq),
>> you people who have my teaching (tôrâ) in your hearts;
> do not fear the reproach of others,
>> and do not be dismayed when they revile you.

---

[67] I thus cannot agree with Kuntz, who argues that 51:1–16 is a discrete unit, or with Holmgren, who defines the unit as 51:1–11; cf. J.K. Kuntz, 'The Contribution of Rhetorical Criticism to Understanding Isaiah 51:1–16', in D.J.A. Clines, D.M. Gunn and A.J. Hauser (eds.), *Art and Meaning: Rhetoric in Biblical Literature* (JSOTS 19; Sheffield, JSOT Press 1982), pp. 140–71; F. Holmgren, 'Chiastic Structure in Isaiah li 1–11', *VT* 19 (1969), pp. 196–201. In his commentary at this point Westermann, *Isaiah 40–66*, pp. 232–7 (= German original, pp. 185–91) argues for an unnecessarily elaborate and hypothetical reordering of the verses in 50:10–51:8.

> *For the moth will eat them up like a garment,*
> *and the worm will eat them like wool;*
> *but my deliverance (ṣᵉdāqâ) will be forever,*
> *and my salvation (yᵉšûʿâ) to all generations.*

Here a 'people', not further defined within this paragraph, are promised assurance on the basis of God's everlasting deliverance[68] and salvation. They need have no fear of their opponents, to whom colourful images of destruction are applied. And they have clearly made their own God's righteousness (here the variant form *ṣedeq* is used, perhaps to distinguish in meaning from the *ṣᵉdāqâ* of verse 8) and teaching. So who are they?

The answer to this question seems to vary according to whether we look to the earlier verses of this passage or to the use of similar ideas and phraseology elsewhere in the wider context. Earlier in the passage the imperatives in verse 4 are addressed by God to 'my people' and 'my nation', which naturally makes us think in the first instance of Israel generally, and this seems to gain confirmation from the first section of the passage, where presumably the same group of people are told, 'look to Abraham your father and to Sarah who bore you' (verse 2).

At the same time it is difficult to avoid the impression that there is in our paragraph a conscious echo of the

---

[68] For *ṣᵉdāqâ* with this sense in Deutero-Isaiah, see (*inter alia*) J.J. Scullion, 'ṣedeq-ṣedāqah in Isaiah cc. 40–66 with Special Reference to the Continuity in Meaning between Second and Third Isaiah', *UF* 3 (1971), pp. 335–48; F.V. Reiterer, *Gerechtigkeit als Heil: צדק bei Deuterojesaja. Aussage und Vergleich mit der alttestamentlichen Tradition* (Graz, Akademische Druck-u. Verlagsanstalt 1976); R. Rendtorff, 'Isaiah 56:1 as a Key to the Formation of the Book of Isaiah', in *Canon and Theology: Overtures to an Old Testament Theology* (Edinburgh, T. & T. Clark 1994), pp. 181–9; Reimer, 'צדק '.

third of the so-called Servant Songs which comes in the immediately preceding chapter of the book, in 50:4–9. There too we read of one who is steeped in God's instruction; though the word *tôrâ* itself is not used, the connection is close in general terms, and becomes even more so if we are justified in linking the 'one who is taught' of verse 4 with the 'disciples' (the same, uncommon word is used in the Hebrew in both passages) of 8:16, among whom the prophet's *tôrâ* is to be sealed up.[69] Even more strikingly, however, the prophet there is also faced by adversaries before whom he declares himself to be confident because of God's support, as a result of which 'all of them will wear out like a garment; the moth will eat them up' (50:9; cf. 51:8).[70]

It is not easy to know how exactly we should settle this puzzle. One possibility, however, which can be advanced only tentatively, is to suggest that an answer might be sought along the lines of what was referred to above as the apparent process of 'internalization' which characterizes this passage. That is to say, there is perhaps a theoretical distinction to be drawn between those who are addressed at the start of the passage as pursuing righteousness (again, *ṣedeq* is used rather than *šᵉdāqâ*), which implies that they have not yet found it, and those who by the end of the passage are said to 'know righteousness'. As we have seen, it is this latter group who share most closely the characteristics of the figure in 50:4–9, probably originally the prophet himself. It is attractive to suppose, therefore,

---

[69] For a fuller discussion of this important theme in these passages and elsewhere in Isaiah see my *The Book Called Isaiah*, pp. 94–115.

[70] *'āš*, 'moth', occurs nowhere else in Isaiah (and only twice elsewhere in the Hebrew Bible).

that we have here again an example of that same tension
between empirical Israel and the ideal servant-Israel. The
latter, originally a vision the prophet hoped would be
fulfilled by all the people (chapter 42), was transformed,
even if only temporarily under the pressure of the prevailing circumstances of Jacob/Israel's failure to respond, in
49:1–6, into a role for the prophet himself or else the
prophet together with the group of those who may have
supported him. To such a group the encouragement to
'look to Abraham' would have been entirely appropriate,
'for when he was but one I called him, but I blessed him
and made him many' (verse 2). In other words, there
remained the possibility that this group who were beginning to respond to the preaching of the prophet – pursuing
righteousness and seeking the Lord (verse 1) – could yet be
increased until they embraced the whole of the people, the
nation (verse 4), by making the experience, faith and
confidence of the prophet himself (verses 7–8) their own.
If something like this is along the right lines it implies that
even after the watershed of chapter 49 the prophet has still
not given up on the hope that the original vision might yet
be realized. One way or the other, it certainly looks, on the
basis of verses 7–8, as though the prophet is still wishing
to engage constructively with his people in terms that
border on the ideal.

It is surely significant, then, that sandwiched between
the first and last sections of this passage we find a central
paragraph which returns to the issue of the place of the
gentile nations:

> *Listen to me, my people,*
>   *and give heed to me, my nation;*
> *for a teaching (tôrâ) will go out from me,*
>   *and my justice (mišpāṭ) for a light to the peoples.*

> *I will bring near my deliverance (ṣedeq) swiftly,* [71]
>   *my salvation (yeša') has gone out*
>   *and my arms will rule (šāpaṭ) the peoples;*
> *the coastlands wait for me,*
>   *and for my arm they hope.*
> *Lift up your eyes to the heavens,*
>   *and look at the earth beneath;*
> *for the heavens will vanish like smoke,*
>   *the earth will wear out like a garment,. . .* [72]
> *but my salvation (y^ešû'â) will be forever,*
>   *and my deliverance (ṣ^edāqâ) will never be ended.* (51:4–6)

This paragraph is full of echoes of material we have already studied in some detail, and closer examination suggests that to a large extent it is reaffirming familiar themes, though with one significant variation of its own. The three main passages which invite comparison are 42:1–7, 2:2–4 and the remaining parts of 51:1–8 itself.

With regard to chapter 42 there is a renewed and emphatic assertion here that God's justice (*mišpāṭ*) will 'go out'[73] to the nations/peoples, the latter being further characterized in each passage as 'the coastlands'. Furthermore, this justice is set in parallel with God's 'teaching (*tôrâ*)', and the coastlands are again said to look forward eagerly

---

[71] There is a textual and linguistic problem with this word, which stands either at the start of this line (so BHS) or at the end of the previous verse (so MT). Its meaning is not sufficiently clear to determine which is best, and the 'metrical' issue, though probably favouring the solution adopted by the NRSV, is not finally conclusive either way; our uncertainties over the correct way to evaluate the details of Hebrew poetic composition mean that it is possible to mount a case for either solution. For an attempt (not without its own difficulties) to render according to the Masoretic division, see RV: ' . . . and I will make my judgement to rest for a light of the peoples. My righteousness is near, . . .'. For further details, see the commentaries.

[72] In my opinion, the line rendered in the NRSV as 'and those who live on it will die like gnats' (better, with the margin, 'in like manner') is a later gloss; see my contribution to the forthcoming *Festschrift* for A. Gelston.

[73] This is from the same verb as 'bring forth' in 42:1 and 3.

to its implementation ('wait for . . . hope for').[74] And finally, the anticipated rule of God is characterized as 'a light to the peoples', which is identical, so far as one can judge, with 'a light to the nations' in 42:6 and 49:6. This latter point is of particular importance, of course, because it is one of the main features in 49:1–6 which indicates that the role of the servant there is to continue that of the servant in chapter 42. In addition, in 49:6 it stands in parallel with 'my salvation ($y^e\check{s}\hat{u}'\hat{a}$)', a noun also prominent in our present passage. In short, it is difficult to deny that the nations may here expect to enjoy the same blessings which were envisaged in chapter 42 and reaffirmed in 49:1–6. The identity of the mediator may have changed in this latter passage, but, as we saw, the outcome for the nations was the same.[75]

When discussing 42:1–4, we noted that there were some echoes there of 2:2–4. It is thus not surprising to find that the same is true of the present passage; in fact, the links are even more marked here than they were there. In addition to the use of some of the same loaded vocabulary we should note in particular the clear parallel between 'a teaching will go out from me' in 51:4 and 'out of Zion shall go forth instruction' in 2:3; the parallel is closer in Hebrew than appears from the English translation: the subject is the same in both cases (*tôrâ*, teaching/instruction), as is

---

[74] 'Wait for' is the same in both passages. The positive implications we noted attending this verb apply equally to 'hope', added here in parallel; cf. Van Winkle, 'The Relationship of the Nations', pp. 447–8. Incidentally, it is interesting to note that the verb 'hope for' also occurs in 8:16, a passage with which we have seen there are other close associations here.

[75] Some scholars have used these parallel words, phrases and ideas to argue that either the whole or part of 51:4–6 must be a later interpolation; see the survey of opinions in Schoors, *I am God Your Saviour*, pp. 155–6. The frequency of such allusions back and forth throughout chapters 40–55, however, suggests that this is unnecessary.

the verb (*tēṣē'*, go out/go forth) and the following preposition (*min*, from/out of). Furthermore, in both passages this is followed by the statement that God (or his arms) will 'judge/rule (*šāpaṭ*)' the nations (2:4; 51:5).[76]

Finally, this paragraph is obviously associated by vocabulary links with the remainder of 51:1–8, and here the ending of verses 6 and 8 bear particular comparison:

> *but my salvation will be forever,*
> *and my deliverance will never be ended.* (51:6c)

> *but my deliverance will be forever,*
> *and my salvation to all generations.* (51:8b)

These lines stand as the climax of their respective paragraphs, and their association is underlined by their chiastic structure: salvation . . . deliverance :: deliverance . . . salvation.

On the basis of these three points of connection, we may confidently conclude that Isaiah 51:4–6 reaffirms Deutero-Isaiah's vision of God's purposes for the nations, and further that, within the context of 51:1–8 as a whole, this is brought into close association with his hopes for his people as well. It is also striking that much of the vocabulary in verses 4-5, in particular, is that which we have seen to have royal associations and overtones elsewhere in his work. Ideally, the nations are to be 'ruled' by the same salvific regime which should have characterized the rule of Israel by her kings in the pre-exilic period. Thus far, Deutero-Isaiah seems to be playing his familiar tune.

At this point, however, one major point of distinction emerges to which I have not yet drawn attention. Unlike

---

[76] I have discussed these parallels in greater detail in *The Book Called Isaiah*, pp. 150–2. Some, though not all, have been noted before, of course; see, for example, H. Cazelles, 'Qui aurait visé, à l'origine, Isaïe ii 2–5?', *VT* 30 (1980), pp. 409–20 (418); Werner, *Eschatologische Texte*, p. 158; M.A. Sweeney, *Isaiah 1–4*, pp. 172–3; Clifford, *Fair Spoken and Persuading*, p. 158.

any of the passages we have looked at so far, in this one God affirms that he will act directly in order to effect the results for which he looks. He is clearly the speaker throughout, and he states that he will undertake the tasks which previously were said to be mediated through the servant. This is a variation which should neither be under-estimated nor overestimated.

On the one hand, a major conclusion of our study receives decisive confirmation from this observation. As has been repeatedly emphasized, what matters for this prophet is the task to be undertaken, and the identity of the mediator is wholly subordinate to this. So much so, indeed, that if necessary it seems that God is prepared to do the work himself. Furthermore, since in these chapters there is a considerable emphasis on the fact that God alone is the one who bears the title of king, there seems to be no particular problem with the notion that he will himself undertake the royal task of ruling and bringing justice to the nations.

On the other hand, it would, I think, be a mistake to assume that God has now cast aside all thought of acting through his chosen mediator. In a general sense, there are many passages in Scripture where God is represented as speaking of direct action in contexts where it is made clear that in practical terms he will use human beings to effect his will. A strong hint that the same is true here comes from the emphasis on the 'arm' of the Lord in verse 5 (twice), which in 53:1 seems to be used as a title for the servant.[77] But more particularly, we have seen that this paragraph is embedded in the centre of a passage where the opening and close have much to say about God's people, and to do so in a way which seems deliberately to

---

[77] See in particular Motyer, *The Prophecy of Isaiah*, p. 406.

draw attention to the parallels between their experience, at least potentially, and that of the nations. The context in which God's assertion is set is thus the strongest indication that he has not, in fact, given up on his purpose to use his people, once they have themselves responded to his invitation, as his agents to bring justice and light to the nations. Inevitably in a poetic composition there are loose ends which the reader has to fill in for himself or herself. What makes 51:1–8 so appropriate as an introduction to the climactic section of the work of Deutero-Isaiah is that it draws together his message both to Israel and to the nations to show, by use of comparable vocabulary and phraseology, how closely intertwined their experience should be.[78]

Despite the length of this chapter it has been possible to examine only four passages from Deutero-Isaiah. So rich is this prophet's thought, that it would be possible to devote a whole book, as indeed many others have done, just to filling out the topics which have concerned us here. Enough has been said, however, to justify what have emerged as our principal findings and to demonstrate how they both share, and yet develop in radically new directions, some of the concerns of the first part of the book. In particular, the role of the Davidic king in relation to Israel in 1–39 has been shifted now to Israel in relation to the nations as a whole. The consequent need for the prophet to evoke a response of faith and obedience from his dispirited people occupied much of his concern, and

---

[78] This would, in fact, be even more emphatically the case if, with some commentators, we were to emend 'my nation' in verse 4 to 'O nations', for in that case verses 4–6 would be addressed both to God's people and to the nations at large. While a case can certainly be mounted along various lines for this reading (see, for instance, Schoors, *I am God Your Saviour*, pp. 156–7), it remains, of course, hypothetical and so should not serve as the basis for wider-ranging theories.

indeed led to a development in his understanding of the identity of the servant Israel in the second part of his work. In fact, we may almost speak of a two-way process resulting from this: a 'democratization' of the Davidic role by comparison with the earlier part of the book on the one hand, and a 'privatization' of the role of the servant figure himself on the other. Nothing could make clearer the conclusion that it is the task, not the identity of the one who should fulfil it, which remains paramount and constant throughout. It is thus wholly appropriate that the key passage in 55:3–5, from which we began, should stand at the close of his work and be enclosed within the strongest form of appeal that we find anywhere in his work. The vision is restated in its clearest terms, and is addressed to the thirsty and the weary, to whom abundance and satisfaction are still promised, if only they will listen (55:1–3a). It is followed by the exhortation to 'seek the Lord while he may be found' and to 'call upon him while he is near' (verse 6). The vision may seem too exalted to be grasped or believed, but 'my ways are higher than your ways, and my thoughts than your thoughts' (verse 9). But ultimately, even the recalcitrance of those to whom God offers the inestimable privilege of serving him in this universal role will not thwart his purpose of bringing light and salvation to the ends of the earth, for a word has gone out from God's mouth:

> *it shall not return to me empty,*
> *but it shall accomplish that which I purpose,*
> *and succeed in the thing for which I sent it.* (55:11)

Five

Fourth Variation: the One and the Many

In this final main chapter of our study we shall look at what is generally agreed to be one of the latest parts of the book of Isaiah, namely chapters 56–66. The nature of this material demands a rather different approach to that adopted up until now. So far we have concentrated on what might be called a few cardinal passages, principally those which have traditionally featured in studies of messianism in Isaiah. There is only one of these in the material now under examination, however, so that, without overlooking the one that there is, it seems more profitable to try to gain an impression of what is being done with the themes which have by now become well established. As we have already seen, it is a characteristic feature of the book as a whole that one contributor builds by way of citation and allusion on the work of his predecessor(s), sometimes in agreement, sometimes in development. This is certainly the case in these chapters as well,[1] so that

---

[1]   Cf. the recent detailed study of this phenomenon by W. Lau, *Schriftgelehrte Prophetie in Jes 56–66: Eine Untersuchung zu den literarischen Bezügen in den letzten elf Kapiteln des Jesajabuches* (BZAW 225; Berlin and New York, de Gruyter 1994). Although quite properly Lau does not restrict his investigation to the use of earlier Isaianic material alone, the latter nevertheless emerges as a dominant influence.

inevitably we shall want to know what is made here of such themes as kingship, servanthood, righteousness and justice, and the relation of Israel to the nations.

By analogy with the term Deutero-Isaiah for Isaiah 40–55, 'Trito-Isaiah' has come to be the shorthand scholarly designation for the last 11 chapters of the book since Duhm first proposed about a century ago that a separate author was at work here. Apart from convenience, however, this title is rather less satisfactory. It is true that the chapters appear to be united by presupposing a setting in the post-exilic Jerusalem community, so that their separation from 40–55 may be justified in general terms, but in the view of most modern commentators they are not to be ascribed to the work of a single author.[2] There are a number of significant differences of outlook between various sections, which suggest that we here have something more of an anthology than a single composition. In addition, some parts seem to bear a much closer relation than others to both the thought and the linguistic style of Deutero-Isaiah, so that there are those who have held that he may even be the author of some of the poems, or conversely that they are the work of a close disciple who himself edited the earlier work of his master.

These and other considerations continue to give rise to much discussion with regard to these chapters, and it

---

[2]   This was assumed by Duhm and some of his successors, but was quickly rejected by others. The most sustained advocate of unity of authorship was K. Elliger, *Die Einheit Tritojesaia (Jesaia 56–66)* (BWANT 45; Stuttgart, Kohlhammer 1928); *idem*, 'Der Prophet Tritojesaja', *ZAW* 49 (1931), pp. 112–41; *idem*, *Deuterojesaja in seinem Verhältnis zu Tritojesaja* (BWANT 63; Stuttgart, Kohlhammer 1933).

would take us too far afield to enter such a debate here.[3]
On one point, however, there seems to be a measure of
convergence which may prove to be of help to us, and that
is that chapters 60–62 are closest to the outlook of
Deutero-Isaiah.[4] As such, they are generally agreed to
provide the earliest core of this material (and so, if anything does, to justify the title Trito-Isaiah), with the other
chapters arranged around them having been written either
in extension of them or in debate with them. The most
elegantly simple form of this approach has recently been
advocated by Smith,[5] who positively, by careful analysis of
all the texts, and negatively, by critical interaction with
other scholars, has advocated that virtually the whole of
56–66 can in fact be ascribed along these lines to just two
hands, which he labels TI_1 and TI_2 respectively. Since this
is probably as far as we need to go for our present
purposes, and because Smith has provided an attractive
and believable case for his opinion (something which

---

[3] Among recent major studies, we may note especially P.D. Hanson, *The
Dawn of Apocalyptic* (Philadelphia, Fortress Press 1979[2]); Vermeylen, *Du
prophète Isaïe*, 2, pp. 451–517; S. Sekine, *Die Tritojesajanische Sammlung (Jes
56–66) redaktionsgeschichtlich untersucht* (BZAW 175; Berlin and New York,
de Gruyter 1989); K. Koenen, *Ethik und Eschatologie im Tritojesajabuch: Eine
literarkritische und redaktionsgeschichtliche Studie* (WMANT 62; Neukirchen-
Vluyn, Neukirchener Verlag 1990); O.H. Steck, *Studien zu Tritojesaja* (BZAW
203; Berlin and New York, de Gruyter 1991); B. Schramm, *The Opponents of
Third Isaiah: Reconstructing the Cultic History of the Restoration* (JSOTS 193;
Sheffield, Sheffield Academic Press 1995). Several of these works include
useful surveys of earlier research. Mention should also be made of the work of
W.A.M. Beuken, who has published a substantial commentary in Dutch
(*Jesaja Deel III A/B* [Nijkerk, G.F. Callenbach 1989]), as well as a series of
influential articles in English, some of which will be referred to below. For
more general introductions see, in addition to the commentaries, Blenkinsopp, *A History of Prophecy in Israel*, pp. 242–51; G.I. Emmerson, *Isaiah 56–66*
(OTG; Sheffield, Sheffield Academic Press 1992).
[4] Though he was not the first to advocate this view Westermann's commentary seems to have been particularly influential in establishing it.
[5] P.A. Smith, *Rhetoric and Redaction in Trito-Isaiah: The Structure, Growth
and Authorship of Isaiah 56–66* (SVT 62; Leiden, E.J. Brill 1995).

cannot be said of all redaction-critical studies), I shall adopt it for the time being, and must refer the reader for fuller justification to Smith and those with whom he debates.

Anyone who reads Isaiah 60–62 immediately after 40–55 finds him– or herself on familiar ground, though presupposing a somewhat later setting. This is not simply because of the many verbal and phraseological similarities,[6] but also because of the general compatibility of theme and tone. To a single community, sometimes identified as Zion, there is addressed an unconditional promise of future salvation under the images of light and glory. To this light are attracted not only the returning dispersion of the exiled people, but also the rulers of the gentiles, who both assist the returning Zionists and bring abundant gifts of tribute as an act of homage and recognition of the presence of God with his people. The ruined places will be rebuilt in a new era of security, and those who formerly considered themselves deserted and forsaken will find that their situation has been precisely reversed as they experience the comfort and presence of their God.

While all these points can readily be paralleled in Isaiah 40–55 it is also undoubtedly the case that the selection of themes for inclusion here was heavily influenced by the circumstances of the writer. Westermann, for instance, points out that the marked emphasis on the riches of the

---

[6] Of the many such echoes which might be mentioned, Smith, *Rhetoric and Redaction*, p. 27, singles out the following as especially significant: 60:4/49:18, 22; 60:9/55:5; 60:11/45:1; 60:13/41:19; 60:16/49:26; 62:10/40:3; 62:11/48:20. For further examples and discussion see H. Odeberg, *Trito-Isaiah (Isaiah 56–66): A Literary and Linguistic Analysis* (Uppsala, A. -B. Lindequistska Bokhandeln 1931); W. Zimmerli, 'Zur Sprache Tritojesajas', in *Festschrift für Ludwig Köhler* (Bern, Bäuchler u. Co. 1950), pp. 62–74 = *Gottes Offenbarung: Gesammelte Aufsätze zum Alten Testament* (ThB 19; Munich, Chr. Kaiser Verlag 1963), pp. 217–33; Lau, *Schriftgelehrte Prophetie*.

tribute brought by the gentiles will have been a response to the shortage of luxury goods experienced during the first years after the return from Babylon, while it is likely that the reduced circumstances and political insignificance of that community also influenced our writer to focus on the subservient role of the nations within the nationalist/ universalist balance we examined in the work of Deutero-Isaiah.[7] He was by no means the last reader of a biblical text to highlight those points which seemed most fitting to his situation.

What unites him so strongly to Deutero-Isaiah by contrast with what is to follow, however, is his address to the community as a whole and the fact that his promise to them is unconditional. It is true that the anticipated salvation, which Deutero-Isaiah seemed to tie closely with the fall of Babylon to Cyrus, and the consequent return of the exiles to Zion, is now cast off into a somewhat more indefinite future, but that, in a sense, is precisely the point. In the face of what may at first have seemed like a denial of the promise – a disappointment that the new age did not arrive quite as suddenly as Deutero-Isaiah had envisaged – this prophet nevertheless keeps faith with that promise and reaffirms it without qualification for a new generation. And of course, the centrality of Zion as the point of return for the dispersion and for the homage of the nations makes clear that the overarching vision of 2:2–4 remains in force.

In line with this general characterization we find that the major themes which occupied us in the previous chapter, though not prominent in 60–62, are nevertheless

---

[7] The MT of 60:9 nevertheless includes the balancing thought that 'the coastlands shall wait for me', as at 51:5 (and cf. 42:4). However, a number of commentators emend either to 'for me the ships will be assembled', or to 'the ships of the coastlands will be assembled'.

perfectly compatible with it. Royal language, such as we saw postulated of Israel and the servant in 40–48 in particular, is absent here (though 62:3 is independently indicative), but the theme of the gentile kings bringing their tribute to Zion is certainly suggestive of the status thought to have been enjoyed at the time of the Davidic empire and kept alive in the royal cult thereafter. Accordingly, we hear absolutely nothing of a new monarchy emerging, but rather

> *I will appoint Peace as your overseer*
> *and Righteousness (ṣᵉdāqâ) as your taskmaster.* (60:17)

Similarly, God reaffirms that he 'will make an everlasting covenant with them' (61:8), which sounds like a precise echo of 55:3, and that this is so may be reinforced by the reference in the preceding line to the prologue of Deutero-Isaiah's work ('I will faithfully give them their recompense'; cf. 40:10[8]), so that in this verse we have a reprise of the opening and close of the work of Deutero-Isaiah as a whole.[9] This prophet thus seems to reaffirm Deutero-Isaiah's notion of the transference of the Davidic promises to the community as a whole. Interestingly, this is continued in the next verse (61:9) by the promise extending to 'their seed' (rendered 'their descendants' in the first line and 'a people' in the last line by NRSV), an extension which may not only indicate the slight temporal remove of this renewal of the promise from the time of Deutero-Isaiah, but which may also be an allusion to the 'seed' of the servant in 53:10 (NRSV: 'offspring'), picking up on the

---

[8] Note further that a complete line of this verse is cited at 62:11, indicating its importance for the writer's thought.

[9] Cf. W.A.M. Beuken, 'Servant and Herald of Good Tidings: Isaiah 61 as an Interpretation of Isaiah 40–55', in J. Vermeylen (ed.), *The Book of Isaiah* (BETL 81; Leuven, Leuven University Press and Peeters 1989), pp. 411–42 (430–1).

earlier references in 44:3 and 48:19; the community is regarded without distinction as the company of those who follow the servant and thus inherit the promises intended for him and through him.

Finally, what do these chapters say of our key theme of righteousness and justice? In brief, we find virtually nothing about justice in relation to the nations, which we saw was one of the key characteristics of the development of this theme in Deutero-Isaiah. In fact 'justice (*mišpāṭ*)' is mentioned only once, at 61:8, which we have just considered:

> For I the Lord love justice,
>   I hate robbery and wrongdoing;
>   I will faithfully give them their recompense,
>   and I will make an everlasting covenant with them.

There is some disagreement here as to whether the reference is to Israel's 'justice', in terms of the righting of the wrongs done to her by the nations,[10] or to the need for justice within Israelite society.[11] Either way, however, the statement clearly concerns God's own character, so that it is difficult to tie it in closely to the distinctive Isaianic theme in any but the most general ways.

It goes along with this that the use of 'righteousness (*ṣᵉdāqâ*)' in these chapters is mainly aligned with that which is most characteristic of Deutero-Isaiah, and which we noted above very briefly in our discussion of 51:1–8, namely 'deliverance, victory', a usage which often occurs in parallel with 'salvation (*yᵉšûʿâ* and related forms)'; cf. 45:8; 46:13; 51:5,6,8; also 41:2; 45:21; 48:18; 54:13–14.[12]

---

[10] So the majority of commentators, which may have influenced them to adopt the emendation of the second line (as in NRSV) against the MT, 'robbery with a burnt offering'.

[11] So Beuken, 'Servant and Herald', p. 430.

[12] See above, chapter 4, note 67.

This seems to be the force of 'righteousness' also at 60:17 (parallel with 'peace'); 61:10 (parallel with 'salvation'); 61:11 (cf. the comparable imagery at 45:8); 62:1 (parallel with 'salvation'); and 62:2 (by extension from verse 1, and in parallel with 'glory'). Where the word occurs in its more overtly ethical sense it is postulated of the whole of the future community which is to enjoy God's blessing: 60:21; 61:3. It thus seems once again that the author of these chapters has fastened on a particular (and prominent) theme of Deutero-Isaiah, which suited his purpose of announcing God's promise to his people, but which was quite different from the predominant usage in 1–39. From our particular point of view, therefore, there is little that is new in what we have seen of these chapters beyond the bare fact of the extension of the promise.

There is, however, one passage[13] which stands at the centre of this material to which I have not yet referred directly, but which has the claim above all others in the last part of Isaiah to be considered a cardinal messianic passage, namely 61:1–3a.[14] In the light of the general conclusions we have reached so far these verses clearly deserve closer attention:

> *The spirit of the Lord God is upon me,*
>   *because the Lord has anointed me;*
> *he has sent me to bring good news to the oppressed,*

---

[13] Against the proposal of Motyer, *The Prophecy of Isaiah*, that there is a major messianic figure in these chapters under the guise of the 'anointed conqueror', see Schultz, 'The King in the Book of Isaiah'.

[14] It is, in fact, difficult to be sure just where this unit ends. Many commentators run it on to the end of verse 3, while the NRSV seems to include verse 4, and a case can be made for continuing to verse 7, after which there is a clear change of speaker. For our present purposes it is the self-presentation of the speaker at the start of the passage which is of chief importance, and there is a convenient syntactic break in the middle of verse 3 which seems to join 3*b* at least to verse 4. I shall therefore concentrate on the first syntactic unit in the chapter, as set out above, without resolving the wider issue here.

> to bind up the brokenhearted,
> to proclaim liberty to the captives,
>   and release to the prisoners;
> to proclaim the year of the Lord's favor,
>   and the day of vengeance of our God;
>   to comfort all who mourn;
> to provide for those who mourn in Zion –
>   to give them a garland instead of ashes,
> the oil of gladness instead of mourning,
>   the mantle of praise instead of a faint spirit.

Although this figure is not called a servant, many of the uncertainties that confronted us in discussing the servant of 40–55 are present here too, and they lead to a comparable array of identifications among the commentators. Rather than focusing on this issue in the first instance, let us once again look at the allusions in these verses which point to the possible role model for the speaker as he describes himself and his task.

First, the opening reference to the Spirit being upon him seems to be a clear allusion to the endowment of the servant in 42:1, and we saw there that, among other possible allusions, there was probably a specific reference to the new David of 11:1. In both these earlier occurrences endowment with the Spirit was explicitly to prepare the figure in question to exercise a judicial role. That is not so obviously the case here, though it would be possible to see in the continuation of the passage a description of part of the royal task of defending the cause of the poor and disadvantaged.

Influenced, no doubt, by what is to follow, most commentators prefer to see in this phrase a reference to a prophetic role. In part, this may simply be because it is the most obvious interpretation for a first-person reference in a prophetic book, though that argument carries less weight in a passage such as this where references to previous written texts are so prominent. More specifically, Westermann, for instance, finds an even closer parallel in Micah 3:8, 'I am filled . . . with the spirit of the Lord, . . . to declare . . .'. He observes, furthermore, that although the pre–exilic classical prophets normally avoided appealing to their endowment with the Spirit, there was an older tradition relating to the seers where it was quite normal (Numbers 24:2; 2 Samuel 23:2),[15] and Whybray reminds us that this was picked up in particular by the exilic prophet Ezekiel.[16]

It seems, therefore, that this introductory phrase is too ambiguous in itself to draw any firm conclusions of this sort. Perhaps it would be preferable to say, in view of the phrase's most obvious point of immediate reference, that the speaker is marking himself out as in the succession not just of the old established offices of king or prophet, but of the newer role of servant, a role which in itself, as we have seen, combined elements of both the earlier ones.

Secondly, the reference to being 'anointed' by the Lord seems to be truly innovative in this context so far as the book of Isaiah is concerned. As we saw in our first chapter the noun is used of Cyrus in Deutero-Isaiah in connection with his role as conqueror of Babylon and as liberator of Israel. In view of the tasks entrusted to our present figure in the following lines it is surprising that the possibility has generally been ignored that he is here claiming to take over those parts of Cyrus' role which still remained to be fulfilled. That seems to me to be the obvious implication.

---

[15] Westermann, *Isaiah 40–66*, p. 365 (= German original, p. 291).
[16] Whybray, *Isaiah 40–66*, p. 72 (commenting on 42:1). See further K.W. Carley, *Ezekiel among the Prophets: A Study of Ezekiel's Place in Prophetic Tradition* (SBT, 2nd series 31; London, SCM Press 1975), pp. 23–37.

The reason for this neglect is once again that the commentators have usually been too quick to try to accommodate all that is said in this passage to one specific office. Outside Isaiah, of course, anointing is mostly associated with the king, and on some occasions this is also explicitly associated with the Spirit, as here; see, for instance, 1 Samuel 16:13; 2 Samuel 23:1–2. However, since it is considered that the present figure is not depicted in royal terms,[17] it is suggested that the reference to being anointed should be understood metaphorically.[18] We also read once of prophetic anointing (1 Kings 19:16), interestingly enough in terms of Elisha as Elijah's successor, a succession which we saw in chapter two also furnished one of the only two precise verbal parallels for the expression of the endowment with the Spirit in Isaiah 11:2. It would be attractive, but probably taking the force of allusion too far, to suggest that our figure too was conscious of standing in a fixed line of succession, possibly that of the servant of 40–55. Had that been so, however, we might have expected him to say that the Spirit of the Lord 'rested' upon him. Finally, high priests were anointed (it is not certain when this custom began), but despite one

---

[17] There are some exceptions to this rule, but they have not carried conviction with the majority; see, for example, H. Gressmann, *Der Ursprung der israelitisch-jüdischen Eschatologie* (FRLANT 6; Göttingen, Vandenhoeck & Ruprecht 1905), pp. 261–2; G. Widengren, *Sakrales Königtum im Alten Testament und im Judentum* (Stuttgart, Kohlhammer 1955), pp. 57–8; Ringgren, *The Messiah in the Old Testament*, pp. 33–4.

[18] E.g. 'The second line uses the word "to anoint" in a non-literal and transferred sense, something like "to give full authorization"' (Westermann, *Isaiah 40–66*); 'this is obviously to be taken metaphorically' (Whybray, *Isaiah 40–66*)); 'just as the anointing of Cyrus in 45:1 is metaphorical, so too is the servant's anointing metaphorical and not literal' (P.A. Smith, p. 25); similar remarks may be found in most commentaries.

recent proposal[19] it seems unlikely that that is of relevance in the present context.

It appears, therefore, that the most plausible point of association for the reference to anointing is to Cyrus, in the sense that this figure is consciously taking over part of his unfinished work. This would help explain the obviously royal overtones of the combining of Spirit and anointing at which most commentators have baulked. It does not, of course, make the speaker a king, any more than the servant of 40–55 was literally a king, but he fulfils some of the same functions. Nor need we conclude that he necessarily identified the servant as Cyrus, as some have done at least with regard to 42:1–4. Rather, a picture begins to emerge of this figure taking over a combination of some of the major actors in Deutero-Isaiah's salvation drama.

Thirdly, the next thing our figure says of himself is that the Lord 'has sent me'. We need not delay long over this, for there is general agreement, which there seems no need to question, that this is particularly characteristic of the call to the prophetic office.[20] It certainly cannot be derived from the royal tradition, and indeed it stands in some

---

[19] P. Grelot, 'Sur Isaïe LXI: la première consécration d'un grand-prêtre', *RB* 97 (1990), pp. 414–31, acknowledging previously H. Cazelles, *Le Messie de la Bible: Christologie de l'Ancien Testament* (Paris, Desclée 1978), p. 156. This view was earlier held by W. Caspari, 'Der Geist des Herrn ist über mir', *NKZ* 40 (1929), pp. 729–47.

[20] Beuken, 'Servant and Herald', p. 415, lists the following references: Moses in Exodus 3:14–15; 4:13,28; 5:22; 7:16; Samuel in 1 Samuel 15:1; 16:1; and also Isa. 6:8; Jer. 1:7; 19:14; Ezek. 2:3–4; 3:5–6; Hag. 1:12; Zech. 2:12 [ET, 8]; Mal. 3:1 (there are some inaccuracies in Beuken's list as printed, which I have here corrected). Smith, *Rhetoric and Redaction*, p. 24, also adds 2 Kings 2:2–6; Jer. 7:25; 25:17; 26:12–15; Zech. 2:15 [ET, 11]; 4:9; 6:15. Koenen, *Ethik und Eschatologie*, p. 104, emphasizes in particular the importance of the construction with dependent infinitives following in this connection, while Beuken, 'Servant and Herald', pp. 416–17, observes that strings of infinitives also characterize the servant's task in 42, 49 and 50.

tension with it, since 'anointing' is generally to a perma-
nent office, whereas 'sending' implies a specific task.[21] The
uneasy juxtaposition of the two verbs here, therefore, is a
further indication that we should hesitate before trying to
press all the characteristics of this speaker into a single
institutional mould.

It is likely that the prominence of the theme of 'sending'
in the commissioning of Isaiah himself in 6:8 may have
been particularly influential here,[22] especially in view of
the links between that chapter and Isaiah 40 (itself recalled more than once in our present passage, as we shall
see) which suggest that Deutero-Isaiah's commissioning
was understood as in some sense an extension of that of
his eighth-century predecessor.[23] In addition to what has
already been noted, therefore, the character depicted in
Isaiah 61 also claims prophetic status for himself, and in
particular that he stands in continuity with the prophet(s)
of the earlier parts of the book such as he will have known
it.

Fourthly, we come now to what the speaker is commissioned to do. Basing ourselves on the usual line in two
halves of Hebrew poetry this may be summed up by the
initial infinitive in each case: 'to bring good news . . . to
proclaim . . . to proclaim . . . to comfort'. The first of these
is given a prominence in the Hebrew that is not obvious in
translation in that it stands in front of its main verb,

---

[21] Cf. Westermann, *Isaiah 40–66*, pp. 365–6 (= German original, p. 291).

[22] Cf. P.B. Wodecki, '*šlḥ* dans le livre d'Isaïe', *VT* 34 (1984), pp. 482–8.

[23] Cf. C.R. Seitz, 'The Divine Council: Temporal Transition and New Proph-
ecy in the Book of Isaiah', *JBL* 109 (1990), pp. 229–47; *idem*, 'How is the
Prophet Isaiah Present in the Latter Half of the Book? The Logic of Chapters
40–66 within the Book of Isaiah', *JBL* 115 (1996), pp. 219–40; R. Albertz, 'Das
Deuterojesaja-Buch als Fortschreibung der Jesaja-Prophetie', in E. Blum, C.
Macholz and E.W. Stegemann (eds.), *Die Hebräische Bibel und ihre zweifache
Nachgeschichte: Festschrift für Rolf Rendtorff zum 65. Geburtstag* (Neukirchen-
Vluyn, Neukirchener Verlag 1990), pp. 241–56.

literally, 'to bring good news to the oppressed he has sent
me'. Likewise, the second infinitive, 'to proclaim', is emphasized by the fact that it is repeated at the start of the
third line as well, and the fourth infinitive, 'to comfort', is
also singled out by virtue of the fact that it is amplified not
just by one balancing half-line but by an additional complete line as well.[24] All these infinitives relate to verbs of
speaking, which again tends to point in the direction of
prophecy.

'To bring good news (*l\u1d49baśśēr*)' is a prominent verb in
Deutero-Isaiah. In 41:27[25] God says that he is going to
'give to Jerusalem a herald of good tidings (*m\u1d49baśśēr*)'.
This is the climax of one of the trial speeches directed
against the idols in which particular reference is made to
the exploits of Cyrus. The good news in question, therefore, is the very heart of this prophet's message, and it is
directed to Jerusalem, which here stands in parallel with
Zion. At 52:7 we find the verb used twice, somewhat
obscured in the NRSV rendering:

> *How beautiful upon the mountains*
>   *are the feet of the messenger* (mᵉbaśśēr) *who announces peace,*

---

[24] Something seems to have gone wrong with the text of the start of verse 3,
which slightly obscures this otherwise balanced structure. The correct solution to the problem is not agreed, but if, for instance, the words translated 'to
provide for those who mourn in Zion' is bracketed as an exegetical gloss on
the preceding 'all who mourn' (roughly, 'to be applied to those who mourn in
Zion'), then the poetic balance of the remainder is neatly restored; cf. K.
Koenen, 'Textkritische Anmerkungen zu schwierigen Stellen im Tritojesajabuch', *Biblica* 69 (1988), pp. 564–73 (567–8).
[25] The first half of this verse is textually very obscure. An attempt to defend the MT has recently been made by J.G. Janzen, 'Isaiah 41:27: Reading
הנה הנומה in 1QIsaᵃ and הנה הנם in the Masoretic text', *JBL* 113 (1994), pp.
597–607. Most commentators are convinced that emendation is called for, and
many proposals have been made, without any of them securing widespread
assent, which suggests that we may not yet have got to the bottom of the
problem. Fortunately, most are happy to accept the second half of the verse,
which is the one which principally concerns us, without alteration.

> who brings good news (mᵉbaśśēr),
>   who announces salvation,
>   who says to Zion, "Your God reigns."

As we have mentioned more than once previously this introduces a major (if not *the* major) climax of the whole of Deutero-Isaiah's work. It is noteworthy that, as at 41:27, this good news is relayed by some unidentified messenger to Zion. Finally, it is difficult to overlook the close connection in both language and thought between this verse and one in the prologue, namely 40:9:

> Get you up to a high mountain,
>   O Zion, herald of good tidings (mᵉbaśśeret);
> lift up your voice with strength,
>   O Jerusalem, herald of good tidings (mᵉbaśśeret),
>   lift it up, do not fear;
> say to the cities of Judah,
>   "Here is your God!"

As indicated above,[26] it is probable that the NRSV rendering is justified here, so that Zion/Jerusalem becomes herself the herald rather than the recipient of good tidings. To that extent, there is a distinction between this verse and 41:27 and 52:7. It is striking, however, that there is a very ancient and widespread alternative tradition of interpretation, going back at least as far as the LXX, which would make Zion/Jerusalem the recipient of the good news, and this is familiar to us from Handel's *Messiah* (but not the AV!): 'O thou that tellest good tidings to Zion'. It would not be at all surprising if Trito-Isaiah already understood the word in this sense in view of its use later in Deutero-Isaiah. Although a case can certainly be made out for the view that this 'herald of good tidings' is a covert reference

---

26   See chapter 4, note 60.

to Deutero-Isaiah himself,[27] it is not explicitly stated in the text. Rather, we may suppose that our later prophet saw here an additional role being portrayed in the work of his predecessor and that, like the others we have already examined, he absorbed it into his own new persona.

Fifthly, the verb 'to proclaim ($q\bar{a}r\bar{a}'$)', which as we have seen now comes twice in the description of this character's task is, of course, extremely common, so that we should be cautious about building too much upon it. Nevertheless, in view of the links already beginning to be established between this passage and the opening of Deutero-Isaiah's work (and there is more to follow), it is at the very least tempting to suppose that another specific reference is intended here, for the same verb comes no less than four times in 40:2–6, where it is rendered by the NRSV as 'cry' (verse 2), 'cries out' (verse 3), 'cry out!' and '(what) shall I cry?' (both in verse 6). The imperative in verse 2 is plural (as are the other imperatives in this and the previous verse), and this is now generally agreed to point to a scene in the heavenly court or 'divine council' where, as in other portrayals of such a setting, such as Isaiah 6 itself, there is a dialogue between and commands issued to God's attendant ministers. If that is right, as seems most probable, then the voice of one crying out in verses 3–5 and the dialogue about what to cry in verses 6–8 should no doubt be seen in the same context. Of course, we cannot be sure that this will still have been understood by the time of

---

[27]   Cf. R.W. Fisher, 'The Herald of Good News in Second Isaiah', in J.J. Jackson and M. Kessler (eds.), *Rhetorical Criticism: Essays in Honor of James Muilenburg* (Pittsburgh, The Pickwick Press 1974), pp. 117–32. Fisher includes a useful survey of the versional, grammatical and contextual evidence relevant to 40:9. His conclusion is the opposite of that which the feminine forms in this verse seem to me to demand.

Trito-Isaiah; in due course, the plural came to be understood as an address to the priests (so the LXX) or to the prophets (so the Targum). The most that we can suggest, therefore, is that whoever he thought was entrusted with this message, he understood it as now being taken over by the character depicted in 61:1–3.

Sixthly, 'to comfort (*naḥēm*)' is the last in this series of emphasized infinitives, and in view of what we have already seen the suggestion is obvious that it should be related to the very first words of Isaiah 40: 'Comfort, O comfort my people'. This indication of its importance to Deutero-Isaiah is reinforced by the fact that the verb recurs a number of times in his work, namely at 49:13; 51:3,12,19; 52:9; 54:11, and it is further of interest to note that in all these cases there is reference in the immediate context to Zion/Jerusalem. (The same was true, it will be recalled, of bringing good news.) This, no doubt, explains why it does not occur in the first half of the work (40–48) apart from the prologue, in which Zion/Jerusalem is also prominent.

To sum up on these three verbs ('to bring good news', 'to proclaim' and 'to comfort'), we have seen that they all appear together in the prologue of Deutero-Isaiah, that in at least two cases they are also of thematic importance in the rest of Isaiah 40–55, and that in these same two cases they are closely associated with comfort/good news for Zion/Jerusalem. Interestingly, none of them is used to describe the work of the servant in the servant passages as usually designated,[28] even though, as we saw, there were significant allusions to this material at the start of the passage, and some more evidence to the same effect will be presented shortly. The impression continues to build up

---

[28]   The verb translated '(not) cry' in 42:2 is different: *ṣā'aq*.

of a character who somehow gathers to himself every available role in Deutero-Isaiah related to the work of announcing and inaugurating God's salvation.

Seventhly, in this final section I want simply to give an indication of some of the possible points of reference within Deutero-Isaiah for the remaining phraseology in Isaiah 61:1–3 which describes those to whom this figure ministers. In general, enough has already been seen to justify the view that the author was working particularly with this body of material in mind, so that even casual references may potentially be of significance. On the other hand it should be recognized that individual words which lack the kind of wider contextual support we have presented up till now cannot carry the same weight even in a cumulative case such as the present one. It therefore seems best simply to lay out the evidence and to leave readers to judge which, if any, is of particular significance. Nothing in my case as a whole stands or falls on the following comparisons.

'The oppressed': this noun (*'ānāw*) does not occur anywhere else in Isaiah 40–66, but its related adjective *'ānî* is used in Deutero-Isaiah in the plural as a description of exiled Israel: 41:17 ('the poor'); 49:13 ('his suffering ones'); and in the singular as a description of the present afflicted state of Zion/Jerusalem: 51:21 ('you who are wounded'); 54:11 ('afflicted one'). 'The captives (*šᵉbûyīm*)': words from this root are also used generally for the people in their Babylonian captivity: 49:24,25 ('captives') as well as specifically for daughter Zion: 52:2 ('captive'). 'The prisoners (*'ᵃsûrîm*)': the same word is used at 42:7 and 49:9 for those whom the servant is to release from prison, presumably an image for the Babylonian exile. 'Release': the form of this word in the MT (*pᵉqaḥ-qôaḥ*) is unusual, and has occasioned much debate. However it is to be explained, it is clearly to be derived from the verb *pqḥ*, 'to open', and as such it is reminiscent of 42:7 and 20. 'The year of the Lord's favour': as many commentators recognize, there seems to be an allusion here to 49:8, 'in a time of favour I have answered you'. At the very end of our passage the author uses an extremely rare word to describe the condition of those whom he is addressing, 'faint (*kēhâ*)' (of spirit). This may therefore be a conscious echo of the use of the same word to describe those to whom the servant ministers in 42:3 (NRSV: 'dimly burning').[29]

This list does not, of course, include all the terms found in 61:1–3, and the way some of those which are included is applied is somewhat different. For instance, it is possible that the use of 'liberty (*d^erôr*)' may point towards a more economic and social than political form of freedom from oppression.[30] This, however, is only to be expected, for the audience is now back in the land, not in exile in Babylon. The significant point is that the author seems consciously to want to address them in terms familiar from Deutero-Isaiah. They are the same community as that to which the promise was originally delivered, and he reapplies that same promise to them even in their changed circumstances. Within this, parts of the message as given here seem to coincide with the role of the servant, even though the servant passages by no means cover all the points of possible comparison. It seems reasonable to conclude that

---

[29] In the light of this, Koenen, *Ethik und Eschatologie*, p. 106, sees a further connection between the 'brokenhearted' of 61:1 and the fact that the servant will not 'break', but rather strengthen, the 'bruised reed'. See too K. Pauritsch, *Die neue Gemeinde: Gott sammelt Ausgestossene und Arme (Jesaia 56–66). Die Botschaft des Tritojesaia-Buches literar-, form-, gattungskritisch und redaktionsgeschichtlich untersucht* (AnBib 47; Rome, Biblical Institute Press 1971), p. 110.

[30] Even this is not universally accepted, however. Whybray, *Isaiah 40–66*, p. 241, thinks that the word is used 'metaphorically of the coming of "liberation" of the community from its frustrations'.

he expects to complete the as yet unfinished work of the servant, just as we have already seen that he expects to complete parts of the work of Cyrus.

We are now in a position to step back slightly and to draw some conclusions about 61:1–3 as a whole. There is a danger in the procedure we have adopted of going through word by word to search for possible antecedents for the author's phraseology of turning the whole into no more than a pastiche. That would be a great mistake, however, and we need do no more than point out that we have not covered every part of this passage in our analysis, nor have we taken into account material which may have been influenced from elsewhere. Rather, our concern has been exclusively with examining the variations he has introduced to some of the themes which have occupied us previously, and there has been no intention in this to deny that the whole is greater than the sum of its parts. Only a full exegesis of the passage could do justice to this, and that has not been attempted here. Nevertheless, some significant results for our more restricted concern have emerged.

As with the remainder of Isaiah 60–62, this passage is addressed to the whole community, not just to the oppressed or faithful within it.[31] Like Deutero-Isaiah before him he uses a variety of terms to describe this community, some more literal, others more metaphorical. Indeed, it would seem that between the two writers some terms have changed sense in this regard precisely because Trito-Isaiah

---

[31] This has been most recently carefully defended by Smith, *Rhetoric and Redaction*, pp. 25–6. In further support of this conclusion Smith points to the last lines of verse 3 (which we have not considered above), which precisely echo the promise of 60:21, itself clearly addressed to all Zion's people. The same point may additionally be made by comparing 61:4 with 49:8 (and cf. 44:26).

wishes to indicate that he has the same basic audience in
view. To this community he affirms that the same promise
of salvation is applicable, even though they have not yet
seen it fully realized in the way they may initially have
been led to believe it would be. It remains open for a more
indeterminate future. Finally, and from our point of view
most importantly, he takes to himself the task of proclaiming the future fulfilment of all the as yet unrealized tasks
entrusted to a variety of figures in Deutero-Isaiah: Cyrus,
the servant, the herald of good news, God's ministers in
the heavenly court and the prophet himself.

Within this, two points deserve particular attention.
First, it is striking that there is no reference here to the
ministry to the nations, which we saw was such a prominent part of Deutero-Isaiah's mission.[32] Although he draws
on all parts of his predecessor's work it seems that he
focuses in particular on the mission to Zion/Jerusalem,
which dominates the prologue, and then chapters 49–55 of
Deutero-Isaiah. The need for a transition to this preliminary task, before the gentiles could be addressed, was
discussed in the previous chapter in connection with
49:1–6, and of course it should not be overlooked that
elsewhere in 60–62 the nations come into sharper focus,
but at this particular point it is the needs of his own
community that dominate. To this extent we see here
something of a return to the concerns of the pre-exilic
period, where we argued that the ideal king's role, so far as
Isaiah was concerned, was to attend to the establishment

---

[32]   There may, however, be an oblique reference in the phrase 'the day of
vengeance of our God' (61:2), as argued by H.G.L. Peels, *The Vengeance of
God: The Meaning of the Root NQM and the Function of the NQM-Texts in the
Context of Divine Revelation in the Old Testament* (*OTS* 31; Leiden, E.J. Brill
1995), pp. 164–70.

of justice and righteousness within Israel, and where his relationship with the foreign nations was not considered. Secondly, it is striking that nearly all the verbs which describe his task – the long list of infinitives following 'he has sent me to . . .' – are verbs of speech rather than action. This is part of the reason why most commentators have regarded his role as primarily prophetic, and this may be justified to the extent that it is not clearly stated that he himself will personally accomplish all that yet remains to be done. Despite this, however, it is noteworthy that no other agent of the actions is referred to either. Westermann may therefore be correct in stating that 'in and through this proclaiming he is to effect a change on those to whom he is sent' (p. 366).

I conclude, therefore, that the figure depicted in Isaiah 61:1–3 is what may be called a composite character, a bringing together into one of all those whom God had earlier said he would use for the salvation of his people. In that sense he may be called truly messianic, and it was surely no accident that Jesus was reported as citing this passage at the initiation of his public ministry (Luke 4:16–21). In an earlier chapter I wrote somewhat critically of those who take various cardinal 'messianic' passages and make an amalgam of them to produce one single portrait. Should any such wish to respond to my criticism they could hardly do better than to refer to this passage for a biblical precedent for their approach. The difference between us, however, would remain that in doing so there is still the danger of overlooking the distinctive emphases of each passage taken on its own terms. But I readily concede that we see here an outstanding example of the desire of one, who came late in the development of such hopes, to see realized by one messianic figure all the promises of God which still had an open future.

With the hindsight of some two-and-a-half millennia we may feel able to pause in wonder at the heights to which such a lofty vision elevates us. At the time, however, there was no such privilege, and the question could not long be delayed: why is God not moving to implement his promises? How long must we wait? The inclusion of an older lament to that effect at 63:7–64:12[33] demonstrates that this soon became a pressing issue for those who pondered the implications of Trito-Isaiah's reprise of his predecessors' encouragements. The remaining chapters of Isaiah 56–66, which should probably be dated shortly after 60–62, give indications of a number of strategies adopted to ameliorate this sense of dissonance between the promise and the reality.[34] These may be categorized under three or four main heads.

First, there was a recognition that the fault lay not with God, but with the people, and so the hunt was on to identify and then to eradicate the particular failings in conduct which had led to the delay. Among the topics mentioned in this regard are profaning the sabbath (56:2–8; 58:13–14), illicit cult practices (57:3–13; 65:3–7), a wrong attitude to fasting (58:1–9), general forms of iniquity, including injustice, violence and deceit (59:1–15), dietary offences (65:4; 66:17) and an improper understanding of sacrifice (66:3–4). This catalogue of failings, both general and specific, reintroduces a note not heard in the book of Isaiah since pre–exilic times. It is noteworthy

---

[33] I have defended this understanding of the passage in 'Isaiah 63,7–64,11: Exilic Lament or Post–Exilic Protest?', *ZAW* 102 (1990), pp. 48–58. For the most recent full study, see I. Fischer *Wo ist Yahwe? Das Volksklagelied Jes 63,7–64,11 als Ausdruck des Ringens um eine gebrochene Beziehung* (Stuttgart, Verlag Katholisches Bibelwerk GmbH 1989).

[34] See R.P. Carroll, *When Prophecy Failed: Reactions and Responses to Failure in the Old Testament Prophetic Traditions* (London, SCM Press 1979), esp. pp. 152–6.

too, especially in chapters 58–9, that by way of verbal allusion it is specifically the promises of 60–62 which are thus being made conditional, for instance, 'If ... if ..., then your light shall rise in the darkness, and your gloom be like the noonday' (58:9b–10; cf. 60:1–3), and 'If ... if ... if ..., then ... I will feed you with the heritage of your ancestor Jacob' (58:13–14; cf. 62:8–9).[35]

This approach to the problem of the delay in the advent of the day of salvation is encapsulated in the first verse of this section of the book as a whole:

> *Thus says the Lord:*
>   *Maintain justice (*mišpāṭ*), and do what is right (*ṣᵉdāqâ*),*
> *for soon my salvation (*yᵉšûʿâ*) will come,*
>   *and my deliverance (*ṣᵉdāqâ*) be revealed.* (56:1)

There is clearly a subtle play on words here, for which the preceding chapters have prepared us.[36] In the second half of the verse deliverance (*ṣᵉdāqâ*) and salvation (*yᵉšûʿâ*) continue the vocabulary of promise from Isaiah 40–55 as taken up also in 60–62, noted on pp. 173–74 above. But this is now made conditional upon the exercise of justice (*mišpāṭ*) and 'what is right (*ṣᵉdāqâ*)'. It is true that salvation is announced as a spur to right conduct, but the wider context makes clear that there is a close link of dependency between the two. This use of the verbal pair so familiar from Isaiah 1–39 points firmly to the ethical and religious sense of *ṣᵉdāqâ*. In the earlier chapters it was particularly associated with the role of the king in establishing the kind of society as a whole for which God looked. Here, however, it is being transferred to an obligation laid upon each individual member of society and is

---

[35] For further examples see Smith, *Rhetoric and Redaction*, pp. 97–127.
[36] See especially Rendtorff, 'Isaiah 56:1'.

interpreted in terms of personal conduct rather than primarily a general social term. In line with this justice (*mišpāṭ*) is no longer associated with the role of Israel towards the nations, as it was in Deutero-Isaiah, but is again a personal obligation concerning inner–communal relationships.

The theme of this verse is taken up repeatedly in the following chapters, nowhere more markedly than in chapter 59.[37] Justice and righteousness may still be symbols of salvation, but now they are no longer 'near', as in 56:1 (*qārôb*; NRSV, 'soon'), but 'far (*rāḥaq/rāḥôq*)' (59:9, 11 [parallel with 'salvation'] and 14 ['at a distance']). The reason for this is that the people do not practise justice and righteousness in ethical terms (see the references to these qualities in verses 4, 8 and 15), as the varied catalogue of all manner of iniquities mentioned throughout the chapter makes clear. Consequently (verses 16–20) God himself will put on the armour of righteousness and salvation and will move into action, but now with a new result. There will indeed be redemption in Zion, but it will be only for those who 'turn from transgression' (verse 20), while there will be wrath and requital repaid to those who remain as his adversaries and enemies (verse 18). The first response to the perceived delay in the arrival of the day of salvation, therefore, was to reinterpret some of the central terms of Isaiah's legacy away from their corporate sense towards a more individual application.

The second response arises directly out of this, and indeed we have already begun to see something of it at the end of chapter 59. The heirs of the promise are no longer the community as a whole, but only those individuals who

---

[37] See in part D. Kendall, 'The Use of Mišpaṭ in Isaiah 59', *ZAW* 96 (1984), pp. 391–405.

meet the specified conditions. As a consequence we begin
to find a sharp distinction being drawn between the faithful and the wicked, both groups being defined by a number of characteristic terms.

The most striking illustration of this process is the fact
that the servant of Isaiah 40–55 seems to have turned into
'servants' in these final chapters.[38] There is certainly a
pointer towards this theme in 54:17, and it makes an early
appearance in Trito-Isaiah at 56:6 (see below). Furthermore, Beuken has argued in particular that the many
allusions to the fourth Servant Song in the following
chapters are also related. It is, however, in chapter 65 that
the theme comes to prominent and overt expression, the
word 'servants' occurring there no less than seven times
(verses 8, 9, 13 [three occurrences], 14, 15).

A sharp distinction is drawn in this chapter between
those who are addressed directly by the prophet on the
one hand and God's servants on the other. They shall eat,
drink, rejoice and sing for gladness of heart (verses

---

[38]   This has, of course, been commented on by others before; see especially K.
Jeppesen, 'From "You, My Servant" to "The Hand of the Lord is with My
Servants": A Discussion of Is 40–66', *SJOT* 1990/1, pp. 113–29; W.A.M. Beuken,
'The Main Theme of Trito-Isaiah: "The Servants of YHWH"', *JSOT* 47 (1990),
pp. 67–87; *idem*, 'Isaiah Chapters lxv–lxvi: Trito-Isaiah and the Closure of the
Book of Isaiah', in J.A. Emerton (ed.), *Congress Volume, Leuven 1989* (SVT 43;
Leiden, E.J. Brill 1991), pp. 204–21; Schramm, *The Opponents of Third Isaiah*,
pp. 158–9; J. Blenkinsopp, 'The "Servants of the Lord" in Third Isaiah: Profile
of a Pietistic Group in the Persian Epoch', *PIBA* 7 (1983), pp. 1–23. Blenkin-
sopp sets the issue in a broader, sociological context, which in itself is helpful.
His 'sectarian' interpretation may, however, be a little premature if the
material is to be dated to the earliest days of the post–exilic period. See too A.
Rofé, 'Isaiah 66:1–4: Judean Sects in the Persian Period as Viewed by Trito-
Isaiah', in A. Kort and S. Morschauser (eds.), *Biblical and Related Studies
Presented to Samuel Iwry* (Winona Lake, Ind., Eisenbrauns 1985), pp. 205–17,
and 'The Onset of Sects in Postexilic Judaism: Neglected Evidence from the
Septuagint, Trito-Isaiah, Ben Sira, and Malachi', in J. Neusner *et al.* (eds.), *The
Social World of Formative Christianity and Judaism: Essays in Tribute to
Howard Clark Kee* (Philadelphia, Fortress Press 1988), pp. 39–49.

13–14), whereas 'you' will be hungry, thirsty, put to shame, cry out for pain of heart, and wail. 'Your' name will become a curse, whereas 'to his servants he will give a different name' (verse 15). The distinction between the groups is so clear at this point in the chapter that we must obviously read the more ambiguous sections in its light.

The chapter begins by castigating a 'people' for a variety of iniquities, primarily cultic, which illustrate that they did not seek or call on God's name, even though he was willing to be sought and found by them. Verses 1–2 (and see too verse 12) thus clearly show by verbal allusion that this people have not heeded the exhortations of chapter 55. As the chapter continues, however, it emerges that this indictment does not apply to everybody without distinction, for there is another 'people' who have sought the Lord, and their destiny is the reverse of that reserved for the majority:

> *Thus says the Lord:*
> *As the wine is found in the cluster,*
>   *and they say, "Do not destroy it,*
>   *for there is a blessing in it,"*
> *so I will do for my servants' sake,*
>   *and not destroy them all.*
> *I will bring forth descendants from Jacob,*
>   *and from Judah inheritors of my mountains;*[39]
> *my chosen shall inherit it,*
>   *and my servants shall settle there.*

---

[39] A case can be made for revocalizing this word as a singular, 'my mountain' (see verse 11 following). This is apparently presupposed by 1QIsa^a (note the form of suffix on the following word) and the LXX (though the addition of the adjective 'holy' there suggests assimilation to the use of the phrase in 56:7; 57:13; 65:11,25; cf. J. Ziegler, *Untersuchungen zur Septuaginta des Buches Isaias* [Münster, Verlag der Aschendorffschen Verlagsbuchhandlung 1934], p. 79); cf. Hanson, *The Dawn of Apocalyptic*, p. 142; Koenen, *Ethik und Eschatologie*, p. 181, note 141.

Sharon shall become a pasture for flocks,
　　and the Valley of Achor a place for herds to lie down,
　　for my people who have sought me.
But you who forsake the Lord . . .
I will destine you to the sword . . . (65:8–12)

Here, then, we have a group who are to be distinguished from the chapter's main addressees, who can also be referred to as 'my people', and who are further defined as 'my servants' and even 'my chosen' (plural). The language is very much that with which we are familiar from Deutero-Isaiah, but it is now transferred from the collective singular usage to that of a plurality of individuals. Unlike the majority they have indeed 'sought' the Lord (verse 10), and as a result they will inherit God's mountain (there is a probable allusion to 54:17 here; see too 57:13).[40] The reference to their 'descendants' (literally 'seed') in verse 9 also ties up with the promises as reaffirmed in 61:9, discussed above (pp. 172–73). The same sharp division is apparent when the servants recur for the last time in 66:14: 'the hand of the Lord is with his servants, and his indignation is against his enemies'.

Although more could undoubtedly be said in amplification of this theme, such elaboration is not necessary, since the point is well recognized by others. As Schramm summarizes:

> What we are witnessing here is a major transition in the theology of the Hebrew Bible. Salvation is no longer conceived purely in

---

[40]　Smith, *Rhetoric and Redaction*, p. 141, makes a further nice point of detail in this connection. Seeing this passage as a whole as a response to the lament of 63:7–64:12 he writes, 'The cry "we are all your people (עמך כלנו)" (64:8 [ET, 9]) is refuted by vv. 8–9, in which "the whole (הכל)" is set over against the faithful remnant'. On the relation of chapter 65 to the preceding see also, for example, E.C. Webster, 'The Rhetoric of Isaiah 63–65', *JSOT* 47 (1990), pp. 89–102; more elaborately, Steck, *Studien zu Tritojesaja*, pp. 217–28.

national terms. The content of such designations as 'YHWH's people', 'YHWH's chosen', 'YHWH's servants' and בני ישראל [the children of Israel], has been radically altered, and one's membership in בני ישראל is no longer simply a matter of birthright. Only those who properly adhere to the cult of YHWH, as this cult is understood by the author, are to be considered 'YHWH's servants', while those who engage in cultic acts like those described in 65.1–7, 11b, and 57.3–13 and so on are to be excluded. In other words, the content of the terms 'YHWH's chosen', 'YHWH's servants' and 'YHWH's people' has become almost exclusively theological. This theological transition is clearly expressed in 65.13–16 where the twin proclamation of salvation and judgment cuts right through the heart of the restoration community. It is exactly as Hanson has stated: 'The glorious promises of Second Isaiah which applied to the servant Israel have been narrowed to a small segment within Israel, and the classical forms of the judgment and salvation oracles have been fused to account for the new division within the people'.[41]

If this second way of handling the delay in the implementation of God's promise is widely recognized, the third is less so, though it both relates to it and also answers the question: what becomes of Deutero-Isaiah's vision for the future of the nations now that Israel as a whole can no longer function as a royal mediator between them and God?

The answer to this question is by no means as negative as might at first be supposed. In fact, the prophet applies to the nations the same criteria for entry into God's new community as he does to the people of Israel themselves: it will be by way of individual faithfulness.

This comes to expression, in particular, in the first paragraph of Isaiah 56–66. In chapter 56 the general condition of justice and righteousness, which we noted earlier, is first amplified in terms of sabbath observance

---

[41] Schramm, *The Opponents of Third Isaiah*, pp. 158–9, citing Hanson, *The Dawn of Apocalyptic*, p. 153.

(verse 2). Immediately, however, the author goes on to include the foreigner and the eunuch within his rubric, both categories previously excluded from the heart of the Israelite cult. The foreigners who may be included are defined as those who are 'joined to the Lord' (verse 3, and cf. 6),[42] while what this entails is spelt out more fully with regard to the eunuchs: 'who keep my sabbaths, who choose the things that please me and hold fast my covenant' (verse 4). Similar language is later used of the foreigners too, 'who keep the sabbath and do not profane it, and hold fast my covenant' (verse 7), so that clearly no distinction should be drawn between them.

Similarly, comparable promises are addressed to them both, and these echo promises made elsewhere to the community of the faithful. To the eunuchs

> *I will give, in my house and within my walls,*
>   *a monument and a name*
>   *better than sons and daughters;*
> *I will give them an everlasting name*
>   *that shall not be cut off.* (56:5)

This clearly echoes the concluding promise of Deutero-Isaiah (55:13, where the NRSV's 'memorial' is literally 'a name'), and there may well also be an allusion to 62:2 (see too 65:15). The foreigners too will have an honourable place in the worship of the temple:

> *to minister to him, to love the name of the Lord,*
>   *and to be his servants, . . .*
> *these I will bring to my holy mountain,*
>   *and make them joyful in my house of prayer;*

---

[42] For this relatively rare word as an expression for proselytes who adopt the faith of Israel, see D. Kellermann, 'לוה', *TDOT* 7 (Grand Rapids, Eerdmans 1974–), pp. 475–6. It occurs elsewhere in Isaiah at 14:1, a verse as close to the thought and language of Deutero-Isaiah as it is possible to get; see *The Book Called Isaiah*, pp. 165–7.

and their burnt offerings and their sacrifices
  will be accepted on my altar;
for my house shall be called a house of prayer
  for all peoples. (56:6–7)

Noteworthy here, of course, is the reference to the foreigners as 'his servants', suggesting a close association with the circle of ideas we discussed previously, but in addition we should not fail to overlook that the promise of 61:6 to the community of Israel is also reflected here, that the presence at God's holy mountain is paralleled in 57:13 (and cf. 65:9, 11,25), and that the theme of joy for the saved people of God is pervasive in Deutero-Isaiah. It is thus difficult to see any distinction in this writer's thought between the status of faithful Israelites and faithful foreigners; the terms of membership of the new community have been completely recast. The last verse of the passage neatly sums up the point:

Thus says the Lord God,
  who gathers the outcasts of Israel,
I will gather others to them,
  besides those already gathered. (56:8)

In the light of the preceding context, it seems clear that the 'others' referred to here do not mean more outcasts of Israel, but rather gentiles who will come to join with the gathered of Israel in the temple which is to be a 'house of prayer for all peoples'.

This remarkable paragraph, it may be suggested, provides a most interesting variation on the theme of the nations' position in relation to God and to Israel. In Deutero-Isaiah we saw that his much-praised universalism had to be understood within a framework established by Israel's position of particular favour, and at the start of the present chapter it soon became clear that there was a

danger here of that being misunderstood. In the circumstances of the first return it was almost inevitable that the
tension of privilege and service should tend to be resolved
in favour of privilege alone. By wrestling with the problem
of non-fulfilment as a whole, however, this slightly later
writer moved to a position in which conduct by the
individual became decisive in determining who should
now be classed as God's servant(s). What seems at first like
a loss of nerve (and in many respects is) led in the mind of
at least one inspired writer to the development of an
alternative vision which equally has attractions of its own,
namely that if acceptance into the 'true' community is a
matter of conduct rather than birth, then nothing need
prevent the gentile from standing on an equal footing with
the Jew. If the terms were not so wildly anachronistic one
might almost be tempted to find here justification for both
Catholic and Protestant theology, not as diametrically
opposed, but as variations on a single underlying theme –
or perhaps better in this instance, a passacaglia.

There is one final response to the problem of unfulfilled
promise which receives attention in these closing chapters
of Isaiah. It is, in effect, a development of one of the three
already studied, and that it was therefore probably
adopted later in chronological terms is supported by its
use elsewhere in one of the latest parts of the book as a
whole, as well as in some parts of subsequent Jewish
literature. As we have so often found in the course of our
study there are elements of both continuity and innovation.

It was observed above that there is a shift in perspective
from the anticipation of the fulfilment of God's promise
being 'near' to being 'far'. At the very end of the book this
is taken even further, for the fulfilment is here situated
beyond the process of purgatory judgment which the need

to separate between the faithful and the apostates has led us to expect. This radical shift in perspective has interesting ramifications for our major topics.

Isaiah 66:18–24 is a complex passage, partly in prose and partly in verse, and there are aspects of its interpretation in terms of detail which cannot all be debated here. Let us begin by noting, however, some of the main points of association with what has already been discussed. First, the sharp distinction between the faithful and the apostates is maintained here, and their eventual fate is contrasted in the starkest possible terms. The faithful are promised that 'your descendants (seed) and your name [will] remain' (66:22). Both these terms have cropped up repeatedly in the previous chapters, and the fact that the promise is to the coming generations alone suggests that fulfilment is being cast off into an indefinite future. As for 'the people who have rebelled against me', by contrast, their fate is depicted in gruesome terms in 66:24, with no further hope of reversal. Secondly, some of the representatives of the nations are promised a peculiarly honoured (indeed, unprecedented) place within the Jerusalem cult, as priests and Levites (verse 21). This is reminiscent of what was promised to the foreigners and eunuchs in 56:3–8, though, if anything, it goes even further in terms of status. And thirdly, still in connection with the nations, the remainder of what is said about them in this paragraph points clearly to a fulfilment of some of the major themes of Deutero-Isaiah. In line with 40:5 they 'shall see my glory' (verse 18),[43] while later an unspecified 'they' will 'declare my glory among the nations', so that

---

[43]   Note too that in 40:5 God's glory will be seen by 'all flesh (NRSV: all people)', which becomes something of a *Leitwort* in the closing verses of the book; cf. 66:16,23,24.

those who 'have not heard of my fame or seen my glory' may also be included (verse 19). The result will be that they will assist the return of the diaspora to 'my holy mountain Jerusalem' (verse 20), as envisaged in such passages as 43:6 and 49:2–3 (and cf. 60:4–16).

On the other hand, there are some important ways in which this passage differs from what precedes it.[44] In particular, it is noteworthy that there is a return here to referring to 'the nations' and 'the Israelites' as complete entities (verses 18 and 20), which at first sight seems to go back on the individualizing tendency so marked in other parts of 56–66. Two related reasons probably account for this. In the first place, since it is virtually certain that this passage was written specifically for its present literary setting, the events described here are envisioned as taking place after the definitive judgment on 'all flesh' in verses 14–16.[45] All those who survive this are, *ipso facto*, righteous or faithful, so that there is no longer any point in drawing a distinction between the faithful and the apostates within each single community. In the second place, and in connection with this, verse 22 indicates that the state of salvation which these verses anticipate follows the

---

[44] On this basis, Davies argues against many other commentators that 66:18–24 cannot come from the same redactor as 56:3–7. He summarizes the differences thus: 'the former is concerned with the here and now, who may be admitted to worship in the rebuilt temple, and with the treatment of individuals, while the latter embodies a future expectation and a visionary programme for the end of time which applies to Israelite and Gentile communities', a summary very much in line with our own findings; cf. G.I. Davies, 'The Destiny of the Nations in the Book of Isaiah', in J. Vermeylen (ed.), *The Book of Isaiah* (BETL 81; Leuven, Leuven University Press and Peeters), pp. 93–120 (117), followed by Smith, *Rhetoric and Redaction*, pp. 167–71.

[45] Indeed, Beuken, 'Isaiah Chapters lxv–lxvi', argues that the closing passage begins at verse 15 itself, and not verse 18, as most others suppose.

creation of the new heavens and the new earth. It is thus a properly eschatological hope that sets it apart from all that has preceded in which the hopes were vested in an intra-historical salvation. Whereas the creation of the new heavens and new earth in 65:17 was a symbol for the dawn of the age of salvation,[46] here it is an event that precedes the age which 'your descendants' are to enjoy. The return to referring to Israel and the nations as complete wholes is thus far from a recovery of the earlier catholic vision, but is rather an indication that the realization of the promise is separated from history and projected forwards into the *eschaton*.

With that, of course, we are fast approaching the world of apocalyptic. So far as the book of Isaiah is concerned chapters 24–7 reflect a closely comparable circle of ideas, for there too we begin with the desolation of earth and heaven (24:1–4) and the anticipation of the day when 'the Lord of hosts will reign on Mount Zion and in Jerusalem, and before his elders he will manifest his glory' (24:23). Although, as we have seen, there are lines of continuity which lead into this world from the old, it reaches beyond the confines of king, messiah and servant which have been determinative for our discussion, so that to enter further into it would lead us too far away from our dominant concerns. The book of Isaiah does not yet extend to the period when within the kingdom of God there was again found space for an earthly representative. Rather, the book

---

[46]   Cf. Westermann, *Isaiah 40–66*, p. 408 (= German original, p. 324), who comments in relation to 65:17–18 that 'new' here 'means the miraculous transformation, as again in Deutero-Isaiah (42.9; 43.19; 48.6). The words, "I create anew the heavens and the earth", do not imply that heaven and earth are to be destroyed and in their place a new heaven and a new earth created – this is apocalyptic, Rev. 21.1; II Peter 3.13, and the addition in Isa. 66.22. Instead, the world, designated as "heaven and earth", is to be miraculously renewed."

concludes closer to the outlook with which it began, where the Lord sits enthroned, high and lofty, where 'the whole earth is full of his glory', and where the prophet cries out in wonder, 'my eyes have seen the King, the Lord of hosts!' (6:1,5).

Six

Recapitulation

During the course of the previous study a number of passages in Isaiah relevant to the theme of king, messiah and servant have been analysed. It will be obvious that it has sometimes been necessary to be selective, and some readers will perhaps be disappointed that no attention has been given to so familiar a passage as Isaiah 53. What has determined our choice throughout, however, has been the contribution each passage might make to what early emerged as an underlying theme, namely the role of some human figure in the establishment of God's ideal society, based on the principles of justice and righteousness. In this way there was a hope that, in addition to arriving at a better understanding of the passages themselves, it might also be possible to contribute to the recent resurgence of interest in the literary connections between the various parts of the book. Clearly, in order to satisfy this latter requirement it was necessary to concentrate on material where there was the best hope of finding such associations.

Another limitation which needs to be recognized is that the analysis has been severely exegetical. Although there has been some attention to historical context I have said virtually nothing about the currently fashionable trend of seeking out the social setting of the various passages. This is by no means because I do not recognize the value and importance of such work; indeed, it is essential for a full understanding of biblical literature. However, since our primary interest has been centred on the possible literary connections between texts composed over an extended period of time by different authors, it has seemed preferable to concentrate on the task in hand rather than to be distracted by attending to every possible alternative avenue which might in theory be explored.

With these restrictions acknowledged, however, there are nevertheless some interesting conclusions which have emerged. Since in the course of the discussion I have already tried to give summaries of the main findings relevant to each individual text, the time has come to take a step back and reflect briefly on the wider picture, to try to see the shape of the wood rather than merely of the individual trees.

Within what may reasonably be reconstructed of the work of Isaiah of Jerusalem himself we found indeed a coherent hope – or perhaps better, demand – for a king who would act as God's appointed agent in the proper regulation of Israelite or Judean society. Although inevitably Isaiah looked primarily to the Davidic family to undertake this task, we found that the identity of the king was emphatically subordinated to the role, and that he seemed to envisage the possibility that the ideal king would come either from some collateral branch of the Davidic family or even, possibly, from elsewhere. Contrary to the widespread opinion that his 'messianic' hope (however defined) was deeply rooted in God's inalienable promise to David in what might be called a biological sense, it would appear that he interpreted that promise rather differently, appealing to it only in so far as it contributed to his more fundamental concerns.

In this connection, it is therefore significant that the chapter which focuses most explicitly on 'the house of David', namely Isaiah 7, is, I argued, not an early part of some hypothetical Isaiah Memoir, but rather a later reflection upon the fate of the Davidic dynasty, somewhat akin to the Hezekiah narratives in Isaiah 36–39. Although it need not be doubted that it rests on a tradition which stretches back to the time of the prophet, it would be difficult now to disentangle Isaianic from later material; the chapter as a whole is too much of a unity expressing its own later viewpoint to make such speculations reliable. And the infant Immanuel himself, of course, is not provided with any specific family tree.

The relative freedom Isaiah showed towards the earlier Davidic tradition was found to be equally well attested when we entered the very different world of Isaiah 40–55. The theme of a royal mediator of God's justice was certainly present, but it was transferred now to the completely new context of Israel among the nations. And even within these chapters the picture did not remain constant, but a development could be traced in the prophet's thinking. Still maintaining the underlying theme he nevertheless allowed the failure of many of his hearers to respond to his vision to reshape his perception of the identity of the mediator. Once again, therefore, the task to be undertaken was the overriding consideration, and the person or group who might do this could be changed or modified if circumstances so required.

Finally, the concluding chapters, 56–66, demonstrated yet further development. Although on the one hand the various salvific figures which might be read out of 40–55 were drawn together in the one figure of 61:1–3, on the other hand the community in view was no longer Israel as a single whole, nor the nations *en bloc*, but rather a congregation of individuals made up of any, whether Jew or gentile, who responded in faith and obedience to the prophetic word.

The consequence of these findings is that we may speak of both continuity and discontinuity in the presentation of our theme in the book of Isaiah. It has been usual in the past to concentrate attention upon the identity of the character who is variously presented as king, servant or Messiah. In my opinion, however, this is clearly a mistake. We have found abundant evidence, in fact, for a change of identity between one passage and another, most notably in the transfer of the Davidic covenant to the people of Israel as a whole in chapters 40–55.

A more profitable approach to the issue of continuity, therefore, is by attention to the role which needs to be performed. Here too there are certainly differences to be noted, for instance whether it is an inner-Israelite or a universal role. But our contention has been that what gives the role a fundamental unity and hence continuity are the principles upon which it is based. These were outlined in the first chapter, where the attempt was made to relate the nature of God's ideals for society to his own character. Since he is 'the high and lofty one', this includes an unashamedly hierarchical element but, in contrast with the usual feudal way in which this has been worked out throughout history, here the direction of concern is reversed. Those in positions of leadership retain their privileged position only for so long as they work for the good of those further down in the hierarchy. The term 'servant king' is by no means inappropriate.

What the book of Isaiah illustrates, therefore, is the outworking of that role in a variety of different contexts.

For Isaiah himself it meant attention to the needs of his own people in Judah and Jerusalem. For later writers the concern could shift to the relation between Israel and the nations or to the emerging 'congregational' understanding of the people of God. In each case, there are some notable similarities between the descriptions of the mediator, such as endowment with the Spirit (11:2; 42:1; 61:1), so that there is a strong probability that the later writers worked in conscious knowledge of their predecessors' work. But that is not to say that they were all trying to portray different aspects of a single character. Rather, they were far more contextually aware as they identified the type of mediator necessary to fulfil the fundamental task of inaugurating God's justice in the world and circumstances of their varied times.

It is in this way, I suggest, that we too should approach these texts from a Christian perspective. As was outlined in chapter four there is more than one way in which it is possible to argue that Jesus 'fulfilled' these prophecies. Rather than seeing them as narrowly predictive it may be argued that he too reflected on the role Isaiah had envisaged and that in the changed circumstances of his situation he adopted the role of the mediator. Furthermore, the New Testament writers presented him in that light, citing from the earlier writings to indicate that fact, just as the later contributors to the book of Isaiah themselves cited and alluded to the presentations of those who had preceded them. If there is any 'predictive' element to be discerned it is in the task to be undertaken, not the person who will do it.

Such a reading, however, does not exhaust the text, for it remains open. So long as the world denies the principles of divine justice, using privilege for exploitation rather than service, so long does the need remain for individuals and communities who will act as mediators of God's justice. How that should be done will vary through time, space and circumstance, just as the book of Isaiah itself demonstrates. The result of such an interpretation, however, is not to remove the impact of the text by contextualizing it in the ancient world alone, but to liberate it to address the church of today with its abiding, yet renewed, challenge.

Bibliography

Ackroyd, P.R., 'Isaiah 36–39: Structure and Function', in W.C. Delsman *et al.* (eds.), *Von Kenaan bis Kerala: Festschrift für Prof. Mag. Dr. Dr. J.P.M. van der Ploeg O.P. zur Vollendung des siebzigsten Lebensjahres am 4. Juli 1979* (AOAT 211; Kevelaer, Butzon & Bercker/Neukirchen–Vluyn, Neukirchener Verlag 1982), pp. 3–21 = *Studies in the Religious Tradition of the Old Testament* (London, SCM Press 1987), pp. 105–20.

Albertz, R., 'Das Deuterojesaja-Buch als Fortschreibung der Jesaja-Prophetie', in E. Blum, C. Macholz and E.W. Stegemann (eds.), *Die Hebräische Bibel und ihre zweifache Nachgeschichte: Festschrift für Rolf Rendtorff zum 65. Geburtstag* (Neukirchen–Vluyn, Neukirchener Verlag 1990), pp. 241–56.

Alt, A., 'Jesaja 8,23–9,6. Befreiungsnacht und Krönungstag', in *Festschrift Alfred Bertholet, zum 80. Geburtstag gewidmet* (Tübingen, J.C.B. Mohr 1950), pp. 29–49 = *Kleine Schriften zur Geschichte des Volkes Israel 2* (Munich, C.H. Beck 1953), pp. 206–25.

Anderson, B.W., '"God with Us" – In Judgment and in Mercy: The Editorial Structure of Isaiah 5–10(11)', in G.M. Tucker, D.L. Petersen, and R.R. Wilson (eds.), *Canon, Theology, and Old Testament Interpretation: Essays in Honor of Brevard S. Childs* (Philadelphia, Fortress Press 1988), pp. 230–45.

Barstad, H.M., *A Way in the Wilderness: The "Second Exodus" in the Message of Second Isaiah* (JSS Monograph 12; Manchester, University of Manchester 1989).

—— 'The Future of the "Servant Songs": Some Reflections on the Relationship of Biblical Scholarship to its own Tradition', in S.E. Balentine and J. Barton (eds.), *Language, Theology and the Bible: Essays in Honour of James Barr* (Oxford, Clarendon Press 1994), pp. 261–70.

Bartelt, A.H., 'Isaiah 5 and 9: In– or Interdependence?', in A.B. Beck *et al.* (eds.), *Fortunate the Eyes That See: Essays in Honor of David Noel Freedman in Celebration of His Seventieth Birthday* (Grand Rapids, Eerdmans 1995), pp. 157–74.

Barth, C., ' יחל ', *TDOT* 6 (Grand Rapids, Eerdmans 1974–), pp. 49–55.

Barth, H., *Die Jesaja-Worte in der Josiazeit: Israel und Assur als Thema einer produktiven Neuinterpretation der Jesajaüberlieferung* (WMANT 48; Neukirchen–Vluyn, Neukirchener Verlag 1977).

Beuken, W.A.M., 'Mišpāṭ. The First Servant Song and its Context', *VT* 22 (1972), pp. 1–30.

—— *Jesaja Deel III A/B* (Nijkerk, G.F. Callenbach 1989).

—— 'Servant and Herald of Good Tidings: Isaiah 61 as an Interpretation of Isaiah 40–55', in J. Vermeylen (ed.), *The Book of Isaiah* (BETL 81; Leuven, Leuven University Press and Peeters 1989), pp. 411–40.

—— 'The Main Theme of Trito-Isaiah: "The Servants of YHWH"', *JSOT* 47 (1990), pp. 67–87.

—— 'Isaiah Chapters lxv–lxvi: Trito-Isaiah and the Closure of the Book of Isaiah', in J.A. Emerton (ed.), *Congress Volume: Leuven 1989* (SVT 43; Leiden, E.J. Brill 1991), pp. 204–21.

Bewer, J.A., 'Two notes on Isaiah 49.1–6. 1. The text-critical value of the Hebrew MS. Ken. 96 for Isaiah 49.3', in S.W. Baron and A. Marx (eds.), *Jewish Studies in Memory of George A. Kohut 1874–1933* (New York, The Alexander Kohut Memorial Foundation 1935), pp. 86–8.

Bickert, R., 'König Ahas und der Prophet Jesaja. Ein Beitrag zum Problem des syrisch-ephraimitischen Krieges', *ZAW* 99 (1987), pp. 361–84.

Blenkinsopp, J., 'The "Servants of the Lord" in Third Isaiah: Profile of a Pietistic Group in the Persian Epoch', *PIBA* 7 (1983), pp. 1–23.

—— *A History of Prophecy in Israel from the Settlement in the Land to the Hellenistic Period* (London, SPCK 1984).

—— 'Second Isaiah – Prophet of Universalism', *JSOT* 41 (1988), pp. 83–103.

Boer, P.A.H. de, *Second-Isaiah's Message* (*OTS* 11; Leiden, E.J. Brill 1956).

Bonnard, P.-E., *Le Second Isaïe, son disciple et leurs éditeurs: Isaïe 40–66* (EB; Paris, Gabalda 1972).

Brettler, M.Z., *God is King: Understanding an Israelite Metaphor* (JSOTS 76; Sheffield, Sheffield Academic Press 1989).

Brown, W.P., 'The So-Called Refrain in Isaiah 5:25–30 and 9:7–10:4', *CBQ* 52 (1990), pp. 432–43.

Brunner, H., 'Gerechtigkeit als Fundament des Thrones', *VT* 8 (1958), pp. 426–8.

Budde, K., 'Ueber das siebente Capitel des Buches Jesaja', in *Études archéologiques, linguistiques et historiques dédiées à Mr. le Dr. C. Leemans, à l'occasion du cinquantième anniversaire de sa nomination aux fonctions de Directeur du Musée archéologique des Pays-Bas* (Leiden, E.J. Brill 1885), pp. 121–6.

—— 'Zwei Beobachtungen zum alten Eingang des Buches Jesaja', *ZAW* 38 (1919–20), p. 58.

—— *Jesaja's Erleben: Eine gemeinverständliche Auslegung der Denkschrift des Propheten (Kap 6,1–9,6)* (Gotha, Leopold Klotz Verlag 1928).

Carley, K.W., *Ezekiel among the Prophets: A Study of Ezekiel's Place in Prophetic Tradition* (SBT, 2nd series 31; London, SCM Press 1975).

Carroll, R.P., *When Prophecy Failed: Reactions and Responses to Failure in the Old Testament Prophetic Traditions* (London, SCM Press 1979).

Caspari, W., 'Der Geist des Herrn ist über mir', *NKZ* 40 (1929), pp. 729–47.

Cazelles, H., 'De l'idéologie royale', *JANES* 5 (1973), pp. 59–73.

—— *Le Messie de la Bible: Christologie de l'Ancien Testament* (Paris, Desclée 1978).

—— 'Qui aurait visé, à l'origine, Isaïe ii 2–5?', *VT* 30 (1980), pp. 409–20.

Chisholm, R.B., 'Structure, Style, and the Prophetic Message: An Analysis of Isaiah 5:8–30', *BibSac* 143 (1986), pp. 46–60.

Clements, R.E., *Isaiah 1–39* (NCB; Grand Rapids, Eerdmans/ London, Marshall, Morgan & Scott 1980).

—— '"A Remnant Chosen by Grace" (Romans 11:5): The Old Testament Background and Origin of the Remnant Concept', in D.A. Hagner and M.J. Harris (eds.), *Pauline Studies: Essays Presented to Professor F.F. Bruce on his 70th Birthday* (Exeter, Paternoster/Grand Rapids, Eerdmans 1980), pp. 106–21.

—— 'The Prophecies of Isaiah and the Fall of Jerusalem in 587 B.C.', *VT* 30 (1980), pp. 421–36.

—— 'Beyond Tradition-History: Deutero-Isaianic Development of First Isaiah's Themes', *JSOT* 31 (1985), pp. 95–113.

—— 'Patterns in the Prophetic Canon: Healing the Blind and the Lame', in G.M. Tucker, D.L. Petersen, and R.R. Wilson (eds.), *Canon, Theology, and Old Testament Interpretation: Essays in Honor of Brevard S. Childs* (Philadelphia, Fortress Press 1988), pp. 189–200.

—— 'The Immanuel Prophecy of Isa. 7:10–17 and Its Messianic Interpretation', in E. Blum *et al.* (eds.), *Die Hebräische Bibel und ihre zweifache Nachgeschichte: Festschrift für Rolf Rendtorff zum 65. Geburtstag* (Neukirchen–Vluyn, Neukirchener Verlag 1990), pp. 225–40.

—— *Old Testament Prophecy: From Oracles to Canon* (Louisville, Westminster John Knox Press 1996).

Clifford, R.J., 'Isaiah 55: Invitation to a Feast', in C.L. Meyers and M. O'Connor (eds.), *The Word of the Lord Shall Go Forth: Essays in Honor of David Noel Freedman in Celebration of his Sixtieth Birthday* (Winona Lake, Ind. Eisenbrauns, 1983), pp. 27–35.

—— *Fair Spoken and Persuading: An Interpretation of Second Isaiah* (New York, Paulist Press 1984).

Conrad, E.W., 'The Community as King in Second Isaiah', in J.T. Butler, E.W. Conrad and B.C. Ollenburger (eds.), *Understanding the Word: Essays in Honor of Bernhard W. Anderson* (JSOTS 37; Sheffield, Sheffield Academic Press 1985), pp. 99–111.

—— 'The Royal Narratives and the Structure of the Book of Isaiah', *JSOT* 41 (1988), pp. 67–81.

—— *Reading Isaiah* (Minneapolis, Fortress Press 1991).

Crüsemann, F., *Studien zur Formgeschichte von Hymnus und Danklied in Israel* (WMANT 32; Neukirchen-Vluyn, Neukirchener Verlag 1969).

Davies, G.I., 'The Destiny of the Nations in the Book of Isaiah', in J. Vermeylen (ed.), *The Book of Isaiah* (BETL 81; Leuven, Leuven University Press and Peeters 1989), pp. 93–120.

—— *Hosea* (OTG; Sheffield, Sheffield Academic Press 1993).

Day, J., *God's Conflict with the Dragon and the Sea: Echoes of a Canaanite Myth in the Old Testament* (UCOP 35; Cambridge, Cambridge University Press 1985).

—— *Molech: A God of Human Sacrifice in the Old Testament* (UCOP 41; Cambridge, Cambridge University Press 1989).

Dietrich, W., *Jesaja und die Politik* (BEvTh 74; Munich, Chr. Kaiser Verlag 1976).

Donner, H., *Israel unter den Völkern: Die Stellung der klassischen Propheten des 8. Jahrhunderts v. Chr. zur Aussenpolitik der Könige von Israel und Juda* (SVT 11; Leiden, E.J. Brill 1964).

Driver, G.R., 'Isaiah i–xxxix: Textual and Linguistic Problems', *JSS* 13 (1968), pp. 36–57.

—— 'Isaiah 6:1 "his train filled the temple"', in H. Goedicke (ed.), *Near Eastern Studies in Honor of William Foxwell Albright* (Baltimore and London, Johns Hopkins 1971), pp. 87–96.

Duhm, B., *Das Buch Jesaia* (HKAT; Göttingen, Vandenhoeck & Ruprecht 1892; 1922⁴).

Eaton, J.H., 'The King as God's Witness', *ASTI* 7 (1970), pp. 25–40.

—— *Kingship and the Psalms* (SBT, 2nd series 32; London, SCM Press 1976; 2nd edition, Sheffield, Sheffield Academic Press 1986).

—— *Festal Drama in Deutero-Isaiah* (London, SPCK 1979).

Eissfeldt, O., 'The Promises of Grace to David in Isaiah 55:1–5', in B.W. Anderson and W. Harrelson (eds.), *Israel's Prophetic Heritage: Essays in Honor of James Muilenburg* (London, SCM Press 1962), pp. 196–207 = 'Die Gnadenverheissungen an David in Jes 55, 1–5', in *Kleine Schriften*, 4 (Tübingen, J.C.B. Mohr 1968), pp. 44–52.

Elliger, K., *Die Einheit des Tritojesaia (Jesaia 56–66)* (BWANT 45; Stuttgart, Kohlhammer 1928).

—— 'Der Prophet Tritojesaja', *ZAW* 49 (1931), pp. 112–41.

—— *Deuterojesaja in seinem Verhältnis zu Tritojesaja* (BWANT 63; Stuttgart, Kohlhammer 1933).

Emerton, J.A., 'The Textual Problems of Isaiah v 14', *VT* 17 (1967), pp. 135–42.

—— 'Review of Mettinger, *A Farewell to the Servant Songs*', *BiOr* 48 (1991), cols. 626–32.

Emmerson, G.I., *Isaiah 56–66* (OTG; Sheffield, Sheffield Academic Press 1992).

Eslinger, L., 'The Infinite in a Finite Organical Perception (Isaiah vi 1–5)', *VT* 45 (1995), pp. 145–73.

Evans, C.A., *To See and Not Perceive: Isaiah 6.9–10 in Early Jewish and Christian Interpretation* (JSOTS 64; Sheffield, Sheffield Academic Press 1989).

Fey, R., *Amos und Jesaja: Abhängigkeit und Eigenständigkeit des Jesaja* (WMANT 12; Neukirchen–Vluyn, Neukirchener Verlag 1963).

Fischer, I., *Wo ist Yahwe? Das Volksklagelied Jes 63,7–64,11 als Ausdruck des Ringens um eine gebrochene Beziehung* (Stuttgart, Verlag Katholisches Bibelwerk GmbH 1989).

Fisher, R.W., 'The Herald of Good News in Second Isaiah', in J.J. Jackson and M. Kessler (eds.), *Rhetorical Criticism: Essays in Honor of James Muilenburg* (Pittsburgh, The Pickwick Press 1974), pp. 117–32.

Gelston, A., 'Isaiah 52:13–53:12: An Eclectic Text and a Supplementary Note on the Hebrew Manuscript Kennicott 96', *JSS* 35 (1990), pp. 187–211.

Gibson, J.C.L., *Davidson's Introductory Hebrew Grammar: Syntax* (Edinburgh, T. & T. Clark 1994).

Gitay, Y., *Prophecy and Persuasion: A Study of Isaiah 40–48* (FThL 14; Bonn, Linguistica Biblica 1981).

Goldingay, J., 'The Arrangement of Isaiah xli–xlv', *VT* 29 (1979), pp. 289–99.

Gordon, R.P. (ed.), *"The Place Is Too Small For Us": The Israelite Prophets in Recent Scholarship* (Winona Lake, Ind., Eisenbrauns 1995).

Gossai, H., *Justice, Righteousness and the Social Critique of the Eighth-Century Prophets* (New York, Peter Lang 1993).

Gottwald, N.K., 'Immanuel as the Prophet's Son', *VT* 8 (1958), pp. 36–47.

Gray, G.B., *A Critical and Exegetical Commentary on the Book of Isaiah I–XXVII* (ICC; Edinburgh, T. & T. Clark 1912).

Greenfield, J.C., 'Ba'al's Throne and Isa 6:1', in A. Caquot, S. Légasse and M. Tardieu (eds.), *Mélanges bibliques et orientaux en l'honneur de M. Mathias Delcor* (AOAT 215; Kevelaer, Butzon & Bercker/Neukirchen–Vluyn, Neukirchener Verlag 1985), pp. 193–8.

Grelot, P., 'Sur Isaïe lxi: la première consécration d'un grand-prêtre', *RB* 97 (1990), pp. 414–31.

Gressmann, H., *Der Ursprung der israelitisch-jüdischen Eschatologie* (FRLANT 6; Göttingen, Vandenhoeck & Ruprecht 1905).

Groves, J.W., *Actualization and Interpretation in the Old Testament* (SBLDS 86; Atlanta, Scholars Press 1987).

Gunkel, H. and Begrich, J. *Einleitung in die Psalmen: Die Gattungen der religiösen Lyrik Israels* (Göttingen, Vandenhoeck & Ruprecht 1933).

Haag, H., *Der Gottesknecht bei Deuterojesaja* (EF 233; Darmstadt, Wissenschaftliche Buchgesellschaft 1985).

Hammershaimb, E., *Some Aspects of Old Testament Prophecy from Isaiah to Malachi* (Copenhagen, Rosenkilde og Bagger 1966).

Hanson, P.D., *The Dawn of Apocalyptic* (Philadelphia, Fortress Press 1979[2]).

Haran, M., 'The Literary Structure and Chronological Framework of the Prophecies in Is. xl–xlviii', in *Congress Volume, Bonn 1962* (SVT 9; Leiden, E.J. Brill 1963), pp. 127–55.

Harrelson, W., 'Nonroyal Motifs in the Royal Eschatology', in B.W. Anderson and W. Harrelson (eds.), *Israel's Prophetic Heritage: Essays in Honor of James Muilenburg* (London, SCM Press 1962), pp. 147–65.

Hasel, G., 'צעק', *TDOT* 4 (Grand Rapids, Eerdmans 1974–), pp. 112–22.

Hayes, J.H. and Irvine, S.A. *Isaiah, the Eighth-Century Prophet: his Times and his Preaching* (Nashville, Abingdon Press 1987).

Heider, G.C., *The Cult of Molek: A Reassessment* (JSOTS 43; Sheffield, Sheffield Academic Press 1985).

Herder, J.G. von, *Vom Geist der Ebräischen Poesie, 2: Eine Anleitung für die Liebhaber derselben und der ältesten Geschichte des menschlichen Geistes* (Leipzig, J.R. Barth 1825[3]).

Hermisson, 'Israel und der Gottesknecht bei Deuterojesaja', *ZThK* 79 (1982), pp. 1–24.

—— 'Einheit und Komplexität Deuterojesajas: Probleme der Redaktionsgeschichte von Jes 40–55', in J. Vermeylen (ed.),

The Book of Isaiah (BETL 81; Leuven, Leuven University Press and Peeters 1989), pp. 287–312.

Höffken, P., 'Notizen zum Textcharakter von Jesaja 7,1–17', *ThZ* 36 (1980), pp. 321–37.

Høgenhaven, J., *Gott und Volk bei Jesaja: Eine Untersuchung zur biblischen Theologie* (AThD 24; Leiden, E.J. Brill 1988).

Holladay, W.L., *Isaiah: Scroll of a Prophetic Heritage* (Grand Rapids, Eerdmans 1978).

Holmgren, F., 'Chiastic Structure in Isaiah li 1–11', *VT* 19 (1969), pp. 196–201.

Hurowitz A., 'Isaiah's Impure Lips and their Purification in Light of Akkadian Sources', *HUCA* 60 (1989), pp. 39–89.

Irvine, S.A., *Isaiah, Ahaz, and the Syro-Ephraimitic Crisis* (SBLDS 123; Atlanta, Scholars Press 1990).

—— 'The Isaianic *Denkschrift*: Reconsidering an Old Hypothesis', *ZAW* 104 (1992), pp. 216–31.

Irwin, W.H., *Isaiah 28–33: Translation with Philological Notes* (Biblica et Orientalia 30; Rome, Biblical Institute Press 1977).

Janzen, J.G., 'Isaiah 41:27: Reading הנה הנומה in 1QIsa[a] and הנה הנם in the Masoretic Text', *JBL* 113 (1994), pp. 597–607.

Jensen, J., *The Use of* tôrâ *by Isaiah: His Debate with the Wisdom Tradition* (CBQMS 3; Washington, D.C., The Catholic Biblical Association of America 1973).

Jeppesen, K., 'From "You, My Servant" to "The Hand of the Lord is with My Servants": A Discussion of Is 40–66', *SJOT* 1990/1, pp. 113–29.

Jeremias, J., 'מִשְׁפָּט im ersten Gottesknechtslied', *VT* 22 (1972), pp. 31–42.

Jones, D.R., 'Isaiah – II and III', in M. Black and H.H. Rowley (eds.), *Peake's Commentary on the Bible* (London, Nelson 1962), pp. 516–36.

Joüon, P., *A Grammar of Biblical Hebrew* (translated and revised by T. Muraoka; Rome, Pontifical Biblical Institute 1993[2]).

Kaiser, O., *Der Königliche Knecht: Eine traditionsgeschichtlich-exegetische Studie über die Ebed-Jahwe-Lieder bei Deuterojesaja* (FRLANT 70; Göttingen, Vandenhoeck & Ruprecht 1959).

—— *Der Prophet Jesaja, Kapitel 13–39* (ATD 18; Göttingen, Vandenhoeck & Ruprecht 1973) = ET, *Isaiah 13–39: A Commentary* (OTL; London, SCM Press 1974).

—— *Das Buch des Propheten Jesaja, Kapitel 1–12* (ATD 17; Göttingen, Vandenhoeck & Ruprecht 1981⁵) = ET, *Isaiah 1–12: A Commentary* (OTL; London, SCM Press 1983).

Kaiser, W.C., 'The Unfailing Kindnesses Promised to David: Isaiah 55.3', *JSOT* 45 (1989), pp. 91–8.

—— *The Messiah in the Old Testament* (Grand Rapids, Zondervan 1995).

Kaplan, M.M., 'Isaiah 6 1–11', *JBL* 45 (1926), pp. 251–9.

Kaufmann, Y., *The Religion of Israel from its Beginnings to the Babylonian Exile* (New York, Schocken Books 1972).

Kayatz, C., *Studien zu Proverbien 1–9: Eine form– und motivgeschichtliche Untersuchung unter Einbeziehung ägyptischen Vergleichsmaterials* (WMANT 22; Neukirchen–Vluyn, Neukirchener Verlag 1966).

Kellermann, D., ' לוה ', *TDOT* 7 (Grand Rapids, Eerdmans 1974–), pp. 475–6.

Kendall, D., 'The Use of Mišpaṭ in Isaiah 59', *ZAW* 96 (1984), pp. 391–405.

Kiesow, K., *Exodustexte im Jesajabuch: Literarkritische und motivgeschichtliche Analysen* (OBO 24; Freiburg, Universitätsverlag/Göttingen, Vandenhoeck & Ruprecht 1979).

Kilian, R., *Die Verheissung Immanuels Jes 7,14* (SBS 35; Stuttgart, Verlag Katholisches Bibelwerk 1968).

—— *Jesaja 1–39* (EF 200; Darmstadt, Wissenschaftliche Buchgesellschaft 1983).

—— *Jesaja 1–12* (DNEB 17; Würzburg, Echter Verlag 1986).

Kissane, E.J., *The Book of Isaiah*, 1 (Dublin, The Richview Press 1941).

Klein, H., 'Freude an Rezin', *VT* 30 (1980), pp. 229–34.

Koch, K., ' אהל ', *TDOT* 1 (Grand Rapids, 1974–), pp. 118–30.

—— *Die Propheten*, 1: *Assyrische Zeit* (Stuttgart, Kohlhammer 1978; 1995³) = ET, *The Prophets*, 1: *The Assyrian Period* (London, SCM Press 1982).

Koenen, K., 'Textkritische Anmerkungen zu schwierigen Stellen im Tritojesajabuch', *Biblica* 69 (1988), pp. 564–73.

—— *Ethik und Eschatologie im Tritojesajabuch: Eine literarkritische und redaktionsgeschichtliche Studie* (WMANT 62; Neukirchen–Vluyn, Neukirchener Verlag 1990).

Kratz, R.G., *Kyros im Deuterojesaja-Buch: Redaktionsgeschichtliche Untersuchungen zu Entstehung und Theologie von Jes 40–55* (FAT 1; Tübingen, J.C.B. Mohr [Paul Siebeck] 1991).

Kraus, H.-J., *Psalmen, 2. Teilband: Psalmen 60–150* (BKAT 15/2; Neukirchen–Vluyn, Neukirchener Verlag 1978[5]) = ET, *Psalms 60–150: A Commentary* (Minneapolis, Augsburg 1989).

Kruse, H., 'David's Covenant', *VT* 35 (1985), pp. 139–64.

Kuntz, J.K., 'The Contribution of Rhetorical Criticism to Understanding Isaiah 51:1–16', in D.J.A. Clines, D.M. Gunn and A.J. Hauser (eds.), *Art and Meaning: Rhetoric in Biblical Literature* (JSOTS 19; Sheffield, JSOT Press 1982), pp. 140–71.

Laato, A., *Who is Immanuel? The Rise and the Foundering of Isaiah's Messianic Expectations* (Åbo, Åbo Academy Press 1988).

—— 'The Composition of Isaiah 40–55', *JBL* 109 (1990), pp. 207–28.

—— *The Servant of YHWH and Cyrus: A Reinterpretation of the Exilic Messianic Programme in Isaiah 40–55* (ConB, OT series 35; Stockholm, Almqvist & Wiksell International 1992).

Lau, W., *Schriftgelehrte Prophetie in Jes 56–66: Eine Untersuchung zu den literarischen Bezügen in den letzten elf Kapiteln des Jesajabuches* (BZAW 225; Berlin and New York, de Gruyter 1994).

L'Heureux, C.E., 'The Redactional History of Isaiah 5.1–10.4', in W.B. Barrick and J.R. Spencer (eds.), *In the Shelter of Elyon: Essays on Ancient Palestinian Life and Literature in Honor of G.W. Ahlström* (JSOTS 31; Sheffield, JSOT Press 1984), pp. 99–119.

Lindblad, U., 'A Note on the Nameless Servant in Isaiah xlii 1–4', *VT* 43 (1993), pp. 115–19.

Lohfink, N., '"Israel" in Jes. 49, 3', in J. Schreiner (ed.), *Wort, Lied und Gottesspruch: Beiträge zu Psalmen und Propheten. Festschrift für Joseph Ziegler* (FzB 2; Würzburg, Echter Verlag 1972), pp. 217–29.

Marti, K., *Das Buch Jesaja* (KHAT 10; Tübingen, J.C.B. Mohr [Paul Siebeck] 1900).

Martin-Achard, R., *Israël et les nations: la perspective missionnaire de l'Ancien Testament* (Neuchâtel and Paris, Delachaux & Nestlé 1959) = ET, *A Light to the Nations: A Study of the Old Testament Conception of Israel's Mission to the World* (Edinburgh and London, Oliver and Boyd 1962).

Matheus, F., *Singt dem Herrn ein neues Lied: Die Hymnen Deuterojesajas* (SBS 141; Stuttgart, Verlag Katholisches Bibelwerk 1990).

Merendino, R.P., *Der Erste und der Letzte: Eine Untersuchung von Jes 40–48* (SVT 31; Leiden, E.J. Brill 1981).

Mettinger, T.N.D., *A Farewell to the Servant Songs: A Critical Examination of an Exegetical Axiom* (Lund, CWK Gleerup 1983).

Milgrom, J., 'Did Isaiah Prophesy during the Reign of Uzziah?', *VT* 14 (1964), pp. 164–82.

Moore, S.D., 'Gigantic God: Yahweh's Body', *JSOT* 70 (1996), pp. 87–115.

Motyer, J.A., *The Prophecy of Isaiah* (Leicester, Inter-Varsity Press 1993).

Muilenburg, J., 'The Book of Isaiah, Chapters 40–66', *IB* 5 (New York and Nashville, Abingdon 1956), pp. 381–773.

Müller, H.-P., 'Glauben und Bleiben: Zur Denkschrift Jesajas Kapitel vi 1–viii 18', in *Studies on Prophecy: A Collection of Twelve Papers* (SVT 26; Leiden, E.J. Brill 1974), pp. 25–54.

Na'aman, N., 'The Kingdom of Judah under Josiah', *Tel Aviv* 18 (1991), pp. 3–71.

Niehr, H., 'Zur Intention von Jes 6,1–9', *BN* 21 (1983), pp. 59–65.

—— *Herrschen und Richten: Die Wurzel špṭ im Alten Orient und im Alten Testament* (FzB 54; Würzburg, Echter Verlag 1986).

Nielsen, E., 'Deuterojesaja: Erwägungen zur Formkritik, Traditions– und Redaktionsgeschichte', *VT* 20 (1970), pp. 190–205.

Nielsen, K., *There is Hope for a Tree: The Tree as Metaphor in Isaiah* (JSOTS 65; Sheffield, Sheffield Academic Press 1989).

North, C.R., *The Suffering Servant in Deutero-Isaiah: An Historical and Critical Study* (Oxford, Oxford University Press 1956²).

—— *The Second Isaiah: Introduction, Translation and Commentary to Chapters xl–lv* (Oxford, Clarendon Press 1964).

Odeberg, H., *Trito-Isaiah (Isaiah 56–66): A Literary and Linguistic Analysis* (Uppsala, A.-B. Lindequistska Bokhandeln 1931).

Oded, B., 'The Historical Background of the Syro-Ephraimite War Reconsidered', *CBQ* 34 (1972), pp. 153–65.

Oehler, G.F., *Theologie des Alten Testaments*, 2 (Stuttgart, J.F. Steinkopf 1882²).

Ollenburger, B.C., *Zion the City of the Great King: A Theological Symbol of the Jerusalem Cult* (JSOTS 41; Sheffield, Sheffield Academic Press 1987).

Olley, J.W., 'Notes on Isaiah xxxii 1, xlv 19, 23 and lxiii 1', *VT* 33 (1983), pp. 446–53.

Orlinsky, H.M., 'The So-Called "Servant of the Lord" and "Suffering Servant" in Second Isaiah', in H.M. Orlinsky and N.H. Snaith, *Studies on the Second Part of the Book of Isaiah* (SVT 14; Leiden, E.J. Brill 1967), pp. 1–133.

Oswalt, J.N., *The Book of Isaiah Chapters 1–39* (NICOT; Grand Rapids, Eerdmans 1986).

Paul, S.M., 'Deutero-Isaiah and Cuneiform Royal Inscriptions', *JAOS* 88 (1968), pp. 180–6.

Pauritsch, K., *Die neue Gemeinde: Gott sammelt Ausgestossene und Arme (Jesaia 56–66): Die Botschaft des Tritojesaia-Buches literar–, form–, gattungskritisch und redaktionsgeschichtlich untersucht* (AnBib 47; Rome, Biblical Institute Press 1971).

Peels, H.G.L., *The Vengeance of God: The Meaning of the Root NQM and the Function of the NQM-Texts in the Context of Divine Revelation in the Old Testament* (OTS 31; Leiden, E.J. Press 1995).

Pomykala, K.E., *The Davidic Dynasty Tradition in Early Judaism: Its History and Significance for Messianism* (Atlanta, Scholars Press 1995).

Quell, G., 'ἐκλέγομαι , B. Election in the Old Testament', *TDNT* 4 (Grand Rapids, Eerdmans 1964–74), pp. 145–68.

Rad, G. von, 'Es ist noch eine Ruhe vorhanden dem Volke Gottes: Eine biblische Begriffsuntersuchung', *Zwischen den Zeiten* 11 (1933), pp. 104–11 = ET, 'There Remains Still a Rest for the People of God: An Investigation of a Biblical Conception', in *The Problem of the Hexateuch and Other*

Essays (Edinburgh and London, Oliver & Boyd 1966), pp. 94–102.

—— 'Das judäische Königsritual', *TLZ* 72 (1947), pp. 211–16 = ET, 'The Royal Ritual in Judah', in *The Problem of the Hexateuch and Other Essays* (Edinburgh and London, Oliver & Boyd 1966), pp. 222–31.

Reimer, D.J., ' צדק ', in W.A. VanGemeren (ed.) *The New International Dictionary of Old Testament and Exegesis*, 3 (Carlisle, Paternoster Press 1997), pp. 744–69.

Reiterer, F.V., *Gerechtigkeit als Heil:* צדק *bei Deuterojesaja. Aussage und Vergleich mit der alttestamentlichen Tradition* (Graz, Akademische Druck-u. Verlagsanstalt 1976).

Renaud, B., 'La Forme poétique d'Is 9, 1–6', in A. Caquot, S. Légasse and M. Tardieu (eds.), *Mélanges bibliques et orientaux en l'honneur de M. Mathias Delcor* (AOAT 215; Kevelaer, Butzon & Bercker/Neukirchen-Vluyn, Neukirchener Verlag 1985), pp. 331–48.

Rendtorff, R., 'Isaiah 56:1 as a Key to the Formation of the Book of Isaiah', in *Canon and Theology: Overtures to an Old Testament Theology* (Edinburgh, T. & T. Clark 1994), pp. 181–9.

Reventlow, H.G., 'Das Ende der sog. "Denkschrift" Jesajas', *BN* 38/39 (1987), pp. 62–7.

Ringgren, H., *The Messiah in the Old Testament* (SBT 18; London, SCM Press 1956).

Ringgren, H., Rüterswörden, U. and Simian-Yofre, H., ' עבד ', *ThWAT* 5 (Stuttgart, Kohlhammer 1970–), cols. 982–1012.

Roberts, J.J.M., 'Isaiah and his Children', in A. Kort and S. Morschauser (eds.), *Biblical and Related Studies Presented to Samuel Iwry* (Winona Lake, Ind., Eisenbrauns 1985), pp. 193–203.

—— 'Isaiah 33: An Isaianic Elaboration of the Zion Tradition', in C.L. Meyers and M. O'Connor (eds.), *The Word of the Lord Shall Go Forth: Essays in Honor of David Noel Freedman in Celebration of his Sixtieth Birthday* (Winona Lake, Ind., Eisenbrauns 1983), pp. 15–25.

—— 'The Divine King and the Human Community in Isaiah's Vision of the Future', in H.B. Huffmon, F.A. Spina and A.R.W. Green (eds.), *The Quest for the Kingdom of God: Studies in*

Honor of George E. Mendenhall (Winona Lake, Ind., Eisenbrauns 1983), pp. 127–36.

'Yahweh's Foundation in Zion (Isa 28:16)', *JBL* 106 (1987), pp. 27–45.

—— 'The Old Testament's Contribution to Messianic Expectations', in J.H. Charlesworth (ed.), *The Messiah: Developments in Earliest Judaism and Christianity* (Minneapolis, Fortress Press 1992), pp. 39–51.

Robinson, H.W., *The Cross in the Old Testament* (London, SCM Press 1955).

Rofé, A., 'Isaiah 66:1–4: Judean Sects in the Persian Period as Viewed by Trito-Isaiah', in A. Kort and S. Morschauser (eds.), *Biblical and Related Studies Presented to Samuel Iwry* (Winona Lake, Ind., Eisenbrauns 1985), pp. 205–17.

—— 'The Onset of Sects in Postexilic Judaism: Neglected Evidence from the Septuagint, Trito-Isaiah, Ben Sira, and Malachi', in J. Neusner *et al.* (eds.), *The Social World of Formative Christianity and Judaism: Essays in Tribute to Howard Clark Kee* (Philadelphia, Fortress Press 1988), pp. 39–49.

Schibler, D., 'Messianism and Messianic Prophecy in Isaiah 1–12 and 28–33', in P.E. Satterthwaite, R.S. Hess and G.J. Wenham (eds.), *The Lord's Anointed: Interpretation of Old Testament Messianic Texts* (Carlisle, Paternoster/Grand Rapids, Baker Books 1995), pp. 87–104.

Schmid, H.H., *Gerechtigkeit als Weltordnung: Hintergrund und Geschichte des alttestamentlichen Gerechtigkeitsbegriffes* (BhistTh 40; Tübingen, J.C.B. Mohr [Paul Siebeck] 1968).

Schoors, A., *I am God your Saviour: A Form-Critical Study of the Main Genres in Is. xl–lv* (SVT 24; Leiden, E.J. Brill 1973).

Schramm, B., *The Opponents of Third Isaiah: Reconstructing the Cultic History of the Restoration* (JSOTS 193; Sheffield, Sheffield Academic Press 1995).

Schultz, R., 'The King in the Book of Isaiah', in P.E. Satterthwaite, R.S. Hess and G.J. Wenham (eds.), *The Lord's Anointed: Interpretation of Old Testament Messianic Texts* (Carlisle, Paternoster/Grand Rapids, Baker Books 1995), pp. 141–65.

Scott, R.B.Y., 'The Book of Isaiah, Chapters 1–39', *IB* 5 (New York and Nashville, Abingdon 1956), pp. 151–381.

Scullion, J.J., 'ṣedeq–ṣedāqah in Isaiah cc. 40–66 with Special Reference to the Continuity in Meaning between Second and Third Isaiah', *UF* 3 (1971), pp. 335–48.

Seebass, H., ' בחר ', *TDOT* 2 (Grand Rapids, Eerdmans 1974 –), pp. 73–87.

Seitz, C.R., 'The Divine Council: Temporal Transition and New Prophecy in the Book of Isaiah', *JBL* 109 (1990), pp. 229–47.

—— *Zion's Final Destiny: The Development of the Book of Isaiah. A Reassessment of Isaiah 36–39* (Minneapolis, Fortress Press 1991).

—— *Isaiah 1–39* (Louisville, John Knox Press 1993).

—— 'How is the Prophet Isaiah Present in the Latter Half of the Book? The Logic of Chapters 40–66 within the Book of Isaiah', *JBL* 115 (1996), pp. 219–40.

Sekine, S., *Die Tritojesajanische Sammlung (Jes 56–66) redaktionsgeschichtlich untersucht* (BZAW 175; Berlin and New York, de Gruyter 1989).

Seux, M.-J., *Épithètes royales akkadiennes et sumériennes* (Paris, Letouzey et Ane 1967).

Sheppard, G.T., 'The Anti–Assyrian Redaction and the Canonical Context of Isaiah 1–39', *JBL* 104 (1985), pp. 193–216.

Skinner, J., *The Book of the Prophet Isaiah Chapters xl–lxvi* (CBSC; Cambridge, Cambridge University Press 1917).

—— *Prophecy and Religion: Studies in the Life of Jeremiah* (Cambridge, Cambridge University Press 1922).

Smelik, K.A.D., 'Distortion of Old Testament Prophecy. The Purpose of Isaiah xxxvi and xxxvii', in A.S. van der Woude (ed.), *Crises and Perspectives: Studies in Ancient Near Eastern Polytheism, Biblical Theology, Palestinian Archaeology and Intertestamental Literature* (*OTS* 24; Leiden, E.J. Brill 1986), pp. 70–93.

Smith, M.S., 'Divine Form and Size in Ugaritic and Pre-exilic Israelite Religion', *ZAW* 100 (1988), pp. 424–7.

Smith, P.A., *Rhetoric and Redaction in Trito-Isaiah: The Structure, Growth and Authorship of Isaiah 56–66* (SVT 62; Leiden, E.J. Brill 1995).

Smothers, T.G., 'Isaiah 15–16', in J.W. Watts and P.R. House (eds.), *Forming Prophetic Literature: Essays on Isaiah and the Twelve in Honor of John D.W. Watts* (JSOTS 235; Sheffield, Sheffield Academic Press 1996), pp. 70–84.

Snaith, N.H., 'The Servant of the Lord in Deutero-Isaiah', in H.H. Rowley (ed.), *Studies in Old Testament Prophecy Presented to Professor Theodore H. Robinson* (Edinburgh, T. & T. Clark 1950), pp. 187–200.

—— 'Isaiah 40–66: A Study of the Teaching of the Second Isaiah and its Consequences', in H.M. Orlinsky and N.H. Snaith, *Studies on the Second Part of the Book of Isaiah* (SVT 14; Leiden, E.J. Brill 1967), pp. 135–264.

Stamm, J.J., 'La prophétie d'Emmanuel', *RHPhR* 23 (1943), pp. 1–26.

—— 'Die Immanuel-Weissagung. Ein Gespräch mit E. Hammershaimb', *VT* 4 (1954), pp. 20–33.

—— 'Neuere Arbeiten zum Immanuel-Problem', *ZAW* 68 (1956), pp. 46–54.

—— 'Die Immanuel-Weissagung und die Eschatologie des Jesaja', *ThZ* 16 (1960), pp. 439–55.

—— 'Die Immanuel-Perikope im Lichte neuerer Veröffentlichungen', *ZDMG.S* 1 (1969), pp. 281–90.

—— 'Die Immanuel–Perikope. Eine Nachlese', *ThZ* 30 (1974), pp. 11–22.

Steck, O.H., 'Bemerkungen zu Jesaja 6', *BZ* N.F. 16 (1972), pp. 188–206.

—— 'Rettung und Verstockung: Exegetische Bemerkungen zu Jesaja 7.3–9', *EvTh* 33 (1973), pp. 77–90.

—— 'Beiträge zum Verständnis von Jesaja 7,10–17 und 8,1–4', *ThZ* 29 (1973), pp. 161–78.

—— *Studien zu Tritojesaja* (BZAW 203; Berlin and New York, de Gruyter 1991).

—— *Gottesknecht und Zion: Gesammelte Aufsätze zu Deuterojesaja* (FAT 4; Tübingen, J.C.B. Mohr [Paul Siebeck] 1992).

Sweeney, M.A., 'Textual Citations in Isaiah 24–27: Toward an Understanding of the Redactional Function of Chapters 24–27 in the Book of Isaiah', *JBL* 107 (1988), pp. 39–52.

—— *Isaiah 1–4 and the Post–Exilic Understanding of the Isaianic Tradition* (BZAW 171; Berlin and New York, de Gruyter 1988).

—— 'A Philological and Form-Critical Reevaluation of Isaiah 8:16–9:6', *HAR* 14 (1994), pp. 215–31.

—— *Isaiah 1–39, with an Introduction to Prophetic Literature* (FOTL 16; Grand Rapids, Eerdmans 1996).

Thompson, M.E.W., 'Isaiah's Ideal King', *JSOT* 24 (1982), pp. 79–88.

Tidwell, N.L., 'My Servant Jacob, Is. xlii 1: A Suggestion', in *Studies on Old Testament Prophecy* (SVT 26; Leiden, E.J. Brill 1974), pp. 84–91.

Tomes, R., 'The Reason for the Syro-Ephraimite War', *JSOT* 59 (1993), pp. 55–71.

Tsevat, M., ' בחן ', *TDOT* 2 (Grand Rapids, Eerdmans 1974–), pp. 69–72.

Van Winkle, D.W., 'The Relationship of the Nations to Yahweh and to Israel in Isaiah xl–lv', *VT* 35 (1985), pp. 446–58.

Vermeylen, J., *Du prophète Isaïe à l'apocalyptique: Isaïe, i–xxxv, miroir d'un demi–millénaire d'expérience religieuse en Israël* (EB; 2 vols.; Paris, Gabalda 1977–8).

—— 'Le Motif de la création dans le Deutéro-Isaïe', in P. Beauchamp (ed.), *La Création dans l'Orient Ancien* (LecD 127; Paris, Cerf) 1987), pp. 183–240.

Volz, P., *Jesaja II* (KAT 9; Leipzig, A. Deichertsche Verlagsbuchhandlung D. Werner Scholl 1932).

Walsh, J.P.M., *The Mighty from their Thrones: Power in the Biblical Tradition* (Philadelphia, Fortress Press 1987).

Waltke, B.K. and O'Connor, M., *An Introduction to Biblical Hebrew Syntax* (Winona Lake, Ind. Eisenbrauns, 1990).

Watts, J.D.W., *Isaiah 1–33* (WBC 24; Waco, Word Books 1985).

Webster, E.C., 'The Rhetoric of Isaiah 63–65', *JSOT* 47 (1990), pp. 89–102.

Wegner, P.D., *An Examination of Kingship and Messianic Expectation in Isaiah 1–35* (Lewiston, NY, Mellen Biblical Press 1992).

—— 'A Re-examination of Isaiah ix 1–6', *VT* 42 (1992), pp. 103–12.

Weinfeld, M., 'ברית', *TDOT* 2 (Grand Rapids, Eerdmans 1974–), pp. 253–79.

—— '"Justice and Righteousness" – משפט וצדקה – The Expression and its Meaning', in H.G. Reventlow and Y. Hoffman (eds.), *Justice and Righteousness: Biblical Themes and their Influence* (JSOTS 137; Sheffield, Sheffield Academic Press 1992), pp. 228–46.

Werlitz, J., *Studien zur literarkritischen Methode: Gericht und Heil in Jesaja 7, 1–17 und 29, 1–8* (BZAW 204; Berlin and New York, de Gruyter 1992).

Werner, W., *Eschatologische Texte in Jesaja 1–39: Messias, Heiliger Rest, Völker* (FzB 46; Würzburg, Echter Verlag 1982).

—— 'Vom Prophetenwort zur Prophetentheologie. Ein redaktionskritischer Versuch zu Jes 6,1–8,18', *BZ* N.F. 29 (1985), pp. 1–30.

Westermann, C., *Das Buch Jesaja, Kapitel 40–66* (ATD 19; Göttingen, Vandenhoeck & Ruprecht 1981⁴) = ET, *Isaiah 40–66: A Commentary* (OTL; London, SCM Press 1969).

Whybray, R.N., *Isaiah 40–66* (NCB; Oliphants 1975).

Widengren, G., *Sakrales Königtum im Alten Testament und im Judentum* (Stuttgart, Kohlhammer 1955).

Wilcox, P., and Paton-Williams, D., 'The Servant Songs in Deutero-Isaiah', *JSOT* 42 (1988), pp. 79–102.

Wildberger, H., 'Die Neuinterpretation des Erwählungsglaubens Israels in der Krise der Exilzeit', in H.J. Stoebe (ed.), *Wort–Gebot–Glaube: Beiträge zur Theologie des Alten Testaments: Walter Eichrodt zum 80. Geburtstag* (ATANT 59; Zürich, Zwingli 1970), pp. 307–24.

—— *Jesaja, 1. Teilband: Jesaja, Kapitel 1–12* (BKAT 10/1; Neukirchen–Vluyn, Neukirchener Verlag 1980²) = ET, *Isaiah 1–12: A Commentary* (Minneapolis, Fortress Press 1991).

—— *Jesaja, 2. Teilband: Jesaja 13–27* (BKAT 10/2; Neukirchen–Vluyn, Neukirchener Verlag 1978).

—— *Jesaja, 3. Teilband: Jesaja 28–39. Das Buch, der Prophet und seine Botschaft* (BKAT 10/3; Neukirchen–Vluyn, Neukirchener Verlag 1982).

Williamson, H.G.M., '"The Sure Mercies of David": Subjective or Objective Genitive?', *JSS* 23 (1978), pp. 31–49.

—— *1 and 2 Chronicles* (NCB; Grand Rapids, Eerdmans/ London, Marshall, Morgan & Scott 1982).

—— 'The Concept of Israel in Transition', in R.E. Clements (ed.), *The World of Ancient Israel: Sociological, Anthropological and Political Perspectives* (Cambridge, Cambridge University Press 1989), pp. 141–61.

—— 'The Prophet and the Plumb-Line: A Redaction-Critical Study of Amos vii', in A.S. van der Woude (ed.), *In Quest of the Past: Studies on Israelite Religion, Literature and Prophetism* (*OTS* 26; Leiden, E.J. Brill 1990), pp. 101–21.

—— 'Isaiah 63,7–64,11: Exilic Lament or Post-Exilic Protest?', *ZAW* 102 (1990), pp. 48–58.

—— 'First and Last in Isaiah', in H.A. McKay and D.J.A. Clines (eds.), *Of Prophets' Visions and the Wisdom of Sages: Essays in Honour of R. Norman Whybray on his Seventieth Birthday* (JSOTS 162; Sheffield, Sheffield Academic Press 1993), pp. 95–108.

—— *The Book Called Isaiah: Deutero-Isaiah's Role in Composition and Redaction* (Oxford, Clarendon Press 1994).

—— 'Isaiah xi 11–16 and the Redaction of Isaiah i–xii', in J.A. Emerton (ed.), *Congress Volume, Paris 1992* (SVT 61; Leiden, E.J. Brill 1995), pp. 343–57.

——'Synchronic and Diachronic in Isaian Perspective', in J.C. de Moor (ed.), *Synchronic or Diachronic? A Debate on Method in Old Testament Exegesis* (OTS 34; Leiden, E.J. Brill 1995), pp. 211–26.

—— 'Isaiah and the Wise', in J. Day, R.P. Gordon and H.G.M. Williamson (eds.), *Wisdom in Ancient Israel: Essays in Honour of J.A. Emerton* (Cambridge, Cambridge University Press 1995), pp. 133–41.

—— 'Hezekiah and the Temple', in M.V. Fox *et al.* (eds.), *Texts, Temples, and Traditions: A Tribute to Menahem Haran* (Winona Lake, Ind., Eisenbrauns 1996), pp. 47–52.

—— 'Relocating Isaiah 1:2–9', in C.C. Broyles and C.A. Evans (eds.), *Writing and Reading the Scroll of Isaiah: Studies of an Interpretive Tradition* (Leiden, E.J. Brill, forthcoming).

Willis, T.M., 'Yahweh's Elders (Isa 24,23): Senior Officials of the Divine Court', *ZAW* 103 (1991), pp. 375–85.

Wodecki, P.B., '*šlḥ* dans le livre d'Isaïe', *VT* 34 (1984), pp. 482–8.

Wolf, H.M., 'A Solution to the Immanuel Prophecy in Isaiah 7:14–8:22', *JBL* 91 (1972), pp. 449–56.

Wong, G.C.I., *The Nature of Faith in Isaiah of Jerusalem* (unpublished PhD thesis, Cambridge, 1994).

Würthwein, E., 'Jesaja 7,1–9. Ein Beitrag zu dem Thema: Prophetie und Politik', in *Theologie als Glaubenswagnis: Festschrift zum 80. Geburtstag von Karl Heim* (Hamburg, Fur'he-Verlag 1954), pp. 47–63 = *Wort und Existenz: Studien zum*

Alten Testament (Göttingen, Vandenhoeck & Ruprecht 1970), pp. 127–43.

Young, E.J., *The Book of Isaiah*, 3 vols. (Grand Rapids, Eerdmans 1965–72).

Ziegler, J., *Untersuchungen zur Septuaginta des Buches Isaias* (Münster, Verlag der Aschendorffschen Verlagsbuchhandlung 1934).

Zimmerli, W., 'Zur Sprache Tritojesajas', in *Festschrift für Ludwig Köhler* (Bern, Baüchler u. Co. 1950), pp. 62–74 = *Gottes Offenbarung: Gesammelte Aufsätze zum Alten Testament* (ThB 19; Munich, Chr. Kaiser Verlag 1963), pp. 217–33.

—— *Ezechiel, 1. Teilband: Ezechiel 1–24* (BKAT 13/1; Neukirchen-Vluyn, Neukirchener Verlag 1969) = ET, *Ezekiel 1: A Commentary on the Book of the Prophet Ezekiel, Chapters 1–24* (Hermeneia; Philadelphia, Fortress Press 1979).

Name index

Scriptural references